D1564881

AN INTRODUCTION TO THE PHILOSOPHY OF PHYSICAL EDUCATION AND SPORT

Robert G. Osterhoudt

Arizona State University

ISBN 0-87563-148-7

Published by
STIPES PUBLISHING COMPANY
10-12 Chester Street
Champaign, Illinois 61820

DEDICATION

To my mother and father,

Rita E. and Clarence B. Osterhoudt

with love and gratitude

ACKNOWLEDGMENTS

The publication of this volume marks the fulfillment of many creative ambitions for me. And it gives remembrance of those who contributed so much to the formulation of those ambitions, and of those most instrumental in fashioning the capabilities to see such ambitions successfully through. Not the least of those who on both counts have made me much of what I am and want to be are the most memorable of my teachers and coaches: Dr. Wilbert Bolton, Dr. Benton Bristol, Mr. David Clemson, Mr. John Doolittle, Mr. Norman Gordon, Mr. Jackson Horner, Mr. William Long, Dr. Chauncey Morehouse, Dr. Richard Nelson, Mrs. Maretta Rice, Dr. Richard Schacht, Dr. Harold Schilling, and Mr. Walter Weaver. Also fondly and gratefully remembered are the administrative chairs I have served in various professional capacities: Dr. John F. Alexander, Dr. Warren P. Fraleigh, Dr. Eloise M. Jaeger, Dr. Matthew G. Maetozo, Dr. Thomas D. McIntyre, Dr. James E. Odenkirk, Dr. William J. Stone, and Dr. Mary L. Young. Three remarkable persons among all of the remarkable others have had the greatest influence, however: Dr. Guy M. Lewis, Dr. John A. Lucas, and Dr. Earle F. Zeigler. Professors Lewis and Lucas were variously my professors, advisors, and sources of personal and professional inspiration through baccalaureate and Master's degree experiences at the Pennsylvania State University. At a most impressionable and otherwise crucial time as well, they provided the most remarkable model of genteel scholarship that I could have hoped for. Professor Zeigler was my professor and Doctor's advisor at the University of Illinois, and in that capacity put up with more nonsense than should have reasonably been expected of anyone. My respect for him and his judgment grows daily--his genius has fully dawned on me, I suppose we could say. The debt owed the lot of these wonderfully sensitive, talented, and devoted persons cannot be repaid in orthodox terms. They were not teachers and scholars by default, as many seem to be these days. Their reward is found in the depth of genuine insight they give to their students, and in the quality of effort they exact from them. No one of them was in the least timid about the importance of either. That is significantly why they have given so much, and why they are so widely admired and well, if belatedly, remembered.

I want also to remember here: my students, colleagues, and friends at the Pennsylvania State University, Lock Haven State College University of Illinois, State University College at Brockport, University of Minnesota, St. Olaf College, and Arizona State University; those who have assisted so ably in the typing and proofing of the final manuscript, Ms. Susan Bandy, Mrs. Shirley Cooper, Mrs. Mary Cosette, Ms. Kathryn Cowdery, Mrs. Barbara Duffy, Mrs. Ida McGuiness, and Mrs. Helen Schatzlein; and my consulting editor at

Stipes Publishing Company, Mr. Robert A. Watts, whose patience, understanding, and assistance were all above and beyond the ordinary. Finally, I need to recollect with love and grateful appreciation the impressive tolerance and support that my wife, Kerry, and children, Kris, Nicole, and Kirk, have given over the past fifteen years. They have done all the good and proper things, and the book would not have been possible without them. The book is dedicated, however, to my parents, Rita E. and Clarence B. Osterhoudt, who have made all those many contributions to my progress that good parents make to their childrens' development. Regrettably, those contributions go all too infrequently unnoticed or unthanked. I want to correct an earlier error in this direction with this dedication. Though all of these persons, and others, have influenced the writing of the book, the book (in particular its errors) is not theirs, but mine. Though it is doubtlessly much less than they would have it be, it is the best of which I am now capable.

CONTENTS

PREFACE

Physical education and sport are no strangers to the odyssey of human history. They have been a part of, and an influence on most every culture and time. Accordingly, quite a great deal has been thought and written about them. Surprisingly little of this thought and writing has been of an authentic and systematic philosophic character, however. The literature devoted to a philosophic examination of physical education and sport is, therefore, somewhat limited; and it is also somewhat recent. The advancing, formal interest in these activities in the twentieth century, however, has brought with it a commensurate advance both in the volume and in the quality of philosophic thought concerning them. This latter advance is largely the result of an increasing accommodation of issues which concern physical education and sport to genuinely philosophic treatments of them. Not until the past several decades have the merits of a philosophy of physical education and sport been very much recognized. Not until the past several decades has it been very much recognized that a fully adequate account of the most fundamental nature and significance of these activities depends necessarily on a philosophic treatment of them. It is through, and only through a philosophic examination of these activities that our understanding of, and appreciation for them can be made complete. For it is only through the philosophic that the unity and ultimate significance of the more particular forms of understanding physical education and sport (like biological, psychological, sociological, and historical such forms) can be shown. It is only through such an examination that a satisfactorily intelligent and sensitive practice of them--an enlightened and compassionate action with respect to them-- can be plausibly expected.

The basic intent of this volume is to give an introductory account of the philosophy of physical education and sport as it variously and necessarily takes on the character of philosophy in general. The philosophy of physical education and sport is itself conceived here as a participant in the general domain of philosophy, and so as comprehensible only in the context of this domain. The book thereby aims at a distinctly philosophic treatment of physical education and sport, overcoming the tendency to reduce such a treatment to natural or social scientific explanations, or to dogmatic (unargued proclamations of opinion) or apologetic (unargued exhortations to believe or do something) appeals. Caution is taken throughout to assure that sufficient attention is given both to the rigors of philosophy as such, and to what these rigors here make their object of inquiry, physical education and sport. Only in this way can we be said to be talking about the philosophy of physical education and sport in the best and most instructive sense.

In working out the detail of this intent, the text argues from general to particular insight, from philosophic matters in general, to philosophic matters with respect to physical education and sport in particular. As such, it begins with an examination of the nature, significance, and method of philosophy, and the major philosophic concepts and issues. These discussions systematically provide the general foundations for what follows. From these, it passes to an account of the concepts and issues of the philosophy of physical education and sport. This account shows the historical development and the basic character of the discipline with respect to concepts and issues, as well as catalogs and abstracts the most accomplished contributions to its essay and dissertation literature concerning concepts and issues. The text then turns to a somewhat less direct, but nonetheless helpful treatment of the major philosophic systems, periods, and figures, and their implications for physical education and sport. As in the case of the earlier account of the concepts and issues of the philosophy of physical education and sport, a discussion of the most prominent essay and dissertation contributions to the literature concerning such implications is included. The volume concludes with some reflections on consensus which effectively attempt to demonstrate the unity of the disparate insights which have gone before.

In this way the general philosophic ground of matters pertaining to the philosophy of physical education and sport in particular, is made systematically and "comprehensively" explicit throughout. Given the basic intent of the volume, this "making" is thought preferable to its major alternative, which would have such ground flowing tacitly into and out of the discussion without explicit attention, and so perniciously without sufficient notice or defense. The insights of the philosophy of physical education and sport are thereby presented within the full context of their general philosophic residence, and not as fragmented bits of knowledge isolated from this context. The text is, in fact, organized around this "logical necessity", which is importantly taken to coincide with psychological and pedagogical exigency.

The essay, dissertation, and book contributions to the literature concerning the philosophy of physical education and sport which have been selected for review in the body and in the appendices of the volume were not unproblematically chosen, nor were they in every case unproblematically classified. The works which have not come in for review (but which have been nevertheless included in the Bibliography, which itself includes a fairly exhaustive listing of the literature) are simply too impressive, and the works which have been reviewed are simply too diverse and complex for this to have been otherwise. I consider the works which have been selected for review the most genuinely philosophic, elegant, and instructive pieces in the English literature concerning the philosophy of physical education and sport. An incisive discussion of the other-than-English literature can be found in Hans Lenk's Leistungssport: Ideologie oder Mythos? In any case the systematic overview of the works discussed here ought to show the terms of the discipline's development, to demonstrate how far the discipline has progressed (to reveal the current status of the discipline), and to propose what is yet to be done in it (to suggest "all" foreseeable, viable alternatives for its development). And this, in turn, furnishes a spirit of complete inquiry with respect to it, and unveils its merits.

The critical appraisals implied by the selections themselves aside, no critical commentary on the pieces selected is attempted. Nor is such a commentary very much evident in other parts of the book. For, insofar as feasible, it has been written with an intended dispassion; preferring to inform with respect to major alternatives, instead of persuading or indoctrinating to a particular position. This latter would come to an account of one's own view or that of another, and it is my intent here to record what has been formally said by "all" who have given thoughtful and accomplished consideration to the philosophy of physical education and sport. This dispassion allows the beginning student and his professor an integrity and independence of mind so crucial to the development of both, and to the responsible dischange of professorial obligation at this level of instruction--an integrity and an independence frequently denied by less impartial accounts. This is not to advocate that particular allegiances should not be worked toward, and in the end embraced. It is simply to say that it will not be the task of this book to determine what is to be embraced, but rather to reveal the various bases on which such judgments are thoughtfully made.

The works from the literature concerning the philosophy of physical education and sport which are reviewed here are put in the form of abstracts because the literature is not sufficiently well developed to discuss them as profitably in such as a bibliographic essay, or in other less formal and more continuous forms of exposition. In places this makes the book read more like an anthology than an original textbook. This arrangement does, however, systematically get out all of the major issues talked about in the literature, and it provides a concise guide and supplement to a reading of the literature itself. It is also worth saying that this arrangement is not to be thought a suitable substitute for such a reading. A further discussion of the way this literature is to be read, or the instructional uses to which it may be best put is the subject of Appendix B. Appendix C and Appendix D are devoted to abstracts of the major book contributions to the literature concerning the philosophy of physical education and sport, as distinct from the essay and dissertation works referred to in the volume's corpus. These contributions aim at such a wide and diverse comprehension that they cut across the distinctions necessarily preserved in the corpus--some of them consider most all of these distinctions in some degree--and are, therefore, presented separately. Though, of course, they illumine the same issues as do the essays and dissertations, and can be profitably read in some sense with them. Appendix B is again helpful in suggesting the order of such a reading.

The historical significance (which carries with it an important substantive significance as well) of the book resides in its bringing to a close the period of philosophic reflection concerning physical education and sport began by such as Elwood Craig Davis' The Philosophic Process in Physical Education and Earle F. Zeigler's Philosophical Foundations for Physical, Health, and Recreation Education. These works, among the earliest, most accomplished, and most characteristic of their kind, were the first to systematically propose the terms in which an authentically philosophic treatment of physical education and sport is possible and desirable, and the first to synthesize and marshal the prior literature to this end. The period inaugurated by these works thus summed the contributions of an earlier, more primitive inclination, and provided the ground for a further, and yet more, sophisticated development. This latter was set in earnest motion by Howard S. Slusher's Man, Sport and Existence: A Critical Analysis. Though much of the creative spirit of the Slusher piece has gotten itself worked out in some detail in recent years--in fact, the pieces abstracted here are thought the most accomplished products of these workings out--the temperament of the earlier tendency is yet very much in evidence. It is my hope that this volume will bring that temperament substantially to an end, not by extinguishing, so much as by fulfilling it. In this way it can best be thought as completing a foundation for more purely creative efforts; and so, as basically preliminary and transitional.

At bottom this book is about sport. Its interest in such as the body, rules, movement, play, recreation, exercise, dance, and physical education (insofar as these are distinct from sport) extends only so far as these are directly instructive with respect to sport itself. The most helpful of the less direct accounts are cited as references in the pieces of direct appeal. The book's title nonetheless includes fashionable mention of physical education as well. This is in keeping with its preliminary significance, and in recognition of the fact that the development of the philosophy of sport has been intimately connected with the development of philosophic thought concerning physical education. The two have in effect grown up together: if one chooses to talk about this growing up, philosophic discussion about sport cannot plausibly avoid such discussion about physical education as well. The former first appeared as a part of the latter, and has only very recently matured to creative independence, whereby the matter of physical education is recognized as an instance of sport. In an inversion of the earlier view, then, the philosophy of physical education is now best understood as an instance of the philosophy of sport. The basic outline of this notion is argued in Appendix A.

Moreover, the book is as much a reference as an introductory text, but this is typically so of texts which give overview intrepretations of a discipline's basic character and organization. Simply put, this is where one must begin, if making a beginning at all; and this is that to which one must return in renewing an acquaintance with basic precepts after a beginning has been made. It is further the case that few uninitiated readers are likely to profit much from an unaided reading of the book. A fully satisfactory understanding may well wait upon the interpretive assistance of one already familiar with the subject. The book can, therefore, be both taught from and taught with. In any case no introductory textbook of merit fails to provoke the sorts of insight which invite such assistance. Otherwise it would simply not be provocative with respect to the elaborated whole it sketches, or it would be other than introductory.

The most deeply hoped for effect of the book is that it will fashion the sort of intelligence, which grows inexorably into the sort of appreciation, which will, in turn, make the sort of difference in our thought about, and practice of physical education and sport, that this thought and practice so much need at present. This is tantamount to hoping that the attractions of philosophic inquiry in general, and philosophic inquiry with respect to physical education and sport in particular, have been made aptly conspicuous; and that, these attractions will serve as an exhortation to move in the direction of a serious and thoughtful formulation of one's own philosophic vision. The book has been written with the conviction that the promise of a distinctly human fulfillment of physical education and sport depends on an authentic philosophic interpretation of them; and that, through such an interpretation the philosophy of physical education and sport takes its rightful place beside the other departmental philosophies, and beside the other sub-disciplinary aspects of physical education and sport studies.

Robert G. Osterhoudt

Tempe, Arizona
February 14, 1977

CHAPTER I

THE NATURE, SIGNIFICANCE, AND METHOD
OF PHILOSOPHY

The difficulty in determining the nature of philosophy

The formulation of a satisfactory formal definition of philosophy is not easily achieved. The greatest barriers to such a definition reside in the humanistic character of philosophic thought--a character which it shares most fully and importantly with the arts. That is to say, the humanistic reaches of such as philosophy are never other than the expression of uniquely individual personalities, formed as they inevitably are by the vagaries of individual and cultural experience. Philosophic thinking and writing always occur in the circumstance of peculiar individual and cultural conditions. Philosophy is, as it were, invariably shaped, or at least very much influenced by such peculiarities. All philosophy is, therefore, in some measure (though, of course, not totally, nor even primarily as it turns out) autobiographico-culturally specific. One would expect in such circumstance to have as many philosophies as individual philosophers. While this is so in one sense, and this is the sense by which obtaining a general conception of philosophy is made difficult, it is not so in another and more important sense, as will be shown presently. It is this latter sense being the most predominant which allows for a satisfactory general conception of philosophy at all.

The inherent diversity and complexity of philosophy further confound an attempt to characterize it. The widely general perspective of philosophy accounts for much of this. Both its diversity and complexity stem from this generality and all that is included by it; namely, a study of all phenomena more particular than itself--phenomena which it is the basic function of philosophy to examine.

The origin of the term itself is neither fully revealing. 'Philosophy' derives from the classical Greek, '$\phi\iota\lambda\epsilon\iota\nu$' (philein: to treat affectionately, or to love), '$\phi\iota\lambda o\varsigma$' (philos: dear, or friend), '$\sigma o\phi\iota\alpha$' (sophia: wisdom), and '$\sigma o\phi o\varsigma$' (sophos: wise, or clever); thus, '$\phi\iota\lambda o\sigma o\phi\iota\alpha$' (philosophia: philosophy, or the love of wisdom) and '$\phi\iota\lambda o\sigma o\phi o\varsigma$' (philosophos: philosopher, or one fond of wisdom). But the meaning of this love and this wisdom is itself too imprecise and too obscure to provide the basis for erecting a satisfactory formal characterization of philosophy.

For these reasons, and other related though lesser ones, coming upon a notion of philosophy that both allows for its multiple and complex expressions, and accounts for these expressions nonetheless being instances of philosophic reflection in general, is at very least a problematic undertaking. This is not to say, however, that it is an impossible one. In any case, the successful carrying out of such an undertaking seems necessary to securing an adequate understanding of, and appreciation for philosophy generally, and, derivatively, the philosophy of physical education and sport. It is to this that the inquiry now turns.

The nature of philosophy

The intent here is to propose what philosophy is; that is, to demonstrate its essential character, or that which makes it what it is. Most fundamentally, philosophy is that humanistic discipline, that peculiarly human form of knowledge, which obtains a reflective apprehension (or informed understanding) of reality (the whole of what is) in its most general, accessible perspective (or form). The vast generality of the philosophic perspective has been variously signified as eternal, cosmic, universal, and synoptic. Philosophy is, in effect, the most general form of human understanding--the most inclusive perspective possible. It is the notions and principles by which we understand and live the most general and fundamental aspects of our lives.

It seeks to recognize in all things, however disparate and repugnant they may seem at first glance, an underlying relation to one another and ultimately to all other, or the whole of things. It sees the universal in the particular, and so accounts for the many and varied aspects of reality, not as fragmented bits and pieces, but as participants in a synthetic and organic unity of events.

Further helpful in terms of demonstrating the expansive character of the philosphic perspective is a discussion that reveals the more particular perspectives of the other archetypal, or integral disciplines--disciplines which knowledge itself necessarily presupposes. The notion of "the most inclusive perspective possible" in any case implies a relational connection (a comparative stance), as distinct from an independent and isolated status. These other disciplines show themselves in four major categories. From the most particular, repeatable, and readily verifiable, to the most general, unique, and problematically verifiable, these are: the methodological, natural scientific, social scientific, and humanistic forms of understanding. The methodologic sciences concern the means or manner by which all order of events relate. They are the formal ordering principles of reality, which conceive of reality as an empty architectonic. The most prominent of these are:

- 2 -

-<u>logic</u>: concerns the formal relations of ideas.
-<u>language</u>: concerns the formal relations of qualitative expressions.
-and, <u>mathematics</u>: concerns the formal relations of quantitative expressions.

The natural sciences concern the starkly objective character of reality. They fill the empty architectonic of the methodologic disciplines with a stark objectivity, and so conceive of reality as a mosaic of objective events. The most significant of these are:

-<u>physics</u>: concerns the structuro-mechanical character of reality.
-<u>chemistry</u>: concerns the functional, or operational character of reality.
-<u>geology</u>: concerns the physical and chemical characteristics of rocks, minerals, and land, water, and air forms.
-and, <u>biology</u>: concerns the physical and chemical characteristics of plants and animals.

The social sciences concern the conscious, objective character of reality. They endow the stark objectivity of the natural sciences with consciousness, and so conceive of reality as a conscious objectivity. These most importantly include:

-<u>psychology</u>: concerns individual animal behavior.
-<u>sociology</u>: concerns interpersonal, or group animal behavior:
   -<u>political science</u>: concerns governmental institutions.
   -<u>economics</u>: concerns institutions which produce, distribute, and consume goods and services.
   -and, <u>religion</u>: concerns institutions which reflect on, and practice a relation with divinity.
-<u>geography</u>: concerns the organization of particular events with respect to space.
-and, <u>history</u>: concerns the organization of particular events with respect to time.

And the humanities concern the self-conscious character of reality. They endow the conscious objectivity of the social sciences with self-consciousness, and so conceive of reality as a self-conscious turning of itself back onto itself. The most prominent of these are:

-<u>fine arts</u>: concern the most general order of aesthetic consciousness, or aesthetic self-consciousness:
   -<u>plastic arts</u>: architecture, sculpture, painting.
   -<u>literary arts</u>: literature, drama, poetry.

-<u>theater arts</u>: theater, opera, cinema.
-<u>movement arts</u>: dance, sport.
-and, <u>music</u>.
-and, <u>philosophy</u>: concerns the most general order of
rational consciousness, or rational self-consciousness.

Conspicuous omissions here include sub-disciplines, or more particular aspects of these "pure" forms of understanding (e.g., as in the
case of geometry's relation to mathematics); composites, or combinations of these forms (e.g., as in the case of social psychology's relation to psychology and sociology); and, education, as that discipline
concerned with explaining the teaching and learning of methodologic,
natural scientific, social scientific, and humanistic knowledge.

The progression in these characterizations is from forms of
understanding with comparatively limited perspectives of the world to
which all things appear differentiated, to those forms of understanding
with more expansive perspectives of reality to which things appear
more unified. Simply put, philosophy is the science of the sciences;
that is, it stands at the end of this progression, and is in this sense
the most general of perspectives and ultimate knowledge. It presupposes all other, more particular forms of knowledge and draws these
others into a higher unity. What demonstrates this most persuasively
is the unique capability of philosophy to explain and realize its own
fundamental nature and significance, not to mention the fundamental
nature and significance of the other, more specific disciplines. In
short, it is the only form of knowledge which turns its consciousness
back onto itself so as to reveal its own fundamental character. And
this is at one with revealing the fundamental character of all things.

It is the fullness of philosophy's generality which also signifies
its penetration to the most fundamental, accessible level of reality.
The principles from which philosophic thought is upbuilt are the most
basic principles known--the principles which underlie all knowledge,
and experience. The principles which rest at the foundation of philosophic inquiry are commonly termed first principles, postulates,
axioms, or assumptions, owing to their utterly fundamental character.
Salient examples of these principles include such as, the notion that
the experience of consciousness is sufficient to establish its existence,
that a material world exists apart from consciousness, and that events
are caused to occur as they do. It is such principles which set thought
and experience to moving--which allow it to begin at all. Like all
thinking and experiencing, philosophy cannot begin from nothing. It
takes, and needs to take some notions as given, or as self-evidently
true, as being incapable of further demonstration, for such demonstration by its nature requires the differentiation of a notion into parts by
means of which the notion itself can be explained. But in this latter
instance, the parts are shown to be more primary than that of which
they are parts, in which case the notion or principle itself falls from

- 4 -

its fundamental status. Such principles are those inherent in thought and experience; they are transparent to themselves alone, and so are directly and immediately known. Unlike all other forms of thought and experience, however, the principles which reside at the ground of philosophy are the most basic principles of all.

Though articles of faith after a fashion, these principles are not without windows; that is to say, they are not blind such articles. They may not be rightly posited in the capricious fancy of any moment or inclination whatever. Like all order of responsible idea, they too must stand the test of rigorous examination. In their case, this examination takes the form of showing what can be ultimately made of them; that is, of revealing how completely and plausibly they explain what is and ought to be (or, reality in its most general form--the whole of our thought and experience). Philosophy, then, formally commences with such principles and formally ends with a demonstration of their consequences. This goes on empirically, of course, in a process of mutual refinement between principle and consequence. In this process philosophy looks both beneath our thought and experience so as to unveil that which is presupposed by it, or that which makes such thought and experience possible, and beyond it in order to uncover its ultimate consequence. What has been constructed in this spatial metaphor is better thought of as a circular, than a linear configuration, according to which the insights, or consequences (the ultimate knowledge), to which one comes in the end are nothing more than a "full" elaboration of the first principles which are required for a beginning.

That different philosophers hold to different first principles and see the consequent working out of these principles differently cannot be in serious dispute. It is largely these differences, in fact, which account for the several alternative systems of philosophy. Chapters IV and V will consider the terms of these differences as such.

From this exploration of the nature of philosophy in which it has been said what philosophy is, the discussion gives way easily to a treatment of philosophy's significance. Here the interest is in what philosophy does, and in the benefits of its serious study; that is, in its operational characteristics. This transition occurs unstrained because philosophy's significance is an expression, a concrete working out, of its nature.

The significance of philosophy

To its serious students, philosophy bequeaths an enriched understanding of, and appreciation for the world that cannot be acquired through a study of any other discipline. While this is so, to a degree, of the other archetypal disciplines as well, it is so in the broadest and most important sense of philosophy. Again, the widely synoptic

generality of philosophy is enough to persuade one of this truth. The priceless gifts of philosophic vision and insight enlarge and enrich our thought and experience in a way unmatched by any other form of human understanding; namely, to the fullest, accessible extent. In this enlargement and enrichment, philosophy neither abandons nor opposes the arts and sciences, but sets them in the context of an all-embracing world view. Philosophy consequently functions both as an
√ extension of, and as a basis for all more specific forms of understanding and experience. The issues which it finds at its center simply exceed the scope of issue taken up by such forms. Philosophic inquiry obtains the most general and unifying of visions and insights, and is in this sense the steward of the eternal and universal.

By it, one sees the world through the eyes of some of the world's greatest genius and most creative achievement; a perception that gives an appreciation for the immense differences this genius has made, and serves in significant fashion to inform with respect to the present circumstance. This perception, which has a widely interpersonal influence, also carries with it a compelling personal appeal; in that, it has the high prospect of effecting the thoughts that one holds, the values that one endorses, and the commitments that one chooses to embrace. These enhanced understandings and appreciations also have a curious way of developing a tolerance for all order of responsible idea, even as they are opposed to our own, and a humility over the strengths and weaknesses of our own position. Philosophy gives intelligence, purpose, and direction to our activities and lives, and so leads us to the threshold of our mind and being, stirs us from our dogmatic repose, and delivers us to ourselves. It subjects unreflective and unexamined world views to scrutiny in order to show in what they are recommended and in what they are not, so as to determine in turn the wisdom of holding to them. It makes one aware of the alternative distinctions, boundaries, connections, and possibilities which are requisite to such judgments. And yet even with this, the philosophic quest is never quite finished. Each conclusion seems to give way to further refinement. It is always in any case open to such refinement, and so is always in this sense tentative. It provokes as many questions as answers, and so has its endings, as well as its beginnings, in wonder.

The search for philosophic truth virtually exhausts the reflective faculties in its quest for the fundamental and ultimate nature and significance of reality. It is not surprising, however, that an undertaking of such inherent diversity and complexity, an undertaking which reaches so "high", should be so arduous. It is nonetheless the case that, since the issues it considers are so basic to life and its fulfillment, its arduousness is insufficiently good reason to dissuade from its pursuit. Though an authentic pattern of philosophic thought comes only with great effort, and is discernible only after a prolonged and trying period of study and reflection, the fulfillment of a distinctly human life demands a devotion to it. The gift of philosophy is, therefore,

beastly in respect to what it asks of us, but is exhilarating and re-
warding in respect to what it gives us; and is in any case, "unrefus-
able". To abandon the adventure of ideas which is philosophy is tantamount to abandoning oneself, to abandoning much of what it means
to be a human being, and to fall into what can be variously called
ideology, dogma, propaganda, or truth by fiat. The particular order
of mindlessness which such an abandonment entails throws one either
into nothingness (foundationlessness), or into an unreflective and
apologetic world view, and represents the desolate alternative to philosophy.

     That philosophy has often fallen into such a tyranny of ideas
cannot be effectively denied. The misuses to which philosophy has
been put have been many. Most notable among these are some of the
irresponsible and vile socio-political and theologic uses that have
been made of it. This is to say that it has often-all-too-often been
employed in the service of ends other than searching after the true
character of reality and the most worthy principles of ethico-political
conduct and aesthetic judgment. That this is so, and is so emphatically so, is to call to mind the distinction between what will be hence-
forth called, bad philosophy, or philosophy improperly so-termed,
and true philosophy, or philosophy proper. The latter, unlike the
former, stands characteristically against the likes of capricious, in-
tolerant, parochial, uncritical, undisciplined, and uninformed masquerades for wisdom. In any case, with this, the exhortation to philosophic reflection has been put right; in that, the unfilfilling and so
unsatisfactory character of its alternative has been shown. That is,
an ignorance of philosophy leads us to a groundlessness by which life
proceeds, if it can be said to proceed much at all under such a circumstance, in darkness.

     What remains now, in this introductory treatment of the basic
character of philosophy, is to remark on the method, or way of philosophy. Such an exposition follows nicely the earlier discussions of
philosophy's nature and significance, in that it demonstrates how it is
that philosophy goes about laying claim to its insights.

The method, or way of philosophy

     Much of what has been thus far claimed implies that philosophy
is distinguished by the sorts of ideas which form it, as distinct from
the means or method by which such ideas are obtained and treated. It
has been shown that these ideas are of a uniquely general order; and
it is they, as the 'what' of philosophy, and not its 'how', which serve
to differentiate the philosophic undertaking from others. For the
methods common to philosophy are also used in varying degree by
other disciplines, and enjoy their own integrity. In short, they are
not peculiar to philosophy, and so are not much helpful, let alone

decisive, in demonstrating the basic character of philosophy itself. These methods (most notably, logic, language, and mathematics) suggest only the manner of proceeding, and are not much instructive as to the character of that with which they proceed, or that which is produced as a result of such proceeding. They are, therefore, no more peculiarly philosophic than they are the unique province of any other discipline, save their own. Even at this, however, one acknowledges that content cannot be produced without the use of a method, and that neither can a method be employed without employing it with respect to content. There is nonetheless a distinction to be noticed between method and content. The most obvious and important consequence of this distinction, at least with respect to this discussion, is that an appeal to content allows for an understanding of what philosophy is in a way in which an appeal to method does not. Though there is, therefore, no distinctly philosophic method to talk about here, there nonetheless remain some interesting and revealing things to say about the way of philosophy.

The general manner of philosophic inquiry takes the form of a systematic dialectic; that is, a carefully considered dialogue, conversation, or discourse of ideas engaged in (in the case of philosophy) for the purpose of searching after ultimate truth. As has been implied, the dialectic process itself is not peculiar to philosophy. What makes it philosophic in any significant sense whatever is its use with respect to ultimate truth, and this is a distinction that has more to do with the ideas that comprise philosophy than with the way in which these ideas are obtained and treated. Dialectic itself attempts to clarify, to distinguish, to show up possibilities, and to call attention to relationships. In the case of philosophy it effects an interminable unfolding of thought concerning the nature and significance or reality as such. It takes the form of an impassioned, albeit unappetitive love of ultimate truth.

The two principal stems of the dialectic as it operates with respect to philosophic matters are the speculative and the critical. In its speculative aspect, this general method is primarily synthetic. In this, it postulates first principles and recognizes a system of values. As such, metaphysics and axiology (both of which will be discussed in some detail in Chapter II) are the philosophic sub-disciplines conducted largely in this fashion. Conversely, in its critical aspect, dialectic is primarily analytic. In this, it separates or breaks down the products of synthetic insight. As such, epistemology and the applications of logic to philosophy (both of which will also be discussed in some detail in Chapter II) are the philosophic sub-disciplines conducted largely in this fashion. Of course, the synthetic and analytic necessarily operate together, variously and mutually expanding and refining positions in accord with the faculties inherent to each. Without the speculative, philosophy would be reduced to logic, without the critical, to poetry. Philosophy is wholly neither.

Yet more particular forms of methodologic device operate within the general context of the dialectic and its two stems. Notable philosophic examples include such as Socratic irony, the deductive logic of Aristotle, the methodologic scepticism of Augustine and Descartes, scholastic method of Abelard and Thomas, inductive method of F. Bacon, universal calculus of Leibniz, transcendental method of Kant, pragmatic method of Peirce, descriptive phenomenology of Husserl, hermeneutic phenomenology of Heidegger and Merleau-Ponty, linguistic analysis of Wittgenstein, and symbolic transformation of Cassirer. Even these distinctions, however, are more so a consequence of doctrinal differences than methodologic diversity as such. Insofar as they are relevant to this inquiry, a treatment of them has been reserved for Chapters IV and V.

From this overview treatment of the nature, significance, and method of philosophy, the discussion now goes on to a more particular accounting of the philosophic undertaking in general (and, derivatively, the philosophy of physical education and sport) by stipulating the major concepts and issues of philosophy. Since such concepts and issues are themselves specific workings out of the major philosophic sub-disciplines, they will be taken up here in the context of these sub-disciplines. It is the intent of this commentary to fashion a more complete understanding of, and appreciation for philosophy by giving a more detailed introduction to its consciousness and language, and to offer more complete preparation for the coming discourse on the philosophy of physical education and sport. Discussed here, therefore, are the major concepts and issues of the philosophic sub-disciplines (and so, collectively, philosophy itself): logic, metaphysics, epistemology, axiology, and the departmental philosophies.

CHAPTER II

THE MAJOR PHILOSOPHIC CONCEPTS AND ISSUES

Logic

Though logic is itself a discrete methodologic science, it is
commonly included in discussions concerning philosophic issues.
Much of this is owed to the great and necessary prominence of its use
in philosophy, and much to the related fact, that some of the world's
greatest philosophers are also numbered among its most accomplished logicians. Logic is used with such prominence principally because
it is so suitable to the sorts of operations that are virtually indigenous
to philosophy. To say that it is suitable, however, is not to say that
it is not itself discrete, nor that it is an aspect, or sub-discipline of
philosophy. Logic is much and appropriately used as a method by
philosophy, but it is used as well by all order of other discipline, and
is, therefore, no more philosophic than it is a feature of the other
disciplines in which it finds a prominent use. No discipline, save itself, includes it, yet all apparently presuppose it, or require it for
the progress of their own deliberations. Though not to be confused
with philosophic inquiry, then, it nonetheless has a sharp influence on,
and augments such inquiry. To recount that many eminent philosophers have also made significant contributions to the discipline of logic is not to conflate logic with philosophy, but to recognize that these
thinkers required a more adequate method with which to do their philosophy than was in their time available, and so went about developing
one.

Logic is the methodologic science which explains the means or
manner by which ideas relate one to others. It is the systematic
examination of the relation of ideas, the study of ideal method in
thought, and as such it contains the formal principles of argument.
These principles show ideas as valid or fallacious, and determine the
criteria by which such judgments can be made. The two major forms
of logical inquiry are material (major, or informal) logic and formal
(minor) logic. In its material form, logic is primarily concerned with
the content, or substance, of argument; that is, with that to which
propositions refer. And in its formal part logic examines the form of
propositions, as distinct from their content; that is, it examines how
the different kinds of proposition are constructed and how they relate.
Moreover, these forms of logical thought conduct themselves either
by induction (the formulation of generalizations from particular instances), by deduction (the drawing of inferences from general to particular cases), or by combinations of these in which the inductive and

deductive elements of argument variously and mutually refine one another.

Due to logic's tangential, albeit important, participation in philosophic thought, explicit and formal mention of it as such has been largely excluded from subsequent discussion. In any case, the major concepts and issues of philosophy proper exclude it. The problems central to philosophic reflection, and those consequently given most attention in subsequent discussion are: the form and substance of ultimate reality (studied by the philosophic sub-discipline of metaphysics), knowledge of ultimate reality (studied by the philosophic sub-discipline of epistemology), and value, or significance of ultimate reality (studied by the philosophic sub-discipline of axiology). It is to a consideration of these that the inquiry now moves.

Metaphysics

Metaphysics is that philosophic sub-discipline which examines the form and substance of ultimate reality, or the most general character and content of reality as such. This is distinguished from an investigation of reality under any particular aspect, as in the case of the more specific sciences. Metaphysics is the most general form of philosophic thought, and so tempers all other such forms. It is a knowledge of metaphysical "objects", and value with respect to these "objects", which entertain epistemology and axiology respectively. Metaphysics provides the basis of a world view and the criteria for establishing such a basis. Its three major objects of inquiry, those comprising the form and substance of ultimate reality, include: the cosmos, or universe, or nature (studied by the metaphysical sub-discipline of cosmology), existence, or humanity (studied by the metaphysical sub-discipline of ontology), and God, or divinity (studied by the metaphysical sub-discipline of theology). Also considered is the primary or dominant agent of reality among these (nature, humanity, or divinity), and the consequent relations among them. The concepts and issues of these metaphysical sub-disciplines are now taken up in the following sections.

Cosmology. Cosmology is that metaphysical sub-discipline which examines the form and substance of the cosmos, or natural world. In this, it considers the origin, development and basic character of the natural universe, and the relation of this world to the human and divine circumstance. More specificially, it concerns itself with the following major concepts or issues:

   -the nature of causality in the cosmos
   -the nature of time and space in the cosmos
   -the nature of contingency, or the conditional, and necessity, or the unconditional, in the cosmos

-the nature of evolution and creation in the cosmos
-the nature of constancy (absolutism) and change (relativ-
 ism) in the cosmos
-the nature of purpose, or design (teleology), and mechanism in the cosmos
-the agent of purpose in the cosmos
-and, the nature of quantity (the number of ultimate realities: monism, dualism, pluralism) in the cosmos.

Ontology. Ontology is that metaphysical sub-discipline which examines the form and substance of existence, or the human condition. It
proposes the formal laws, or general principles of being. As such,
it is primarily given to a study of the basic character of humankind
and its relation to the natural and divine orders. More specifically,
it considers the following major concepts or issues:

-the nature of the self--variously construed as primarily
 natural, spiritual, material, functional, social, existential, cultural, or intentional in character
-the relation of mind and body--variously conceived as:
    -different substances affecting one another (inter-
     actionism)
    -different substances not affecting one another, but
     nonetheless harmoniously accompanying one an-
     other (parallelism)
    -mind merely accompanying, but not influencing
     bodily activity (epiphenomenalism)
    -two aspects of a single substance or reality (double
     aspect theory)
    -mind as a natural evolution accompanying body
     (emergence theory)
-and, the problem of freedom--variously conceived as a
 combination of, a mediation between, or an assent to the
 following two strict theses:
    -doctrine of free will: holds that humankind is
     authentically free; that is, capable of genuine
     choice, or able to will the occurrence of particular
     events, as distinguished from alternative such
     events
    -doctrine of determinism: holds that humankind is
     not authentically free, and so not capable of genuine
     choice, as the course of its experience has been
     determined, or established, independently of its
     willing.

Theology. Theology is that metaphysical sub-discipline which examines the form and substance of God, or the divine condition. It shows
the basic character of divinity as singular (monotheism) or multiple
(polytheism), and demonstrates its relation to the natural and human

orders. The most prominent and general forms of theologic view, on which there are many variations, are:

-atheism: denies the existence of God altogether
-transcendentalism: conceives of God as the omniscient and omnipotent creator of all things, but as being utterly distinct from these creations, the natural and human worlds, as in its two major forms:
  -deism: holds that God does not intervene in the created world
  -theism: holds that God compassionately intervenes in, and sustains the created world
-pantheism: argues that God is identical with the natural and human worlds
-and, panentheism: regards God as including, but not being exhausted by the natural and human worlds.

Epistemology

Epistemology is that philosophic sub-discipline which studies knowledge in its most general form; that is to say, knowledge of ultimate reality. More specifically, it examines the origin, nature, and organization of knowledge, and as such stands in an intimate relationship with metaphysics. The general matter of knowledge cannot be, and is not very much separated from the general matter of what is known. Epistemology approaches the threshold of metaphysics in virtue of its concern with the manner in which, and the means by which ultimate reality is apprehended, and knowledge of it organized. In order to satisfy such a concern, this manner, these means, and the terms of this organization must assume the form of a consonant reflection of the realities pointed to by metaphysical discourse. The intimacy of this relation is perhaps best demonstrated by observing that thought and talk about such realities both presuppose and reflect an epistemic position. The most important epistemic issues include: the possibility and limits of knowledge, the origin and instrument of knowledge, the kinds of knowledge, and the problem of truth.

Concerning the possibility and limits of knowledge, several major alternatives suggest themselves:

-agnosticism: holds that indubitable knowledge of reality in any aspect is impossible,
-scepticism: holds that only knowledge of very limited aspects of reality is possible,
-functional knowledge: holds that only knowledge of operational experience is possible,
-and, ultimate knowledge: holds that certitude with respect to "ultimate" reality is possible.

- 13 -

In effect, these alternatives represent a progressively less restrictive order of doubt.

Concerning the origin and instrument of knowledge, the following distinctions are most instructive:

> -empiricism: maintains that knowledge is gained primarily from sense-perceptual experience, and is immediately acquired, or simply found in the agent of knowledge and thereby known by no means
> -rationalism: maintains that knowledge is gained primarily from intellectual, or rational sources, and is mediately acquired, or obtained by means of other ideas
> -intuitionism: maintains that knowledge is gained primarily from intellectual sources, and is immediately acquired
> -and, authoritarianism: maintains that knowledge is gained primarily from sense-perceptual experience, in the form of indisputable, authoritative proclamation and is mediately acquired.

Thus, empiricism and authoritarianism are of the view that the origin and primary instrument of knowledge is sense-perception, whereas rationalism and intuitionism argue that intelligence provides the source and acts as the primary instrument of knowledge. And, knowledge is immediately and passively obtained according to empiricism and intuitionism, and mediately and actively acquired for rationalism and authoritarianism.

The reference to kinds of knowledge is a reference to a posteriori and a priori knowledge. In the case of the former, ideas or propositions are obtained by experience and observation, and so follow such experience, or are posterior to it. Such ideas are empirically or authoritatively known, and may be other than they are, as in the case of colors and shapes of objects. These ideas are matters of fact, or contingent truths, and take either of two forms. They are either problematic, showing knowledge of what is capable of occurring, or assertoric, showing knowledge of what has actually occurred or is actually occurring. In the case of a priori knowledge, ideas or propositions are obtained "independently" of experience and observation, or are prior to it. That is, such ideas are known by the character of intelligence itself, and cannot be other than they are, as in the case of the distinctive features of a rhombus. These are relations of ideas, or necessary, self-evident, tautological, or apodictic truths, in that they show knowledge of what cannot be otherwise.

It is with respect to the problem of truth that epistemology approaches the domain of metaphysics most closely. Truth itself is construed as the relational compatibility of an idea or proposition with a standard of some sort which reveals the validity or invalidity of the original idea or proposition. The different theories of truth arise principally over the different standards with which the original idea or proposition is said to have a relation. The most prominent of these theories are:

-the correspondence theory of truth: maintains that truth presents itself in the relational compatibility between an idea or proposition and the material or intentional object to which it refers
-the coherence theory of truth: holds that truth reveals itself in the relational compatibility between an idea or proposition and a pre-existent system of ideas or propositions (a comprehensive world view)
-the pragmatic theory of truth (functionalism): argues that truth shows itself in the relational compatibility between an idea or proposition and its utility in the world (its problem-solving capability)
-and, the disclosure theory of truth: holds that truth presents itself in the relational compatability between an idea or proposition and that which is immediately given, revealed, or disclosed to one's thought and experience.

Axiology

Axiology is that philosophic sub-discipline which examines the value, or significance of ultimate reality. It is the general theory of value, and as such considers the nature, criteria, and metaphysical status of value. Its connections with metaphysics and epistemology are consequently intimate; in that, its concern is with the purpose of that which constitutes the metaphysico-epistemic realm.

The general nature of value is thought to take two major forms: intrinsic, or consummatory value, and extrinsic, instrumental, or contributory value. In the case of the former, that which is valued at so for its own sake; that is to say, it is valued in-and-for-itself, and so as an end-in-itself. It not only recognizes itself as a distinctive "something" (or entity), but its primary regard for itself is that which goes to distinguish itself as such. The primary regard for this entity therefore resides at its own center, is its own nature, is that which makes it what it is, and so, by this view, it is primarily self-contained and self-sustained. In the case of the latter, that which is valued is so for the sake of the external ends it produces, allows, or encourages. As such, that which is valued is not considered as an end-in-itself, but as a means to the realization of ends without itself. In this instance, the valued entity is not regarded as primarily self-contained and self-sustained, but as an instrument valued for the ends that it effects external, or accidental to its own nature.

The criteria of value has been variously conceived. Most prominent among these conceptions are: voluntarism, which holds that the fulfillment of desire is the primary criterion of value; hedonism, which argues that pleasure is such a criterion; the interest theory, for which interest is primary; the preference theory, for which preference is of principal importance; formalism, for which the form of will and reason is primary; personalism, which is of the view that the unified experience of personality provides such a criterion; evolutionism, for which the experience of edifying the species is primarily significant; and the pragmatic theory, for which the relation of "things" as means to an achieved end is of paramount importance.

Three major alternatives appear with respect to the metaphysical status of value: subjectivism, logical objectivism, and metaphysical objectivism. These attempt to define the general disposition of value in relation to the world view of which it is the axiologic part. In the doctrine of subjectivism, values are conceived as entirely dependent on human experience of them, in which case they are metaphysically independent in all other respects. In logical objectivism values are construed as logical essences; or, as persisting independently of being known and experienced. By this view, they are metaphysically independent in the sense in which they are not located in the world as such, but in a mosaic of laws or principles instead, and metaphysically dependent in the sense in which they are nonetheless located in other than a purely subjective recognition of them. And, in metaphysical objectivism, values are regarded as integral, active, and objective participants in the world (so-termed metaphysical reality), and so are as such metaphysically dependent.

Like metaphysics, axiology is further divided by its three major objects of inquiry: morality (studied by the axiologic sub-discipline of ethics), beauty (studied by the axiologic sub-discipline of aesthetics), and the common good (studied by the axiologic sub-discipline of politics). The concepts and issues of these sub-disciplinary aspects of axiology are now examined in the following sections.

Ethics. Ethics, or moral philosophy, is that axiologic sub-discipline which examines judgments of rightness and wrongness, goodness and badness, virtue and vice with respect to dispositions of actions or states of affairs. It is the study of ideal individual conduct in view of the nature of good and evil--a prescriptive, or normative, as distinct from a merely descriptive account of the principles and substance of moral obligation. Of principal importance among ethical issues are: the nature of the greatest good (the summum bonum, or end of morality), the criteria of moral conduct, the motivation of moral conduct, and the merit of life.

The greatest good is the general axiologic disposition expressed in moral terms. It is the primary axiologic focus with respect to matters moral. The criteria of moral conduct refer to the practical principles of morality, or those by which the concrete moral dimensions of life are directed. These principles are derived from the greatest good, being effectively particular expressions of it, just as the greatest good is itself derived from the primary axiologic focus, and this focus in turn from the metaphysico-epistemic system in which it is a participant. Views concerning the motivation of moral conduct are most commonly distinguished as tending either toward egoism, in which the self-interest of oneself is primary, or toward altruism, in which the self-interest of others is of primary significance. Much of ethical thought has been devoted to a conciliation of these two, in themselves, extreme theses. And, the issue as to the merit of life is usually discussed as inclining either toward,

-optimism, which argues that life, or existence, is generally good and worthy of preservation,
-pessimism, which holds that life, or existence, is generally evil and unworthy of preservation,
-or, meliorism, which withholds absolute judgment on the matter, allowing instead that the worth of life is a function of each person's regard for, and treatment of it.

Aesthetics. Aesthetics, or the philosophy of art, is that axiologic sub-discipline which examines the nature and significance of beauty and the arts. It is a prescriptive, or normative, as distinct from a merely descriptive account of the general principles of ideal form, beauty, and the beautiful, most particularly in the arts. It effectively embodies the standards of aesthetic taste, artistic judgment, and aesthetic value. Most important among the issues that it considers are:

-the metaphysical status of beauty and the arts
-the form, content, and subject matter of the arts
-the criteria of aesthetic judgment, or criticism
-the role of representation in the arts
-the role of contemplation and emotion in the arts
-the role of technique and expression in the arts
-the aesthetic process and product
-artistic media and notative form
-aesthetic intentionality
-artistic greatness
-the role of training, or education in the arts
-the role of the artist, performer, teacher, and audience in the arts
-the aesthetic experience
-the moral, social, political, didactic, and cultural significance of the arts

-and, the <u>nature of, and distinctions among the particular arts</u>: architecture, sculpture, painting, literature, drama, poetry, theater, cinema, opera, dance, and music.

<u>Politics</u>. Politics, <u>social ethics</u>, or <u>social and political philosophy</u>, is that axiologic sub-discipline which examines the moral character of social life and political, or governmental power. It concerns the nature and significance of the socio-political order, and is the study of ideal social and political organization, or the general principles of the common good (the public interest). It studies the terms in which one ought to conduct oneself in relation to social and political institutions. The most general and significant distinction in politics arises between the two most fundamental notions of the common good:

-the <u>natural law, or individualistic thesis</u>: posits the self-evidence of the common good to the individual--the common and individual goods are separable
-and, the <u>organic thesis</u>: posits the inseparability of the common good and the good of the individual--the private and public interests coalesce.

More specifically, politics considers the <u>value of society and the state</u>, the <u>origin, criteria, and locus of law and political power</u>, the <u>limits of law and political power</u>, and the <u>ends of law and political power</u>.

Departmental philosophies

With this, the analysis inherits what impresses at first glance as a paradox. The major concepts and issues of philosophy have been variously trotted out, and conspicuously absent from them are entities which have long been topics of philosophic conversation. Most notable of these are: religion, science, history, education, and physical education and sport. Such entities are examined philosophically by the so-termed departmental, or special philosophies. These philosophic sub-disciplines are, then, genuinely philosophic undertakings, but they are about aspects of reality which are not themselves inherently philosophic. That is to say, they investigate the metaphysical, epistemic, and axiologic status of such aspects, and so systematically consider the issues of these aspects until the most general and fundamental, the philosophic character of those issues is made apparent. These philosophic sub-disciplines are consequently reflective apprehensions of the nature and significance of discrete aspects of reality which are themselves incapable of turning their consciousness back onto themselves so as to unveil their own fundamental character. Such aspects devote themselves to an examination of particular phenomena, and cannot make themselves objects of their own reflection.

This meta-determination is instead and necessarily left to philosophy. These meta-determinations then provide the full foundation for, and the unity of such examinations. As earlier implied, the most important of the departmental philosophies (from among a virtually limitless potential number) are the philosophies of religion, science, history, education, and physical education and sport. A discussion of the major concerns of each follows.

Philosophy of religion. The philosophy of religion entails a philosophic investigation of the whole of the religious phenomenon--of divinity and its psycho-socio-historical implications. It examines the nature and significance of religious experience, knowledge, practice, service, and worship. As such, and insofar as it differs from theology at all, it differs in virtue of its also explaining the general psycho-socio-historical implications of theologic reflection. The major issues of the philosophy of religion most prominently include: the problem of God's existence (a central theologic concern); the relation of God and nature, and God and humanity (also a pivotal matter in theologic inquiry); the relation of religious faith to rational, or philosophic critiques of it (a major epistemic concern); and, the comparative nature and significance of world religions, or religious orders (the primary issue of the philosophy of religion itself).

Philosophy of science. The philosophy of science entails a philosophic investigation into the whole of the scientific (as distinct from, or as standing in relation to the humanistic) phenomenon. It is the systematic examination of the nature and significance of science. Its major issues most importantly include the basic character of scientific method, the fundamental nature and significance of scientific knowledge, and the limits of, and relations among the special sciences (classification of the particular sciences).

Philosophy of history. The philosophy of history entails a philosophic examination of the nature and significance of history. It is a systematic investigation into the whole of the historical phenomenon. Its most significant issues include: the fundamental character of historical method, the basic nature and significance of historical knowledge, and the relation of history to the events and ideas it apprehends.

Philosophy of education. The philosophy of education entails a philosophic examination of the nature and significance of education. It is a systematic reflection on the whole of the educational phenomenon--a reflective apprehension of educational concepts and issues on a philosophical level. Its major issues most importantly include:

> -the relationship of the educational institution to the
> psycho-social, political, economic, and religious orders
> -the fundamental character of educational method, or
> process

-the fundamental character of educational knowledge and
  skill, or product--the problem of the curriculum
-educational values, aims, objectives, and goals
-the nature, significance, and relation of teaching and
  learning
-the nature, significance, and relation of instruction and
  evaluation
-and, the nature, significance, and relation of professional and scholarly activities.

Philosophy of physical education and sport. Like the other departmental philosophies, the philosophy of physical education and sport
entails a philosophic examination of an in-itself non-philosophic aspect of reality. In its case this aspect is physical education and sport.
Such a characterization both calls attention to the genuinely philosophic perspective of the philosophy of physical education and sport, and
recounts the inherently non-philosophic disposition of physical education and sport themselves. The discipline attempts a reflective apprehension of the nature and significance of physical education and
sport; that is, it addresses itself to the metaphysical, epistemic, and
axiologic status of physical education and sport. It studies the concepts, issues, and problems of physical education and sport as such
concepts, issues, and problems are located in, serve to influence,
and are influenced by a world view. Among the more important insights implied by this is that physical education and sport cannot be
understood in a full blown and thereby altogether satisfactory sense
apart from such a study. And that, neither can reality as a whole be
adequately understood in the absence of considering physical education
and sport. The full scope and significance of this recognition will
provide the subject for much of the discussion to follow. In Chapter
III is offered a more detailed accounting of this recognition in terms
of the historical development and the major concepts and issues of the
philosophy of physical education and sport, as well as the extant literature's treatment of these issues.

CHAPTER III

THE CONCEPTS AND ISSUES OF THE PHILOSOPHY OF PHYSICAL EDUCATION AND SPORT

The historical development of the philosophy of physical education and sport

In some form physical education and sport have been a feature of most every known form of cultural life, and have had a part in every major epoch in the history of civilization. They have even significantly influenced many of these forms and periods. They did not much begin to assume their present forms, however, until the mid- to late nineteenth century. A sophisticated literature concerning them as such did not consequently begin to appear until quite recently; its being almost entirely a twentiety century phenomenon. This literature was first devoted to the physiological, then later in turn to the biomechanical, psychological, sociological, and historical perspectives of physical education and sport. The philosophy of physical education and sport is a yet more recent development, about which surprisingly little of an authentic and systematic character has been written. The volume and quality of work concerning it have steadily increased in the past fifty to sixty years, however, during which period serious work with respect to it has been going on. Much of this increase is due to the accelerating respect for, competency in, and accommodation of the best insights of philosophy generally for the purpose of enhancing our understanding of, and appreciation for physical education and sport.

The historical development of the philosophy of physical education and sport can be traced through three substantially distinct eras; here termed the primitive, formative, and creative periods. The first concentrated series of contributions appeared in the early 1920's. Prior to this time several major, and quite a number of lesser philosophic thinkers had given some attention to the likes of physical education and sport, but this attention was most commonly of a cursory and perfunctory character. During these "pre-primitive" periods philosophic reference to physical education and sport usually took the form of a commentary on the biological, military, or educational use of them, or a use of them as mere examples to demonstrate a higher insight. These references consequently never penetrated to the nature or significance of physical education and sport themselves. Most notable among the great philosophic thinkers who have nonetheless mentioned them are: Plato and Aristotle in the ancient world; St. Augustine and St. Thomas Aquinas in the medieval period; Francis Bacon, John

Locke, Jean Jacques Rousseau, and Immanuel Kant in the so-termed
modern period; Friedrich Schiller, Johann Gottlieb Fichte, George W.
F. Hegel, Johann Friedrich Herbart, Friedrich Nietzsche, Jeremy
Bentham, John Stuart Mill, and Herbert Spencer in the period of the
nineteenth century; and, Josiah Royce, Benedetto Croce, Giovanni
Gentile, Henri Bergson, Karl Jaspers, Jean-Paul Sartre, Gabriel
Marcel, Martin Buber, Maurice Merleau-Ponty, Alfred North White-
head, George Santayana, and John Dewey in the twentiety century.

The works of the 1920's referred to above inaugurated the formal and explicit study of the philosophy of physical education and
sport as such. Though in the beginning these works approached true
philosophic rigor only by faint glimpse--that is, they were commonly
unsystematic, imprecise, implicit, somewhat dogmatic, and so primitive in an unavoidable and unperjorative way--they nonetheless represent the first recognitions of a realm worthy of further reflection.
Throughout this period the literature was variously recorded in books,
theses and dissertations, and essays. The first contributions in book
form were Luther Halsey Gulick's A Philosophy of Play, 1920, and
Clark W. Hetherington's School Program in Physical Education, 1922.
Fred M. Schutte's "Objectives of Physical Education in the United
States: 1870-1929", 1930, and Richard A. Larkin's "The Influence of
John Dewey on Physical Education", 1936, were the first theses. And,
George Santayana's "Philosophy on the Bleachers" (an extraordinary
work, which is a part of this period in chronological terms only),
1894, and H. Graves' "A Philosophy of Sport", 1900, were the first
essays. The major pieces of this period were the so-termed "principles and foundations texts", which both gave the philosophy of physical
education and sport its systematic start, and importantly prepared
the way for more refined developments. These texts were taken up
with largely unargued proclamations concerning the general nature of
physical education and sport and espousals as to their most significant
use. Characteristically discussed in such books are the biological,
psychological, sociological, philosophical, educational, curricular,
methodological, and administrative foundations of physical education
and sport. Their principal concern for these foundations are found in
the terms in which they can be applied to fashioning a democratic
school program of physical education and sport. Their philosophic
inclinations were, therefore, more so an apologetic adjunct of the
philosophy of education, than an independent and scholarly examination of physical education and sport themselves. Most notable among
the many works of this type are Charles K. Brightbill's Man and Leisure: A Philosophy of Recreation, Charles C. Cowell's and Wellman
L. France's Philosophy and Principles of Physical Education, Eugen
Matthias' The Deeper Meaning of Physical Education, Charles H.
McCloy's Philosophical Bases for Physical Education, Jay B. Nash's
Physical Education: Interpretations and Objectives, Delbert
Oberteuffer's and Celeste Ulrich's Physical Education: A Textbook
of Principles for Professional Students, Jackson R. Sharman's Modern

Principles of Physical Education, Natalie M. Shepard's Foundations and Principles of Physical Education, Seward C. Staley's Sports Education: The New Curriculum in Physical Education, Agnes Wayman's A Modern Philosophy of Physical Education, and Jesse F. Williams' The Principles of Physical Education. The general character of such works was little more than compounded and repeated through the early 1960's.

With the publication of Elwood Craig Davis' The Philosophic Process in Physical Education in 1961, his Philosophies Fashion Physical Education in 1963, and Earle F. Zeigler's Philosophical Foundations for Physical, Health, and Recreation Education in 1964, however, a new era, the so-termed formative period, was begun. These works were the first of several to synthesize the contributions of the prior literature and to systematically and explicitly propose the terms in which an authentic study of philosophy generally enhances our understanding of, and appreciation for physical education and sport. They surpassed the contributions of the primitive period primarily in virtue of their having achieved a more genuinely philosophic account of physical education and sport. Davis' earliest work, now in its second edition and co-authored by Donna Mae Miller, emphasizes the character of the philosophic process, or the doing of philosophy, as it pertains to the thought and practice of physical education and sport, as distinct from focusing on the products, or wisdom of philosophy. This process is discussed as taking four reflective forms: philosophy as heritage (which provides a guide to the origin and development of human beliefs as embodied in such philosophic systems as idealism, realism, and pragmatism), action (which provides a guide to the analytic and synthetic functions of philosophy), quest (which provides a guide to fundamental values and purposes), and discovery (which provides a guide to the use of the philosophic process). The significance of these forms and their applications to the concepts and issues of physical education and sport is then shown. Davis' other mentioned piece represents the first extensive and systematic assimilation of general philosophic systems to the philosophy of physical education and sport. In this, an anthology, the essential character of aritomism, existentialism, idealism, pragmatism, and realism is discussed and the implications of each for physical education and sport proposed. And Zeigler's memorable book embodies the most comprehensive and systematic general treatment of philosophy's place in, and influence on a serious study and practice of physical education and sport yet achieved. It gives an objective account of the basic nature, tenets, problems, and history of philosophy; then develops a discussion of experimentalism, idealism, naturalism, and realism in philosophy generally, the philosophy of education, and the philosophy of physical education and sport more particularly; and follows this with a treatment of persistent problems in physical education and sport (progress, values, politics, nationalism, economics, methods of instruction, the role of administration, professional preparation, the healthy body,

physical education and recreation for women, dance, the use of leisure, and amateur, semi-professional, and professional sport) as
interpreted and resolved by the philosophic systems earlier cited.
The text concludes with an appeal for philosophic consensus, an explanation of the stages of an individual's philosophic development, and a
compelling exhortation to erect a personal, professional, and general
philosophy. Other major contributions of the formative type are abstracted in Appendix C.

The formative period was both a triumph and an end in itself,
and a transitional stage. It was the former in the sense in which it
summed the contributions of a more basic era and made a substantial
advance on them. It was the latter in terms of its having provided the
foundations for a further leap in the development of the philosophy of
physical education and sport, the so-termed creative period. Though
the bridge between the preliminary inclinations and insights of the
formative period and the advanced inclinations and insights of the
creative era has not yet been fully crossed, it is clear that a substantial progress beyond the formative has occurred. This progress begins in earnest with the 1967 publication of Howard S. Slusher's Man,
Sport and Existence: A Critical Analysis, and is dominated by comprehensive and systematic treatments concerning the nature and significance of physical education and sport, as such treatments are
located in the circumstance of a fully developed world view. The most
extensive, accomplished, and important of these treatments, here
termed the great books of the philosophy of physical education and
sport, exceed the achievements of the primitive and formative periods
(as well as others of the creative era) in both scope and quality of insight, while nonetheless remaining indebted to the achievements of
these earlier developments. Though the first of these works was originally published in the late 1930's, they did not come fully of age until
the appearance of the Slusher treatise. The five pieces which merit
this status most fully are: Eugen Herrigel's Zen in the Art of
Archery, Johan Huizinga's Homo Ludens: A Study of the Play-Element
in Culture, Eleanor Metheny's Movement and Meaning, Howard S.
Slusher's Man, Sport and Existence: A Critical Analysis, and Paul
Weiss' Sport: A Philosophic Inquriy. These are abstracted in Appendix D. Other major contributions of the creative period are variously
abstracted either elsewhere in Chapter III, or in Chapter IV or V.
The fundamentally creative achievements of this period are becoming
increasingly well accepted and prevalent. It is in any case only under
the influence of such achievement that the philosophy of physical education and sport may be plausibly expected to take its place fully beside the other departmental philosophies and the other sub-disciplinary
aspects of physical education and sport studies.

Not until very recently has there been much institutional provision for the study of the philosophy of physical education and sport.
Though professional courses pertaining in some sense to the subject

have been taught since the 1930's, and, professional organizations, symposia, and journals have given varying degrees of attention to it since the 1950's; few of these have been seriously and continuously devoted to such concerns. Most prominent of the professional organizations supporting philosophic work concerning physical education and sport in English have been:

-the American Alliance for Health, Physical Education, and Recreation, which established a History and Philosophy Section (later the Philosophical and Cultural Fuundations Area) in 1959, and which has published some philosophic-tending pieces in its Journal of Physical Education and Recreation and Research Quarterly
-Phi Epsilon Kappa, which has published some philosophic work in its The Physical Educator since the 1950's
-the National College Physical Education Association for Men and the National Association of Physical Education for College Women which have sponsored some philosophic discussions and have jointly published philosophic essays in Quest since 1963
-and, the Canadian Association for Health, Physical Education, and Recreation, which established a Committee on the Philosophy of Sport and Physical Activity in 1972.

The most important symposia giving at least partial attention to the philosophy of physical education and sport have been:

-the meeting of the AAHPER in Atlantic City, New Jersey, March, 1961, where major essays by Elwood Craig Davis ("What Direction Physical Education?"), Roger K. Burke ("Physical Education and the Philosophy of Pragmatism"), Leona Holbrook ("The Philosophy of Realism and Physical Education"), Delbert Oberteuffer ("Idealism and Its Meaning to Physical Education"), and Deobold B. Van Dalen ("Interpretive Summary of Three Philosophies") were presented
-the meeting of the NAPECW in Interlochen, Michigan, June, 1964, where important essays by Eugene F. Kaelin ("Being in the Body"), Seymour Kleinman ("The Significance of Human Movement: A Phenomenological Approach"), and Howard S. Slusher ("The Existential Function of Physical Education") were delivered
-the meeting of the NCPEAM in Portland, Oregon, December, 1970, where significant essays by Warren P. Fraleigh ("Theory and Design of Philosophic Research in Physical Education") and Seymour Kleinman ("Physical Education and Lived Movement") were read
-and, the American Association for the Advancement of Science Symposium (part of which was devoted to "Sport

and Its Participants"), Dallas, Texas, December, 1968; the Conference on Aesthetic Aspects of Sport, Salford, England, July, 1969; the International Scientific Congress of Sport, Munich, West Germany, August, 1972; the Seminar on the Aesthetics of Human Movement, Salford, England, July, 1973; and the First Canadian Congress for the Multi-Disciplinary Study of Sport and Physical Activity, Montreal, Canada, October, 1973.

The first gatherings devoted exclusively and explicitly to a study of the philosophy of physical education and sport, and which were full products of the creative period, were the Symposium on the Philosophy of Sport, Brockport, New York, February 10-12, 1972; the First Canadian Symposium on the Philosophy of Sport and Physical Activity, Windsor, Canada, May 3-4, 1972; and the Symposium on Sport and Ethics, Brockport, New York, October 26-28, 1972. Both Brockport affairs were organized and directed by Warren P. Fraleigh, and the Windsor event by P. J. Galasso. The most significant institutional event in the historical development of the discipline, however, was the founding of the Philosophic Society for the Study of Sport in Boston, Massachusetts, December 28, 1972. The Society is to promote, and to engage in a scholarly, philosophic study of sport, and to provide an ongoing channel of communication among those undertaking such a study. The principal vision for its creation came from Warren P. Fraleigh, who was assisted in the working out and implementation of that vision by P. J. Galasso, Ellen W. Gerber, James W. Keating, Francis W. Keenan, Seymour Kleinman, R. Scott Kretchmar, Hans Lenk, Robert G. Osterhoudt, Paul Weiss, and Richard M. Zaner. The first duly elected or appointed officers of the Society were: Paul Weiss, President; Warren P. Fraleigh, President-Elect; Francis W. Keenan, Secretary-Treasurer; Robert G. Osterhoudt, Editor; and Michel Bouet, R. Scott Kretchmar, Hans Lenk, and Earle F. Zeigler, Members-at-Large. Since this time, Warren P. Fraleigh and Earle F. Zeigler have served as president. The Society conducted its first annual meeting in Brockport, New York, November 1-3, 1973, and its second annual gathering in London, Canada, November 14-16, 1974. It is from these, as well as the earlier Brockport and Windsor meetings, that much of the most significant essay literature has come. Since September, 1974, the Society has also annually published the Journal of the Philosophy of Sport, the first periodical exclusively devoted to the philosophy of physical education and sport.

The basic character of the philosophy of physical education and sport

Now that the historical development of the discipline has been shown, the discourse turns to a demonstration of its basic constitution; that is, to a demonstration of the concepts and issues in which it

consists, or which define it. Such a demonstration provides the basis
for an explicit and systematic overview of it. In Chapter II the philosophy of physical education and sport was characterized as a reflective apprehension, or philosophic examination of the nature and significance of physical education and sport--as a systematic discussion of
matters important to physical education and sport until the metaphysical, epistemic, and axiologic status of such matters is revealed. The
major concepts and issues of the philosophy of physical education and
sport are:

Introductory considerations concerning the philosophy of physical education and sport:

-the nature (delimitations) of philosophic reflection concerning physical education and sport
-the attractions (significance) of philosophic reflection
concerning physical education and sport
-the method of philosophic reflection concerning physical
education and sport

The metaphysical status of physical education and sport: concerned most generally with the essential nature of physical education and sport, as this nature includes, is included by, or is
distinguished from the likes of athletics, camping, dance, exercise, game, health, health education, leisure, movement,
physical culture, physical fitness, physical training, play, outdoor education, recreation, recreation education, safety education, and work; more specifically concerned with:

-the cosmological status of physical education and sport:
concerned most generally with the relation of physical
education and sport to the cosmos, or natural world;
more specifically concerned with:

-the role of causality in physical education and sport
-the role of time and space in physical education and
sport
-the role of contingency and necessity in physical
education and sport
-the role of evolution and creation in physical education and sport
-the role of constancy and change in physical education and sport
-the role of purpose, or design, and mechanism in
physical education and sport
-the agent of purpose in physical education and sport

-the ontological status of physical education and sport: concerned most generally with the relation of physical education and sport to the human condition; more specifically concerned with:

  -the self in physical education and sport
  -the relation of mind and body in physical education and sport
  -the problem of freedom in physical education and sport

-the theologic status of physical education and sport: concerned with the relation of physical education and sport to the divine condition

The epistemic status of physical education and sport:

  -the limits of knowledge concerning physical education and sport
  -the mechanism(s) by which a knowledge of physical education and sport is obtained
  -the organization of knowledge concerning physical education and sport

The axiologic status of physical education and sport: concerned most generally with the value, significance, or purpose of physical education and sport; more specifically concerned with:

  -the ethical status of physical education and sport: concerned most generally with the form and content of moral conduct proper to physical education and sport; more specifically concerned with:

    -the greatest good in physical education and sport
    -the criteria of moral conduct in physical education and sport
    -the motivation of moral conduct in physical education and sport

  -the aesthetic status of physical education and sport: concerned most generally with the form and content of artistic judgment and judgments of beauty proper to physical education and sport; more specifically concerned with:

    -the criteria of aesthetic judgment in physical education and sport
    -the role of contemplation and emotion in physical education and sport

-the role of technique and expression in physical education and sport
-the aesthetic process and product in physical education and sport
-the medium and notative form of physical education and sport
-aesthetic intentionality and physical education and sport:

  -competition and records in physical education and sport
  -violence and deception in physical education and sport

-artistic greatness and physical education and sport
-the role of training in physical education and sport
-the role of the performer, teacher, and audience in physical education and sport
-the aesthetic experience of sport

-the socio-political status of physical education and sport: concerned most generally with the moral form and content of the social and political dimensions of physical education and sport; more specifically concerned with:

  -the relation of physical education and sport to other forms of socio-political institution
  -the general role of law, justice, and political power and organization in physical education and sport
  -physical education and sport and the common good, or public interest

The insights of these perspectives are also commonly invoked in discussions concerning particular forms of existential experience and practically grounded organizational and managerial concerns with respect to physical education and sport; largely as providing the principles and visions which govern such concerns. And, they are used as well in accounts of the historical development of a philosophic concept or issue concerning physical education and sport, and in investigations concerning the philosophic views of selected persons, groups of persons, or institutions with respect to physical education and sport. Such uses are philosophic in only a marginal, secondary, and tangential sense, however, and will not be taken up in detail here. Representative of the former use is Minnie L. Lynn's "Major Emphases in Physical Education in the United States", and typical of the latter is Dale W. Spence's "Analysis of Selected Values in Physical Education as Identified by Professional Personnel". The Lynn study is an historical recollection and descriptive interpretation of the objectives of physical education and sport from their ancient to their modern development--more so an historical than a philosophic undertaking. And the Spence study investigates the values of physical education and sport by surveying the views of several groups of physical educators on the subject--more so a sociologic than a philosophic examination.

What remains of Chapter III is devoted to an account of the extant literature's treatment of the issues cited above; that is, of the introductory considerations concerning the philosophy of physical education and sport, and the metaphysical, epistemic, and axiologic status of physical education and sport. This account will show how far the philosophy of physical education and sport has progressed--it will reveal the present status of the discipline. It will also tacitly demonstrate what yet awaits discovery in the discipline, and so furnish a spirit of complete inquiry with respect to it. These are in any case the only terms in which its present circumstance and foreseeable future possibilities can be very much talked about. The literature chosen for discussion contains the most distinctly philosophic and illuminating English treatments of concepts and issues properly studied by the philosophy of physical education and sport.

Introductory considerations

These considerations are variously concerned with the literature which examines the nature (delimitations), attractions (significance), and method of philosophic reflection with respect to physical education and sport. They are introductory in the sense in which they are metaphilosophic, or concerned with the nature, significance, and method of the philosophy of physical education and sport, as distinct from the nature and significance of physical education and sport themselves.

The nature of philosophic reflection concerning physical education and sport. Works of this type examine the scope, or substantive limits of the philosophy of physical education and sport. The most important of these are Warren P. Fraleigh's "Theory and Design of Philosophic Research in Physical Education", William A. Harper's "Philosophy of Physical Education and Sport (A Review of the Literature)", Hans Lenk's "The Philosophy of Sport", and Robert G. Osterhoudt's "A Descriptive Analysis of Research Concerning the Philosophy of Physical Education and Sport" and "A Taxonomy for Research Concerning the Philosophy of Physical Education and Sport".

Fraleigh distinguishes four types of philosophic reflection concerning physical education and sport: theory building (or the construction of original systems of thought), structural analysis (or the drawing of implications from such general systems to problems of concern to physical education and sport), phenomenology (as a way of philosophizing about physical education and sport; namely, observing the

general features of its experience), and linguistic analysis (as another
way of philosophizing about physical education and sport; namely, in-
quiring into the general features of its language). Harper provides a
brief sketch of the literature devoted to the philosophy of physical education and sport. This sketch discerns two major periods of development: the pre-1963 era dominated by unsystematic ruminations and
so conceived as a mere prologue to the significant literature, and the
post-1963 period in which some sophisticated philosophic work concerning physical education and sport has been done. The discussion
of this latter period's contributions is broken into its two major awak-
enings: the awakening of physical education to philosophy (personal
thought, and the drawing of implications from philosophic systems and
thinkers), and the awakening of physical education to its disciplinary
character (as having movement and sport as its primary objects of inquiry). Lenk classifies, describes, and critically reviews the major
contributions to the literature concerning the philosophy of physical
education and sport. He construes this literature as concerning sport
as: a medium of self-fulfillment, a spontaneous or expressive display
of creative strength and so the foundation of human life, play, an aesthetic phenomenon, ethical training, determination of social status, a
compensatory response and adjustment to the circumstance of industrial life (most importantly including a discussion of Jaspers' views),
a domain of signs, a self-preserving catharsis, a tool in the class
struggle (a means of increasing production and overcoming alienation
--most importantly including a treatment of Marx' views), and narcis-
sistic satisfaction.

Osterhoudt's first work offers a systematic and comprehensive
classification and description of research concerning the philosophy of
physical education and sport, in which the intimate relationship of this
research to developments in philosophy generally and the philosophy of
education is also shown. As in the taxonomy this research is organized as being principally concerned either directly with philosophic
concepts and issues as they pertain to physical education and sport, or
indirectly with such concepts and issues in the form of implying insights from general philosophic systems, periods, and figures for
physical education and sport. In the taxonomy itself the criteria by
which such an organizational schema is established are made explicit.
These criteria are: the categories of the schema must be of a like
order (assuring a common criterion of distinction among them), they
must be clearly distinguished each from the others (assuring their
mutual exclusion), and they must exhaust all extant and foreseeable
contributions to the literature. The taxonomy produced by these criteria is then taken to characterize the scope of the philosophy of physical education and sport.

The attractions of philosophic reflection concerning physical education
and sport. Works of this sort both demonstrate the merits of philosophic reflection concerning physical education and sport, and exhort

- 31 -

to such a reflection. The most notable of these is Earle F. Zeigler's "A True Professional Needs a Consistent Philosophy". Zeigler argues that a sufficiently consistent, and unified, as well as authentically personal view of life, education, and physical education and sport ultimately depends on the development of a general and professional philosophic position. And that, such a position, far from being antipathetic to science, is instead a necessary extension and complement of science--the position that makes our vision of reality generally and physical education and sport more particularly comprehensive.

The method of philosophic reflection concerning physical education and sport. Works of this type characterize the methodologic limits and features of the philosophy of physical education and sport. Principal among them are Drew A. Hyland's "Modes of Inquiry in Sport, Athletics, and Play", Seymour Kleinman's "Toward a Non-Theory of Sport", Frank McBride's "Toward a Non-Definition of Sport", and Robert G. Osterhoudt's "Modes of Philosophic Inquiry Concerning Sport: Some Reflections on Method". Hyland opposes the notion that there is, or can be a single correct method of inquiry for philosophic issues concerning sport, athletics, and play. He considers such a notion a vestigial excess of Cartesianism, which held that there is one method which best suits all modes of inquiry. Preferred instead is the Aristotelian heterogeneity of methodologies, according to which methods are determined by, subordinate to, and as different as the subject matter they treat.

Kleinman's essay attempts to reveal the best method of determining a general, or philosophic understanding of sport. Though of the view that a single correct theory of sport in terms of its substantial content is not possible, Kleinman argues that a single correct method of theorizing with respect to sport is discernible. Three methods are discussed:

> -formal description, by which the individually necessary and collectively sufficient conditions which distinguish sport are stipulated--regarded as a logically vain process, for it demands a "closed" concept (one not open to further modification) of something which is practiced and used as an "open" concept--after an Aristotelian motif
> -logical description, by which the similar conditions under which a term is correctly used are described-- regarded as allowing for a sufficiently open-ended conception of sport, but fashioning only a knowledge of how 'sport' is used and what it does in language--after a Wittgensteinian motif
> -and, phenomenological description, by which the intensity and gratification of the sport experience as lived are described--regarded as allowing for both a sufficiently open-ended view of sport and an account of sport's most

important aspect, its experience--after a Merleau-
Pontyan motif.

This latter method is, therefore, the most preferred. Not discussed
are the terms in which all theories, including philosophic ones, if
they are to fulfill their best expectations as theories, must be in some
measure closed (else they fail to make the distinctions that they set
out to, and fall into referring to everything in general and so to nothing in particular) and in some measure also open (else the ongoing development of human experience be left unrecognized or violated).
Neither discussed are the possible terms of unity among these three
methods, the helpful distinction between the form of a theory (the
conditions which establish its general limits) and its content (those
phenomena which variously fill these limits), nor the terms in which
phenomenological description (as here construed) comes to preferring
literary to philosophic accounts of sport.

The purpose of McBride's essay is to discourage attempts at
defining the concept of sport by showing, through reference to conventional usage, that:

-neither the intension (the criteria which determine a set)
nor the extension (the members of a set) of the concept,
sport, is concise--both are, in fact, vague
-attempts to limit concisely the intension of the concept,
sport, will either fail or end up as stipulative--for one
cannot take a concept that is as a matter of fact (a matter of language and culture) vague and make it precise by
presenting a stipulative account of it
-and, the concept, sport, is ordinarily employed in a wide
variety of ways (it has a wide variety of usages, or meanings); which is to say, it is ambiguous.

The concept, sport, is, therefore, both vague and ambiguous, and to a
a considerable extent; such that, any attempt to strictly define it is
logically vain.

And Osterhoudt shows the variety of distinctions commonly proposed in general discussions about philosophic methodology, as well as
in those concerning methodologic matters of relevance to a philosophic
study of sport. Of greatest importance are the distinction between
substantial knowledge and methodology, the general forms of methodologic device (logic, language, and mathematics), the speculative and
critical functions of philosophy, the nature of dialectic, and classical
formulations of the methodologic process.

The metaphysical status of physical education and sport

Presented here are abstracts of the most accomplished treatments of the metaphysical status of physical education and sport.
More particularly, this section considers the cosmologico-ontologic
and the theologic status of physical education and sport. Cosmological and ontological concerns are considered together because they are
not very much separated in the literature.

The cosmologico-ontologic status of physical education and sport.

Allard, Ronald J. "Sport: Tyranny of the Mind".
Allard construes human existence as consisting in the
opposition of spontaneity and control, subjectivity and objectivity, emotion and reason. The general human and
sporting circumstance is defined as a living in the tension
between these dichotomies. Primary attention is given to
the competitive-cooperative dichotomy, however, which is
seen, in its most fundamental form, as referring to the
relationship of life and death. Professional sport is conceived as predominantly competitive, or work-dominated,
and as demonstrating an external or discontinuitous relation of life and death; and amateur sport is conceived as
predominantly cooperative, or play-dominated, and as
demonstrating an intrinsic or continuitous relation of life
and death.

Broekhoff, Jan. "Physical Education and the Reification of the
Human Body".
This essay traces the Western view of the body and the
profound influence of this view on physical education from
the Greek regard for it and humankind as continuous and
unified with nature, to the medieval and modern view of it
as one among the disparate objects in the world. This
latter objectification, or reification, of the body has had
as its consequence the predominant development of geo-
metrically constructed systems of movement regimen, the
primary objective of which is either to improve the bio-
psychological structure and function of the body, or to
bring the body under fuller control of the mind. Such systems wrongly regard the body, and so in some measure
the self and nature, as utilitarian machinations--a regard
destructive of the body, self, and nature as such.

Coutts, Curtis A. "Freedom in Sport".
Coutts examines the terms in which freedom underlies
man's engagement in sport. By this account freedom takes
three principal forms in sport:

-man is free to participate in sport, or to withhold
participation; that is, a genuine entry into sport
depends on the freedom to choose participation or
its rejection, and the freedom from coercion with
respect to such participation
-man is free to accept or reject the rules which
govern the chosen sport--this is not, however, so
clear, as such rules are evidently what define
particular sports, and a voluntary acting in accord
with them what it means to participate in the sport
governed by them; thus, a free entry into sport apparently entails the free acceptance of its rules
-and, man is free from his mundane existence (most
significantly, the past and prejudice), and free for
self-fulfillment in sport; that is, he finds here the
opportunity to escape the deadening encumbrances
of the everyday, and to be himself.

This latter is the most significant sense in which man is
free in sport, for it is in this sense that the highest calling of human existence is recognized and realized in sport;
that is, the quest to know and fulfill the self. And while
this is done qualitatively away from the mundane, it is
nonetheless done in a transcendent relation with the mundane. Though the elaborate system of rules and regula-
tions which govern sport give the appearance of confine-
ment and undue restriction of freedom, then, they in
genuine actuality provide a well-bounded context in which
to express one's freedom--in which one is both liberated
from the concerns, chaos, ambiguity, and absurdity of the
everyday, and provided a unique opportunity for the location of self. To observe that there are some sports which
provide greater opportunity for the expression of freedom
than others because they have fewer, or less confining
rules--non-game sports more so than individual sports,
and individual sports more so than team sports--is not to
undermine the notion of freedom as principally a function
of one's response to, or mode of awareness within a
mosaic of objective circumstance, but to call to mind that
objective circumstance does have an influence on the
modes of awareness which occur around it, and that such
circumstance is not, therefore, altogether inconsequential
with respect to such modes. Coutts concludes that the
employ of sport as a means to external ends, as distinct
from its being an end in-and-for-itself, is at the basis of
an exploitation and misuse of it, and is empirically equivalent to a denial of freedom, self-fulfillment, and sport
itself.

Ellfeldt, Lois and Metheny, Eleanor. "Movement and Meaning: Development of a General Theory".

In this essay, Ellfeldt and Metheny propose a general theory of movement-kinesthesia as a basic human experience. This theory is developed in the form of the philosophy of symbolic transformation as first advanced by Cassirer and Langer. By this view, human movement kinesthesia is conceived as a somatic-sensory experience given significance, and potentially meaning, by the human mind's symbolic transformation of it. This transformation of somatic-sensory experience into symbolic understanding occurs in three stages or on three levels; the structural, referring to the non-discursive pattern of positional relationships (called the kinestructural level when considering kinesthetic events), the perceptual, referring to a sensory awareness of structural occurrences (called the kinesceptual level when considering kinesthetic events), and the conceptual, referring to a comparably full consciousness of structuro-perceptual occurrences (called the kinesymbolic level when considering kinesthetic events). The basic constitution of these levels and the formal links between them are not discussed.

Fraleigh, Warren P. "The Moving 'I' ".

Fraleigh demonstrates the terms in which self-knowledge, or self-fulfillment is available to participants in sport, dance, aquatics, and exercise. This demonstration is equated to showing the meaning of man as a moving being. In an authentic involvement of these activities, an individual finds an awareness of himself as at once:

-an individual (in some sense different than all others), and as having membership in the human circumstance (in some sense like all others)
-having the lived-body experience of freedom (in which the self is controlled by the exercise of one's free will) and necessity (in which the self is externally controlled or determined)
-an objective I (represented by his actions and a subjective I (represented by his intention)
-and, cooperative (in which one's so-termed opponents are treated with tenderness and conceived primarily as other subjects) and competitive (in which one's opponents are treated with violence and conceived primarily as objects to be overcome).

According to Fraleigh, authentic participants in these activities are edified and fulfilled by these apparently opposing, but nonetheless mutually reinforcing experiences.

Fraleigh, Warren P. "Some Meanings of the Human Experience of Freedom and Necessity in Sport".

In this essay the several senses in which man experiences freedom and necessity in sport, and so the conditional limits of his freedom therein are stipulated. The lived-body experience of necessity in sport is variously construed as:

- -deterministic, in which the body is regarded as a material object, subject to natural law
- -a personal condition of motor inability, by which psychomotor insufficiency invokes failure to perform motor tasks effectively
- -a personal condition of physiological inability, by which physiological insufficiency invokes failure to perform motor tasks effectively
- -and, a restriction on the choice of movements performed by self-chosen rules.

The lived-body experience of freedom in sport is variously construed as:

- -freedom from deterministic necessity, in which the appearance of ephemeral conquest over natural law is achieved
- -freedom for the realization of personal intentions, in which the ability to perform intended skills is secured
- -freedom for creating new personal intentions, in which new intentions arise from the ability to develop new skills
- -and, freedom to be unified, in which the self obtains a harmony or unification with the other than self-- an harmonious acting in accord with that which is within and that which is without self.

Harper, William A. "Human Revolt: A Phenomenological Description".

Much influenced by Camus' treatment of human revolt and Husserl's phenomenological methodology, Harper stipulates the essential structures of human revolt as instanced by sky diving experience. Human revolt is itself characterized as an authentic alternative to the inauthentic rejection of (in the form of a flight from) humanity's evident absurdity. It is effectively a confrontation of, and protest against such a rejection. And it assumes the form of keeping viable the conflict between man's desire to achieve clarity and unity in the world, and the hostile and unreasoning silence of that world with respect to this desire--of rejecting

both hope and suicide, and embracing revolt as an accentuation of the absurd, as a resolute preservation of life as
it goes on beside the irrevocable necessity of death.
Harper concludes that sky diving is particularly full of instructive experiences concerning the absurd and human
revolt.

Harper, William A. "Man Alone".
Harper demonstrates here that opportunities for obtaining
solitude in sport provide a rich resource for seizing an
awareness of one's own unique existence. He laments the
inauthentic state in which contemporary man finds himself.
Making use of Heidegger's "I-they", Marcel's "official
dossier", and Sartre's "good faith-bad faith", Harper
characterizes this state as one in which the "I" has given
way to the "they"; in which the private, unique, and personal have been swallowed up by the public, the anonymous,
and the average; in which the substance of individuals is
understood to have been exhausted by reference to the collection of empirical qualities ascribed to them; and in
which the objective character, instead of the subjective
center of oneself, is taken as representing one's essential
nature. All of this sums to the extinction of man's own being, his uniquely subjective existence. Equating the authentic with the individual and the subjective as he has,
Harper next moves to demonstrate that man can climb out
of his present debilitation only through the cultivation of a
solitary circumstance, as only in such a condition is he a
unity within himself and away from the public determina-
ations. Moreover, sport provides a particularly viable
medium for transcending the deception characteristic of
the everyday, and for recognizing and fulfilling oneself as
a unique, subjective individual. For, in sport one is com-
pelled to accept as utterly personal the freely assumed responsibility for one's performance.

Harper, William A. "Taking and Giving in Sport".
In this essay, the essential nature, or mystery of sport is
revealed by the character of, and relationship between
taking and giving as they occur in sport. Sport is itself
conceived as a distinctly human endeavor grounded in the
discrete but compatibly related experiences of taking and
giving. The experience of taking is further distinguished
in terms of taking-as-doing, taking-as-appropriating, and
taking-as-controlling. In sport, the experience of taking is
more significant than that which is taken. Thus, taking is
significant in virtue of its being a human action or experience of doing, appropriating, or controlling and not in
virtue of its leading to the ownership or possession of

something or someone. The impulse to taking is, therefore, further construed as a desire for power—a will to power over things, others, and self—which commonly results in the sort of embittered partisanship that has become increasingly prominent in sport. Moreover, since the doing, appropriating, and controlling of things or persons are observable acts, the taking aspect of sport is regarded as its public part. Conversely, giving is conceived as a presupposition of taking, as the fundamental complement of taking, and as the private aspect of sport. It is the giving of oneself to sport in the form of freely participating in it. It is that which constitutes one's entry into sport somewhat as the experience of taking constitutes that which is done in sport once entered. This experience of giving in sport is further explained as a form of the human ambition for self-knowledge, or self-realization through activity which requires a symbiotic participation of both the bodily and the intellectual faculties; a form of experience which functions then as the private correlate of taking in sport which has been explained in turn as an expression of the human predilection for power.

Herman, Daniel J. "Mechanism and the Athlete".
This essay traces modern mechanistic tendencies from the physics and mathematics of Descartes to the operant behaviorism of Skinner. That is to say, it follows the development of these tendencies from their expression in the natural, into their expression in the social sciences. Herman holds that the allegiance of these tendencies to the causal principle, and so their rejection of mentalisic, internal, and immeasurable explanations, says much too little of human freedom, self-realization, and the whole of human values. He, therefore, argues against the mechanistic demon, and for a more complete expression of human freedom in, and a less instrumental regard for human life generally, physical education and sport more particularly.

Hyland, Drew A. "Athletic Angst: Reflections on the Philosophical Relevance of Play".
Examined here is the relevance of athletic games to an understanding of man. Hyland uses existential phenomenology, specifically of the sort which Heidegger employs in Being and Time, to reveal the meaning of athletics for human existence. Discussed with respect to the athletic experience are:

-space, not as objective location in the world, but as lived expanse

-time, not as an objective medium, but as lived
possibility
-the ready-to-hand character of athletic equipment,
by which a sensitive intimacy with such equipment
is realized
-Being-towards-death, which points to the radical
finitude of human existence as capsulized in the
limits of athletic contests--to the extraordinary
urgency about such contests which provides the
ultimate possibility of authentic being, of genuine
self-awareness
-and, alienation of self, others, and nature which is
overcome in authentic encounters of the athletic
variety.

Kaelin, Eugene F. "Being in the Body".
This essay argues that minds and bodies, no less than
theories and practices, cannot be separated from the context of direct human involvement. And that, neither are
they substances to be quantified and measured. Effectively, it eliminates the false separation of minded and bodily
activity, and shows up the polar contrast between the
natural or scientific view of the world and the existential-
phenomenological conception of it. Under the sway of
Merleau-Ponty, the natural view of the body is said to conceive of it as a purely physical entity with an objective
spatio-temporal significance only; while the existential-
phenomenological conception construes it in experiential
terms as inseparable from intellectuality, and so with a
subjective and peculiarly human significance. As such,
the phenomenological perspective is suited to enlarge the
horizons of human experience and is appropriate for use
in education and physical education and sport in a way in
which the natural perspective is not. Kaelin regards education and physical education and sport as arts themselves,
which may use technological results, but which are foremostly in pursuit of distinctly human and technologically
inaccessible values. Physical education and sport may
aspire to artistic significance by recognizing and fulfilling
their fundamentally phenomenological grounds--by progressing from their natural possibilities of instrumental
character, to their phenomenological possibilities of intrinsic appeal.

Keating, James W. "Athletics and the Pursuit of Excellence".
Proposed here is a distinction between two characteristically different ways of regarding physical recreation, called by Keating, sport and athletics, and the implications of
these ways with respect to the pursuit of excellence in such

activities. On etymologic, historical, and analytic grounds, sport is characterized as a kind of diversion, a carrying away from work, which has as its primary end fun, pleasure, and delight, and which is dominated by a spirit of moderation and generosity. It is an essentially cooperative form of activity, the prize or end of which is primarily subjective and mutually held. In it, winning is of secondary significance, and excellence is intrinsic. Conversely, athletics is conceived as a contending-for-a-prize, which has as its primary end victory in the contest, and which is dominated by an egoistic spirit. It is an essentially competitive form of activity, the prize or end of which is primarily objective and exclusively held. In it, winning is of primary importance, and excellence is extrinsic. Excellence as entailing a favorable comparison with others, a surpassing of others through victory in the contest, is, therefore, at the center of athletic endeavors.

Keating, James W. "The Heart of the Problem of Amateur Athletics".
In this, Keating again invokes his sport-athletics distinction, as well as characterizes amateurism as that inclination to participate in an activity primarily for the love of such participation, and professionalism as that inclination to participate in an activity primarily for other than its intrinsic appeal. Amateurism is then construed as properly the spirit of sport, and professionalism properly the spirit of athletics. It is further argued that the amateur-professional distinction needs to be retained in order to preserve the two characteristically different forms of expectation concerning physical recreation, and so preserve an equitable opportunity for success and fulfillment within each. The heart of the problem of amateur athletics resides in a failure to recognize these differences.

Kelly, Darlene A. "Phenomena of the Self-Experienced Body".
Examined here is the nature of the phenomenal body as it is self-experienced generally and as it is experienced in sport and dance. Much under the persuasions of Marcel and Merleau-Ponty, the body is discussed as an experience of being oneself (an experience of being a unified being), as an experience of being the completion of one's ideas, and as an experience of being in a spatio-temporal relation with external phenomena. The self-experienced body acts both as an acquirer of knowledge, and as an expressive realization of intentional consciousness and so a communicator of consciousness through observable, symbolic forms of willed movement. Among the most notable of these forms are sport and dance.

Kleinman, Seymour. "The Nature of A Self and Its Relation to An 'Other' in Sport".

With Kierkegaard, Kleinman conceives of the self, not as singularly self-constituted, but as a relationship which relates itself to its own essential self--a relationship which requires encounters with "others" (other persons and things). The sport situation appears alive with possibilities and opportunities for actualizing the self, or becoming a genuine self by relating itself to another, primarily through a sensual (as distinct from an intellectual) dialectic. Sport, virtually by its nature, commits us to a public dialectic with "other", and is as such a dynamically meaningful activity.

Kleinman, Seymour. "Physical Education and Lived Movement".

In this essay, Kleinman emphasizes the primary importance of experience in movement activity. The experience of such activity is called "lived movement", and its significance is taken to reside in its aesthetically and subjectively infectious character, and not in any objective, unlived, unexperienced nexus. Kleinman's brand of phenomenology is more so descriptive than fully philosophic, however, in that it does not show the universal categories of experience with respect to physical education and sport, so much as render the autobiographical terms of such experiences.

Kretchmar, R. Scott. "From Test to Contest: An Analysis of Two Kinds of Counterpoint in Sport".

In this essay, Kretchmar shows the ground of two very different kinds of point-counterpoint, or opposition in sport, opposition by scale (in which one phenomenon differing in degree, as on a scale of 0 to 100, is found) and opposition by cut (in which two mutually exclusive phenomena, as on opposite sides of a 0 point are present). Also demonstrated is the sense in which the latter operates as the presupposition of the former. Counterpoint by cut is taken to be the type of opposition characteristic of tests, and that by scale the type characteristic of contests. The true contraries in the test are the test and oneself, not elements of the test or the testing act--the actor constitutes the "yes," the test the "no". This counterpoint by cut provides a basis for contests in that the contesting impulse to excel another makes no sense in relation to that which is either impossible, and so invulnerable, or a foregone conclusion, and so gratiutous, but is itself independent, from competitive acts. The test's revelations, then, need not stand in relationship to the achievements of another--they are in themselves individual. The transition from test to contest is the change from human singularity to community. It is finding someone else with whom one can share a test. In it, a commitment is made by each side to excel the other--and the drive to excel is an attempt to show difference or disparity. The contraries in this polarity are the opponents themselves--the difference here is a subtle difference in degree, an opposition by scale. Opponents try to do the same thing as one another, only more so--they are essentially alike. Kretchmar also argues that success in relationship to either form of counterpoint does not assure success in the other, and that both are captivating in themselves--both have their own "sweet tension".

Kretchmar, R. Scott. "Ontological Possibilities: Sport as Play".
Demonstrated here are the possibilities of sport being play, or the intelligibility of sport being played. Play and sport are reduced to their most fundamental bases and the relation of these bases shown. The themes of freedom (from worldly concern and for self-fulfillment), intrinsicality (as the basis of play), temporality and spatiality (as suspended present and unique location), and opposition (as a cooperative assisting of, and being assisted by others in obtaining self-fulfillment) are developed in order to demonstrate that play, characteristically unlike work, is not a curtailed thrust toward specific ends, but a spontaneous expression of self. This view of play, as it culminates in the notion of opposition as an expression of self with, and not against the hindrance of so-termed opposing agents and energies, fashions a sympathetic and constructive bond among players (and sportspersons insofar as they adopt the play motif) which is not available to workers. In the case of work, other persons and the activity itself are extrinsically valued and thereby regarded primarily as empirical objects to be vanquished or used in obtaining external ends. Kretchmar concludes that one's lived experience is rarely purely playful or purely work-like, but most commonly an admixture of these--a living in the tension between these.

Kretchmar, R. Scott. "A Phenomenological Analysis of the Other in Sport".
By use of Husserl's phenomenological method, Kretchmar examines the objective and the subjective aspects of sporting experience. By this account, sport entails the notions of:

-opposition, as a being against, which uniquely demands an Other (principally a so-termed opponent,
but also commonly, teammates, officials, coaches,
and spectators), and requires the further notions of
unique spatiality, temporality, variation, and in-
compatibility

-relevant facticity, as a being located in a circumstance of purposeful movement

-and, arbitrariness, as a being engaged in a freely
chosen condition which is not essential to the preservation of life.

Kretchmar, R. Scott and Harper, William A. "Must We Have a
Rational Answer to the Question 'Why Does Man Play?'"

In this essay, the nature of man's impulse to play and his
attempts to explain this impulse are examined. Holding
that play provides the foundation of physical education and
sport, Kretchmar and Harper argue that man intuits play
as an irrational (or arational) activity--as an activity
which precedes, and so is in a sense more fundamental
than rational explanations of it. Play is such a primary
category of life that it cannot be reduced to such explanations, for it cannot be differentiated as these explanations
demand. It can only be pointed to in our experience and
not explained by reasoned argument. This view establishes
the limits of our knowledge concerning the play phenomenon, by concluding that rational accounts of play are spurious impositions on an event of irrational character. The
reality of play is primarily lived; such that, man is in
physical education and sport on grounds independent of the
practical and rational. The major significance of this insight has to do with the terms in which the general cultural
penchant for rationality covers over our primordial urge
to play; that is, it has to do with the inadvisability of
making our playing a function of our understanding of play.
The function of philosophic reflection in this, insofar as it
has a function, must be to employ its rational means for
the purpose of demonstrating the irrationality of play. An
arational phenomenon thereby becomes the object of a
rational process of inquiry, or it becomes the object of no
inquiry at all.

Meier, Klaus V. "Authenticity and Sport: A Conceptual
Analysis".

Meier here examines the possible and actual contributions
of sport participation to the development of personally
meaningful and authentic human existence and freedom.
Heidegger's and Jaspers' delineation of the existential notion of authenticity, as well as other existential elucidations

of the human condition derived from this notion (such as
death, historical determinacy, chance, suffering, struggle, conflict, guilt, communion with nature, communication with others, and solitude), are used in an analysis of
mountain climbing, skiing, surfing, and sport parachuting.
Meier concludes that a confrontation with these activities
unearths possibilities for filling life with significance, that
such a confrontation is conducive to providing an awareness of authentic modes of human existence, and so to
making man fully accessible to himself.

Meier, Klaus V. "Cartesian and Phenomenological Anthropology: The Radical Shift and Its Meaning for Sport".
This essay examines Descartes' dualistic formulation of
the mind-body problem, the terms in which this formulation gives way to the enlightenment of Merleau-Ponty's
monistic conception of man, and the meaning of the radical
shift in these two ontological structures for man's engagement in sport. Descartes' view of the body is objective--
it conceives of the body as a machine working under the
strict dictates of nature's mechanical laws. The phenomenological notion of Merleau-Ponty conceives of man as an
embodied consciousness, as a subjective "lived-body", a
body-subject--as a unity of events in dialectical relationships, and not as a mere union of disparate aspects. By
this view, man does not possess "his" body, but is his body
--he is being a body, not having one. The body is conceived as the locus of a necessary dialectic with the world,
and man himself as a being-in-the-world, and not as a
spiritual thinking substance. Merleau-Ponty's position
allows man engaged in sport to experience his full and
meaningful humanity; whereas, objective approaches are
inappropriate and inadequate to a full comprehension of the
nature of man's embodied being. Under the sway of this
position, sport releases and celebrates the subjectivity of
the participant. It permits man (through concrete inter-
mingling with the world in projects which express his
unique being) to obtain insight into his basic existence as
incarnate consciousness. In this, sport becomes a full and
meaningful human experience, and not a mere mechanical
exercise.

Meier, Klaus V. "An Existential Analysis of Play".
Meier here discusses the play phenomenon as it relates to
the existential features of the human condition. Of principal importance are the possible contributions of play to
the development and living of a personally meaningful and
authentic existence. Shown are the terms in which play

reveals the true nature of man (or restores genuine
awareness and human dignity) by transcending inauthentic
and mechanistic tendencies. Much persuaded by Merleau-
Ponty's phenomenology of the human body, Meier concludes that "through" the play experience man can reject
the world of anonymous humanity (cast off the shroud of
inauthenticity) by direct and intense interaction with others
and the world; and that the openness and awareness acquired "through" human movement, sport, and play provide insight into, are expressions of the basis of human
existence.

Metheny, Eleanor. "Only By Moving Their Bodies".
This essay demonstrates the nature and high metaphysical
status of movement. It conceives of man as a unity between a world of understanding, cognition, intellection, or
subjectivity, and a world of materiality, or objectivity.
Movement is then construed as providing the functional
link between the subjective and objective realms of human
existence. It represents the unity of man in terms of his
dual aspects. Movement thereby performs a crucial function in apprehending the whole of things--it is the singular
means by which the subjective and objective realms are
brought into an intelligible relationship. For, through
movement, the subjective is given objective content and the
objective is given subjective life. Only by bodily movement does one, therefore, discover his existence as at
once a richly punctuated subjectivity and an active objectivity.

Morgan, William J. "Sport and Temporality: An Ontological
Analysis".
The intent of this piece is to exact an ontological account
of sport in terms of its underlying temporal nature. The
notion most fundamentally advanced is that the phenomenon
of sport is rooted in a distinctive form of temporality,
what Heidegger's Being and Time calls human temporality
(by which the intrinsically and authentically human dimensions, the ontologic dimensions of man are realized) as
distinct from being rooted in the classic notion of time
called by Heidegger, world-time (which perceives, not the
internal continuity of temporal stages through which one
lives as an existential being, but focuses instead on the
notion of time as an objective succession of "nows", and
thereby throws the human condition into an ontic, an everyday, an instrumental, and so an inauthentic mode of existence). This position is constructed through discussions
of Heidegger's formulation of the Being-question,
Heidegger's interpretation of the Greeks' conception of

time as world-time, Heidegger's theory of temporality, an analysis of the temporal character of training as the pre-competitive condition of sport, and an analysis of the temporal constitution of sport proper. It concludes that the orthodox view of sport as either embellished work-time or capricious pastime--the product of a world-time conception with respect to it--obscures the fundamental temporal form and thereby the primordial ontological character of sport. If sport is to move in the arena of authentic human event, it must be conceived instead as founded in that temporal mode which allows man to express his essential humanity.

O'Neill, John. "The Spectacle of the Body".
O'Neill argues that nothing is either more expressive than the human body, or more subject to abuse and alienation than the human body. Authentic experience of the body is characterized as a necessary and prominent feature of the good life. And the body is itself regarded as the theater of our individual and social lives, as the material of all spectacles. Moreover, it is only through bodily experience, in particular through activities which significantly engage the body such as sport, that the spectacle of our humanity is observed and claimed. Sport is, in the end, conceived as the spectacular body rites of industrial man.

Paddick, Robert J. "What Makes Physical Activity Physical?"
This essay argues that, 'physical activity' is the best term to describe the focus of physical education, for it is somewhat and appropriately broader than 'sport' and suitably narrower than 'human movement'. Physical activities are conceived as activities involving bodily movements in which success is primarily dependent on these movements, which are themselves in turn valued as such. That is to say, the movements themselves have a special significance in the sense in which they do not in the likes of everyday activities and board and card games. Movements comprising physical activities are usually manifested in active games, sports, and dance because the movements in these forms are valued in this significant way. This argument is preferred over the more commonly invoked one which attempts to distinguish physical activities by contrasting them with mental activities, for the physical and mental are everywhere admixed, and the degree of each in any activity is indeterminate. Paddick concludes that the difference between physical and other activities is not in the movements but in the regard for such; and that, being a physical activity is more crucial for sport than being competitive. He even holds with respect to this latter

that competition, unlike physicality, is not absolutely
necessary to the notion of sport.

Roochnik, David L. "Play and Sport".
In this essay, Roochnik playfully examines the nature of
play and demonstrates the terms in which sport provides
man with such a marvelous place to play. Much against
fashionable notions to the contrary, Roochnik argues that
play is the very opposite of illusion, for it is a deepening
of the experience of the world; it is a stance for all aspects of life, a mode of encountering and immersing oneself in the world and not a pleasurable route away from it.
Moreover, it embodies a unique and extraordinary spatiality and temporality in virtue of its grounding itself, unlike
ordinary life events, in the present as a harmonious product of the past and vision of the future. Roochnik concludes, that this genuine mode of existence becomes most
possible with our bodies, and attributes the long and favorable association of play and sport to the realization of this
possibility.

Santayana, George. "Philosophy on the Bleachers".
It is the intent of this essay to uncover the underlying
force of athletics, the elusive force or fundamental power
of human nature by which we are drawn to athletic enthu-
siasms. Santayana argues against two fashionable views,
one of which explains the spectator's primary attraction to
athletics as a function of indolence, and the other of which
explains the primary concern of the players for athletics
in terms of the need for healthy exercise. The impulse to
athletics is instead more basic and so less conspicuous
than these. Like all other so-termed "powers of the
imagination", or fundamental forms of human activity (or
inclinations to such activity), athletics is taken to have a
deeper basis than the insubstantial character of lassitude
and the utility of exercise. It is conceived as a response
to a natural impulse, and so as existing as an end-in-and-
for-itself. As such, it shares a kind of nobility with the
likes of art, religion, and science, all of which collectively represent the basis of human life. Humanity is characterized by the inclinations to these activities and the responses that are made to them; that is, variously by the
inclinations to aestheticality which culminates most importantly in the arts, to religiosity which culminates most
importantly in religion, to intellectuality which culminates
most importantly in systems of knowledge, or science,
and to physicality which culminates most importantly in
athletics. These inclinations are presupposed by our ex-
perience--they make possible such experience. The more

particular character of athletics is shown by examining its
relationship to war, art, religion, and education. In this,
athletics is evidently regarded as a sublimation of war,
and neither as a preparation for, nor a form of it. Athletics is likened to art and religion in terms of its being a
fundamental expression of our nature, in terms of its
consequently governing our common character, and in
terms of the great aesthetic development of which it is
capable. As such, athletics is an important feature of
education--a major contributor to the full development, to
the liberal education of man. Santayana concludes by
arguing that the chief claim which athletics makes on our
respect concerns its tendency to unite vitality (or intense,
spontaneous, and joyous effort) with disinterestedness (or
selfless devotion). Though this tendency is not very much
cultivated, the possibilities which lie in this direction are
extraordinary, and form the basis of an authentically human regard for, and practice of athletics. Such a regard
and practice make athletics one of the most conspicuous
and promising rebellions against an industrial tyranny
which makes our labor servile and our play frivolous.
This tyranny inverts internal and external values, makes
us a victim of the external, makes us primarily workers,
and so leaves our best thoughts and emotions either unexpressed, or disguised as instruments and so in violation
of themselves.

Schmitz, Kenneth L. "Sport and Play: Suspension of the
Ordinary".
Play is here characterized as the form of free and extraordinary activity; that is, as being freely entered and
maintained, and a suspension of ordinary, everyday, and
natural events, and so as taking on a unique spatio-
temporal character. As such, it is further conceived as a
distinctive way of being-in-the-world, a unique mode of activity which allows man to recover his freedom. Four
varieties of play are distinguished: frolic, or spontaneous
celebration; make-believe, or creativity; sporting skills,
or informal contests; and games, or formal contests. By
this view, sport is fashioned as an extension, or form of
play which emphasizes good performance and the element
of contest. It consequently derives its essential character
and values from play, and finds its full realization much
dependent on a cultivation and promotion of the play spirit.
Schmitz then discusses three prominent abuses by which
the play-element in sport, and so sport itself, is diminish-
ed: an excessive emphasis on winning, an excessive interest in the technologic features of sport, and an excessive
acquiescence to uninformed spectator demands in sport.

Such abuses signify an alienation of sport from its play-likeness, and an alienation of the sportsperson from himself and his so-termed opponent(s).

Sheehan, Thomas J. "Sport: The Focal Point of Physical Education".

Sheehan holds that neither physical fitness, nor social character, nor movement comprise the basic focus of physical education. For, each of these excludes much that has been historically and rightly included by physical education. All of these, no less than others, are instead reducible to sport, which is, therefore, taken as the focal point of physical education, because it is the most fundamental form of activity which includes or entails all that has been properly considered by physical education. Physical education and sport science are, therefore, equated in the end.

Stone, Roselyn E. "Assumptions About the Nature of Human Movement".

Examined here are the general theories of movement advanced by François Delsarte, Émile Jaques-Dalcroze, Rudolf Laban, and Rudolf Bode. In some measure, each of these thinkers regarded movement as a medium for the expression of spirit/soul/self, the harmonization of body and mind, and the communication of the self with other, more synoptic metaphysical entities. To Delsarte is attributed the view that movement frees expressive impulses thereby bringing one into an unobstructed relationship with the Divine--movement thereby effects a unity of Mind, Life, and Spirit. For Dalcroze, movement harmonizes body and spirit so as to create individuality, which is the basis of all art. It is further construed as an idealized form of musical rhythm through which the whole of man's spatio-temporal familiarity is established. Laban's view has movement as a rhythmic relating and balancing of inner efforts to external forces--as an expressive medium by which man's highest and most fundamental inspirations are fulfilled. And for Bode, movement is regarded as an instinctive rhythm which frees the individual toward his fulfillment. Though inconclusively argued, each of these positions draws attention to the high ontological status of movement and its various forms.

Suits, Bernard. "The Elements of Sport".

It is the intent of this essay to advance the thesis that the elements of sport are essentially, if not totally, the same as the elements of game. Stipulated then are the elements

of game, those of sport, and the relation among them.
Suits distinguishes four basic elements in game-playing:

-goals, or ends, as that to be obtained by games:

-lusory goals: winning, or performing successfully against a stipulated standard (e.g.,
winning a 440 yard dash competition, or running 440 yards in 45 seconds)
-pre-lusory goals: the particular end of a
particular game (e.g., crossing the finish
line in the case of a 440 yard dash, or lying
in the jumping pit in the case of high jumping)

-means for achieving these goals, or that by which
these goals are to be achieved:

-lusory means: means which are permitted,
legal, and legitimate in the attempt to achieve
pre-lusory goals (e.g., running the entire
way about the track in an assigned lane in the
case of a 440 yard dash, or leaping over the
crossbar in the case of high jumping)
-illusory means: illicit means, or means not
permitted, legal, and legitimate in the attempt to achieve pre-lusory goals (e.g., running across the infield or in another runner's
path or lane in the case of a 440 yard dash,
or stepping around or beneath the crossbar in
the case of high jumping)

-rules which stipulate the means and ends of particular games:

-constitutive rules: that which defines or sets
out all of the conditions which must be met in
order to participate in a particular game--
they prohibit the use of most efficient in favor
of less efficient means for reaching pre-
lusory ends (as in the examples above whereby the illusory means cited are more efficient
than the lusory ones), an essential feature of
games, which is nonsensical in everyday life;
a fact which may partially explain our attraction to games
-rules of skill: insights or cues which allow
one to effectively participate in a game--
these are not essential to games, but are

usually found in them, and are in any case to be distinguished from constitutive rules

-and, lusory attitude, or the knowing acceptance of constitutive rules just so the activity made possible by such acceptance can occur--this is the attitude without which it is not possible to play a game, the attitude of game-players as such, the attitude which unifies the other elements of game-playing into a single formula which successfully states the necessary and sufficient conditions for any activity to qualify as an instance of game-playing.

Games, then, are attempts to achieve a particular state of affairs (lusory and pre-lusory ends), using only means permitted by rules (lusory means), where the rules prohibit the use of more efficient in favor of less efficient means (constitutive rules), and where such rules are accepted just because they make possible such activity (lusory attitude). They are voluntary attempts to overcome unnecessary obstacles--an absurdity in everydayness. Sport is then understood to be any instance of game which primarily involves skill (as distinct from chance) of a primarily physical (as distinct from intellectual) sort, which enjoys a wide following (historico-culturally stable and interculturally engaging), and which has achieved a certain, historico-culturally determined measure of institutional stability (that is, has gathered about it a cadre of teachers, coaches, athletes, and spectators). It is not altogether clear from this in what terms the likes of dance, nature sports, hunting and fishing, sports with self-propelled mechanical contrivances, sports involving animate non-humans, and sports between animate non-humans figure as possible content for sport. Neither discussed are the multiple pre-lusory ends (or the terms in which such ends must be repeated) of team sports in particular. Suits concludes by arguing that sport, like other prominent leisure interests, is a type of intrinsic good, or play, which gives work its derivative seriousness, as distinct from being a good which receives its purpose from work.

Sundly, Jerry A. "The Desire to Win: A Phenomenological Description".
Sundly uses Husserl's eidetic phenomenology to reveal the ontological significance of the desire to win as it is experienced in sport. The ontological structure of the desire to win is distinguished by its two interdependent aspects, the phenomenon of desire itself, and the object desired. Effectively, this structure comes to the desire to fulfill the

project of winning. The ultimate purpose of this desire is to consciously and freely give a sense of worthwhile being to one's existence. Such being takes the form of unveiling the primal structure of life as grounded in temporality, and of being-for-others and being-for-self.

Weiss, Paul. "Records and the Man".
It is the intent of this essay to offer a general discussion of the nature and significance of athletic records. These records are characterized as objective summaries or symbols of the best that man has yet done under controllable conditions and through the agency of a well trained body. They are indications of man's physical capabilities, and a medium of comparison among men of differing times and places. They are not a common attribute of sport generally, however, as there are some sports which have no records as such. Moreover, these records take a variety of forms, they are not entirely accurate, objective measures of performance, and they do not exhaustively chronicle the occurrences of a sporting event. Concerning this latter quality, Weiss observes that athletic records may be said to provide only partial evidence of what has been done. There are aspects of every sporting event which escape the grasp of measurement, for they occur in circumstances which are concrete, unique, and unrepeatable, they are subject to contingencies (they could have occurred otherwise), and they involve novelties, are affected by luck, beset by obstacles, and benefitted by opportunities. Most notable of those things which athletic records fail to indicate are the qualities requisite to establishing them. They signify what the recordman has done, but not what he is. They have abstracted significantly from the individual and so say little of him. In order to fully understand sport, then, one must go beyond the records to the man. Weiss also discusses his views concerning athletic activity and the engagement of the athlete in that activity. By this account, the athlete seeks the unification of a worthy past and a desirable future in order to attain a maximal present result through the rigorous and dedicated use of an excellent body. The athlete attempts to realize an idealized conception of himself, a view of himself at his utmost, in an objectively judged and severe public test. Participation in activity which gives the phenomenal appearance of sport for purposes of pleasure or relaxation is called inauthentic, or a playing at, and not in sport.

Fraleigh, Warren P. "On Weiss on Records and on the Significance of Athletic Records".

    Fraleigh's response to Weiss holds that it is not reason-
able to expect complete insight from the likes of athletic
records; that, like all such devices, athletic records can
only approximate the actual occurrence of events. Most
important about athletic records, however, is what an interest in keeping them tells us about humankind generally.
Their principal significance resides in their acting as
sources of symbolic meaning which are available and important to us. That is, they satisfy a common and relent-
less search for knowledge of the human condition, of
human status in the world, of self-identity. Effectively,
records in various forms provide such satisfaction by
offering a comparison between oneself, other selves, and
specified standards of performance. Fraleigh also attempts here to clarify Weiss' distinction between the ends
sought by athletes and those sought by musicians, scien-
tists, philosophers, and religious and ethical persons. He
suggests that more so like than unlike these others, the
athlete seeking to achieve the so-termed well-played game
uses his body in greater measure than these others, though
not essentially dissimilar to them; is able to articulate
what a complete and fulfilled life is, though in somewhat
different terms than these others; and is engaged in an essentially cooperative enterprise, also much like these
others. The distinction between athletes and these others,
then, is primarily one of degree, and not one of kind.

Schacht, Richard L. "On Weiss on Records, Athletic Activity
and the Athlete".

    Schacht's response to Weiss argues that it is Weiss' em-
phasis on the "results" of athletic activity, of which athletic records are an instance, which leads him astray.
According to Schacht, the primary significance of athletic
activity has to do with the terms in which it contributes to
a complete and fulfilled life; that is, with the sort of intrinsic joy and satisfaction which come to athletic participants who perform to the best of their ability. The "results" of this activity are, therefore, largely incidental to
its fundamental significance. Weiss' criteria for athletic
activity are consequently too strict, and give insufficient
attention to the intellectual requirements of athletics. In
order to properly understand the nature and significance of
athletic activity as a potentially important component of a
truly human life, one must place this activity in the full
content of what it means to be a human being generally.
Consequently, one must look not merely beyond the record
to the athlete, but beyond the athlete to the man as well.

This view has the virtue of neither dehumanizing athletic activity, nor placing it beyond the reach of all but the very young and the very talented. Concerning athletic records themselves, Schacht concludes that their imprecision, as pointed to by Weiss, is simply the well known case with respect to all historical records, and so says nothing peculiar about their athletic form.

Weiss, Paul. "Strategems and Competition".

Competition is characterized here as a struggle in which men act both with and against one another. The struggle is done with one another insofar as it is done under common, equitable conditions. It is done against one another insofar as each attempts to achieve a result that cannot be achieved by all. Also discussed are strategems and their role in sport. Strategems are construed as attempts to disadvantage an opponent by arousing or sustaining an expectation in him which one is prepared to disappoint. Weiss shows that forms of cooperation and deception improper to the conduct of ordinary events are rightly practiced in sport, for in sport they are misleading only with respect to the place that they occupy beside other equally allowable acts, and not as criminal gestures.

Wenkart, Simon. "The Meaning of Sports for Contemporary Man".

This essay examines the contemporary image of man in regard to his body, as demonstrated most particularly in sporting activity. According to Wenkart, this image develops in the context of an existential act and occurs in the form of an existential experience. An existential act is an event the fundamental constituent elements of which are unified in purpose. The existential experience is then characterized as a distinctive impression of oneness, or unity. By this view, such an experience entails the notions of freedom and intrinsically, and virtually defines authentic human existence. Sport is considered an instance of existential acts insofar as it fashions a oneness within one's body, an integration of self and medium, and an integration of self and the implements of sport by which the external world becomes an extension of one's body and self. As such, sport becomes not so much a conquest over, or a perfunctory use of oneself or others, as an expression and fulfillment of oneself--as the act of a person stepping out of his isolation into existence, into the full experience of one's being in existence.

The theologic status of physical education and sport

Morgan, William J. "An Existential Phenomenological
Analysis of Sport as a Religious Experience".
> Morgan argues that institutional forms of sport cannot be
> equated with the essential nature of sport, for such forms
> are no more than the results of extraneous responses to,
> or extrinsic capabilities of sport proper. Sport is con-
> ceived instead as an aspiration of being itself--being as
> disclosed by conscious experience, as distinct from its
> disclosure by disparate social encounter. And being is the
> fundamental interpretive principle of reality, and so, the
> source and end of all striving, including that form proper
> to sport. Morgan further holds that the true character of
> sport is best revealed and realized by cultivating the
> religious inclinations of being inherent in, and fundamental
> to sport. The religious experience of sport is then defined
> as a self-surrender to being. Also discussed are such
> familiar existential themes as absurdity, anguish, anxiety,
> asociality, boundary situation, choice, despair, emptiness,
> faith, finitude-infinitude, revolt, struggle, and transcen-
> dence as they occur in the religious experience of sport.
> The conclusions of these discussions suggest that the other
> in sport is authentically an object of love, not appropri-
> ation, and that competitive success is most constructively
> regarded as an inward triumph, an integrating and liber-
> ating experience, an opportunity to be what one is most
> fundamentally.

The synthesis of these disparate insights has to do with their
common attempt to capture the essential character of physical education and sport, or an aspect thereof. Such a synthesis shows the high
metaphysical status of physical education and sport--the high place
they enjoy in the entire scheme of things. The singular conclusion to
which all point, insofar as there is such a conclusion, persuades to a
cultivation of this essential character, to a fulfillment of it, and so to
an intrinsic regard for it.

The epistemic status of physical education and sport

Presented here are abstracts of the most accomplished treatments of the epistemic status of physical education and sport. Included are pieces which both draw attention to the intellectual dimension of physical education and show in what this dimension consists.

Brackenbury, Robert L. "Physical Education, An Intellectual Emphasis ?"

In this essay, Brackenbury shows that, though physical education is commonly thought the antithesis of intellectual pursuit, it possesses itself a significantly intellectual dimension. That is, like all meaningful events, even those of a predominantly physical sort, physical education too has much to do with intelligence, and contributes well to the centrally intellectual concerns properly outlined for education. Much of the prevailing misconception about the intellectual dimension of physical education is the consequence of a regrettable and mistaken form of philosophical dualism whereby intellectual and physical events are separated absolutely, and intellectual perspectives are understood to reign over physical ones. To take one's physicality seriously under such a view is either to fall into a form of animality or to conceive of the principal significance of physical engagements as a leading to those of an intellectual order (in which case physicality relinquishes any redeeming intellectual appeal itself). And to take one's intellectuality seriously is to sharply suppress one's enthusiasm for physical involvements. Such a conception persuades against a balanced and harmonious life, as well as against an educationally favorable view of physical education. Conversely, an organismic conception of man by which the physical is inseparable from the intellectual allows for such a life and an academically respectable view of physical education as being more than mere thoughtless movement and a means of preserving or sustaining life-- as being that in which life in part is, and that in which life in part is genuinely enriched.

Fraleigh, Warren P. "Toward a Conceptual Model of the Academic Subject Matter of Physical Education as a Discipline".

It is the intent of this essay to develop a conceptual model of what constitutes the basic perspective and substantive content of physical education as an academic discipline. The perspective is drawn from the examined phenomenon, in this case from human movement called exercise, games, sports, athletics, aquatics, gymnastics, and dance, and it is the intrinsically integrating element of the discipline, or that which defines the discipline in most fundamental terms. The key concepts, or substantive content, of the discipline then flow from, and fill up this perspective. This content consists in the use and meaning of human movement as biological development, as political, social, and economic force, as expression, as learning, and as applied mechanics.

Henry, Franklin M. "Physical Education: An Academic Discipline".

Henry demonstrates the character of physical education as an academic discipline, or an organized body of knowledge collectively embraced in a formal course of learning, and having principally theoretical and scholarly, as distinct from technical and professional significance. The traditional emphasis in physical education has been toward improving its practical, or professional aspect, however, rather than toward the development of an academic discipline. Though devoted to showing the differences between professional and disciplinary matters, Henry nonetheless recognizes their intimate connections. The practical provides the theoretical with content, and the theoretical provides the practical with form, or the principles by which it acts. The two mutually refine one another, and neither would be possible by itself. Moreover, the academic discipline of physical education does not consist of the mere application of other disciplines, but is instead the disciplinary study of certain aspects of such other disciplines as anatomy, physics, physiology, cultural anthropology, history, sociology, and psychology. Also demonstrated is the disposition of physical education as inviting the scholarly treatment of a discrete, unique, and inherent feature of human existence, which cannot be otherwise understood and appreciated. Not very much talked about, however, is the integrating force of this discipline, or the precise terms in which the organization of its knowledge is determined.

Keenan, Francis W. "The Concept of Doing".

Examined here is the Deweyan concept of doing as a general educational activity, and as an activity which operates in physical education, sport, and physical activity. Though commonly overemphasized, even under the guise of Deweyanism, in such as physical education and sport, doing is regarded by Dewey as only the initial, albeit a necessary stage of the learning process. It is the foundation on which all else is learned, but it does not contain all that is to be learned. This stage provides only experiential data and a knowledge of "how to do" things, all of which acts as a mere prelude to achieving the cognitive sorts of understandings Dewey sought foremost in the information and science stages of the curriculum. In the information stage a perceptual awareness and appreciation of the personal and social significance of human activity is obtained. And in the final or science stage, human knowledge culminates in a theoretical awareness of the continuity of human activity. By this account, then, physical education and sport

are assigned a place in the curriculum for intellectual and
social, rather than expedient reasons. Like all curricular
provisions, physical education and sport must pursue an
understanding, a refined conscious experience; they must
promote an intelligence with respect to doing, and not
merely engage in a mindless doing of things.

The axiologic status of physical education and sport

Presented here are abstracts of the most accomplished treatments of the axiologic status of physical education and sport. More
particularly this section considers the ethical, aesthetic, and socio-
political status of physical education and sport.

The ethical status of physical education and sport

Broekhoff, Jan. "Sport and Ethics in the Context of Culture".
Of principal concern here is Huizings's Homo Ludens
segregation of ethics and play, and the consequent separation of ethics and sport (conceived as a contest for
something with all of the characteristics of play).
Broekhoff holds that play in its "transition" to sport comes
to incorporate some features of the work condition, if in
only a secondary way. Despite this incorporation, however, sport (owing to its roots in play) maintains its essentially intrinsic, free, extraordinary, and non-rational
qualities. As such it also stands outside the valuations of
virtue and vice. Even the rules, or laws of sport which
determine its boundaries and the manner of conduct in it
are not construed as moral laws, but as providing the activity with a definition. Insofar as morality enters sport
at all, it enters principally through the uncertainty and
tension which comes from the emphasis that a particular
society places on the winning and losing of sporting contests. And this is more so an entry from without than
from within sport. A discussion of the ethical status of
sport, therefore, leads inexorably to an examination of the
cultural context in which it appears. The greater the emphasis on winning, the greater also is the proclivity of
players to interpret the rules in a strict, legalistic manner, and so to regard them as external sanctions, rather
than exhortations to follow the inner convictions of con-
science. That is, an excessive emphasis on the winning of
sporting events encourages the players to act merely in
accord with the rules, to act out of an inner resolve to take
even "unfair" advantage of a situation insofar as such an
act is not explicitly prohibited by the rules. In such a
circumstance, the spirit of genuine fair play, or good faith

among players is sorrowfully lacking. To consider such
rules as internal sanctions, then, is to show that ethics,
play, and sport are not in every sense separate. In any
case, Huizinga's discrimination between ethics and play is
based on the irreducible character of play and not on play
having nothing whatever to do with ethical inclinations as
such.

Delattre, Edwin J. "Some Reflections on Success and Failure
in Competitive Athletics".
This essay numbers the moments of significance in athletic games--the most satisfying moments when no tolerance for error is possible--among the range of our passionate concerns and so inviting serious philosophic
reflection. In particular, the essay considers the basic
conditions of success and failure in athletics. It holds the
that the two basic conditions of success in competitive
athletics are: 1) the mutual discovery of worthy opponents,
opponents who are capable of generating with us moments
of significance, and 2) an utter respect for the game itself;
that is, players must consider it unworthy of themselves
to deliberately break the rules of the game, and so, abuse
the opponent as means. Only in the face of such intensity
and fairness can the athlete be said to succeed or fail
genuinely. No one can be a success in competitive athletics if he fails to compete, either by avoiding worthy opposition or by cheating. Only under these conditions can
athletics become a form of self-discovery. Obtaining
these conditions entails less emphasis on winning than
commonly ascribed it. To stress victory (though important) to the point of overlooking quality of performance is
to impoverish our sense of success in athletics. This effectively represents a failure to act with respect for the
moral status of persons as ends. Success in competitive
athletics is, therefore, not reducible to winning, nor failure to losing. And satisfaction in victory is warranted
only when we have played well and fairly against a worthy
opponent. Otherwise victory is no genuine achievement at
all, and pride in it is false.

Fraleigh, Warren P. "Sport-Purpose".
It is the intent of this essay to identify some of the problems which arise when sport and purpose are discussed in
relation to one another. Cited are the great diversity of
ideas expressed with respect to this issue, the source
from which purpose is supplied for sport (existential,
metaphysical, and historical sources of purpose), and the
logical relationship between purpose and other purpose-
related terms used in the literature concerning sport

(value, intention, motive, opportunity, interest, and
attraction). Purpose itself, by this view, is historically
grounded and conceived as the reason for which a structured form of human activity exists. The purpose of sport
is to provide equitable opportunity for the mutual testing
of the relative abilities of the participants to move mass
in space and time within the confines of an agreed-upon
set of rules. As such, the purpose of sport, unlike such
as the other purpose-related terms, includes reference to
the basic character of sport itself, and cannot escape such
reference. The purpose of sport, unlike these other
terms, is, therefore, the same for all persons. The differences among persons' axiologic associations with sport
thereby arise with respect to these other concerns, and
not with respect to purpose itself.

Keating, James W. "The Ethics of Competition and Its
Relation to Some Moral Problems in Athletics".
This effort opposes the growing literature which emphasizes the negative aspects of competition, and argues instead for its positive contributions. Competition is characterized as an attempt, according to agreed upon rules,
to get or to keep any thing either to the exclusion of others
or in greater measure than others. It is further interpreted as an ineradicable trait of human nature, and one
that uniquely assists in the establishment and maintenance
of a viable social order. Also distinguished here are
playful activity, as a free and creative activity in which
the primary goal of the participants is to maximize the joy
of the moment, and in which there is no goal outside the
activity itself, and athletics, as physical contests designed
to determine human excellence through honorable victory
in a contest. These two forms of activity are radically
different in terms of their objectives, and since it is their
objectives which determine the moral attitude and conduct
proper to them, the moral attitude and conduct proper to
playful activity cannot also be suitable to athletics. By
this view, playful activity is regarded as an essentially cooperative venture in which the participants seek a mutually
obtainable goal, and which is dominated consequently by a
spirit of generosity and magnanimity. And athletics is
conceived as an essentially competitive undertaking in
which the participants seek a mutually exclusive goal, and
which is dominated consequently by a legalistic and antag-
onistic spirit. Keating concludes that the moral problems
in athletics are largely the result of its highly competitive
nature, the excessive desire for victory encouraged by
that nature, and the improper application of playful expectations to it. Since formal responses to this essay by

Osterhoudt and Sadler focus on its socio-political implications, abstracts of these have been placed in the section of this chapter devoted to the socio-political status of physical education and sport.

Keating, James W. "Sportsmanship as a Moral Category". The intent of this essay is to establish the moral relevancy of sportsmanship by showing that it is neither an all-embracing moral category applying equally to all activities, nor a strict legislative code which merely curtails criminal activities. That is, it is neither indistinct as the first notion implies, nor is it exhausted by a negative signification as is suggested by the second. The fundamental source of confusion over the proper nature and function of sportsmanship concerns the diverse objects, or types of event to which it is applied. This observation then leads to Keating's well known distinction between sport and athletics. On etymologic and other empirical grounds, sport is taken to mean a carrying away from work or a diversion. As such, it has for its end fun, pleasure, and delight, and it is dominated by a spirit of moderation and generosity. Its end is, therefore, subjectively held and mutually obtainable, it is essentially cooperative, in it winning is secondary, excellence is intrinsic, and the spirit of amateurism prevails. This is not to claim that sport is frivolous, capricious, or aimless, a form of activity without constraint and seriousness as some have thought. For it is the serious and arduous standing in viable relation to difficult-to-achieve goals which provides the source of sporting joy, pleasure, and delight. Conversely, athletics is construed as a contending for an objectively held and mutually exclusive prize. It is an essentially competitive activity, in it winning is primary, excellence is extrinsic, and the spirit of professionalism prevails. Sportsmanship is then conceived as conduct and attitude proper to the sportsperson as such. The basic maxim of sportsmanship, therefore, becomes an acting so as to increase the mutual pleasure found in the activity. Misconceptions of sportsmanship are principally the consequence of applying it to types of activity which are not primarily devoted to the mutual satisfaction of pleasure; most notably, to athletics. In its application to the likes of athletics, it acts as a purely legal, as distinct from a fully moral code, and so merely places basic limitations on the rigors of competition—it civilizes athletics and acknowledges human worth and dignity in it. That such limitations are important is not seriously doubted, that they take on a negative signification when the product of sportsmanship's influence is equally apparent.

Pearson, Kathleen M. "Deception, Sportsmanship, and Ethics".

In this essay, Pearson holds that the primary purpose of athletics is to test the skill of one or several individuals against that of another or several other individuals in order to determine the most skillful performer in a well defined activity. Examined within the context of this purpose is a matter of central importance to athletics, deception. Two types of deception in athletics are distinguished, strategic deception and definitional deception. Strategic deception entails the overt deceit of an opponent by encouraging an anticipation of an action which one is prepared to disappoint. The ability to deceive in this way is a major feature of the skill factor in many sports, and as such it significantly augments the purpose of athletic events and so remains altogether within the spirit and rules which define them. This type of deception is very much different than definitional deception. In this, one contracts to participate in one form of activity (as defined by its rules) while deliberately engaging in another. Deliberate fouls, not accidental ones, are instances of such deceit, for they are designed by a free willing participant in an activity to deliberately interfere with the purpose of that activity. These are instances of an active subversion of the rules, and so violations of the basic character of the game, and the game itself. Deception of this sort is thereby unethical and unsportsmanlike, and something to be condemned.

Roberts, Terence J. and Galasso, P. J. "The Fiction of Morally Indifferent Acts in Sport".

It is the intent of this piece to demonstrate that there is no aspect of man's voluntary, conscious, and responsible activity which is not morally endowed. That is, there are no such acts/actions which are morally neutral. And in the more particular case of sport, they argue that such acts/actions are necessarily moral. According to this account, an act/action is any activity or performance which is both voluntarily engaged and consciously deliberated. Also implied by such engagement and deliberation are intention and, therefore, rationality and responsibility. Such acts/actions may be ascribed only to humankind, then, as only man performs from a conception of law and not merely out of a response to natural requirement. This notion which conceives af all acts/actions as either morally right or wrong, and thereby never morally neutral, distinguishes the rational activity of moral intention and conduct from mere bodily movements or other phenomena which occur by empirical fiat. Roberts and Galasso further assert that there are many instances of such acts/ actions in sport, and that a recognition of them as such may promote a more fully and persistently moral disposition with respect to our sporting experience.

Suits, Bernard. "The Grasshopper; A Thesis Concerning the Moral Ideal of Man".

Suits argues here that activities commonly termed work (activities which are only instrumentally valuable to those who engage in them) are self-contradictory in principle, as their formal end is self-extinction. A life of play (activities which are intrinsically valuable to those who engage in them) is consequently conceived as the only justification for work, for it is principally the opportunity to play that work attempts to secure. It is a state of "idleness", or a being at play, that man seeks foremost. It is an acting in accord with this Grasshopperian ideal which is most worthy of human allegiance, for it is by its nature the form of ideal that authentically fulfills. Moreover, game-playing (as an attempt to achieve a specific state of affairs, using only means permitted by rules, where the rules prohibit more efficient in favor of less efficient means, and where such rules are accepted just because they make possible such activity) is construed as the purest form of playful activity. It is regarded as the essential constituent of the moral ideal of man--as that "thing(s)", the only justification for which is that it justifies all else. By this account, then, it is game-playing which makes Utopia intelligible, and which offers the non-Utopian world the salvation of insight into a better order. Despite all of this, however, Suits observes that virtually everyone alive is engaged in the playing of elaborate games, while at the same moment believing themselves to be going about their ordinary affairs. Most are not, therefore, game-players, but think life worth the requisite effort to preserve it, if, and only if, they believe themselves engaged in something "useful". The moral ideal of man thereby recedes into the background, obscured and covered over as it is by its opposite, and remains unexpressed, let alone unfulfilled.

The aesthetic status of physical education and sport

Best, David. "The Aesthetic in Sport".

It is the intent of this essay to sketch the logical relationship between sport and the aesthetic. The aesthetic is itself conceived as a way of perceiving objects or activities, as, therefore, not being a constituent feature of objects or

activities, and as consequently and potentially referring
to aspects of all objects or activities including sport.
Some objects and activities are of more central aesthetic
interest than others, however. Works of art are, perhaps, the most important of these. The fundamental condition for such works is their intrinsicality, or non-
purposiveness; that is to say, the terms in which they are
valued in and for themselves, or the terms in which their
means and ends coalesce. Best distinguishes two types of
sport with respect to this condition, purposive and aesthetic sports. Most sports are purposive, or primarily
directed toward the achievement of external ends, largely
scoring or winning. This type of sporting activity violates
the fundamental condition for art in that its end can be
specified independently of the manner of achieving it.
There are other sports, however, so-termed aesthetic
sports, whose aim cannot be separated from the aesthetic.
Most notable of these are diving, figure skating, and gymnastics. Even in these cases, however, owing to the
persistently objective end of sport, a separation between
means and ends remains. These sports thereby also fail
to meet the necessary condition for art. In these sports,
unlike in art, the performer neither has an opportunity to
express his view of the human circumstance. Best, therefore, concludes that, though most sports are superb aesthetically (they contain and present pleasing patterns of
movement), they are not art. Also proposed is the view
that a totally concise direction towards the functional end
of sporting activity is a requirement for maximum aesthetic satisfaction with respect to such activity. And that,
aesthetic preferences are expressed on these functional
grounds, as evidenced by the preference for running over
race walking, and the preference for flowing, or ballistic
movements as distinct from moving fixations.

Elliott, R. K. "Aesthetics and Sport".
This essay recognizes skill (as expressed in the forms of
swiftness, grace, fluency, rhythm, and vitality) and
dramatic quality as aesthetic features of sport. It does
not, however, conflate sport with drama itself--sport is
not an imitation of life in the same way that drama is
understood to be--nor with any other kind of spectacle
(such as the circus), nor for that matter with art or with
the sort of beauty characteristic of art. The beauty of
sport is more like the beauty of nature than it is like that
of art--it is more so sublime, as being a triumph of the
spirit over great hindrances, than aesthetic in an artistic
way. For every athletic act is primarily for the sake of
victory, and if for beauty at all, only secondarily and

incidentally so. In art, conversely, beauty is aimed at as the primary end.

Fisher, Marjorie. "Sport as an Aesthetic Experience".
Sport is here characterized as an art form, or aesthetic situation, which, like other such forms, has three aspects, the spectator, artist (athlete), and work of art (sport itself). Sport is said to be the object of the spectator's and athlete's devotions, the athlete is said to be the creator of this object, and the spectator is thought an objective observer of this creation. The thought of Martin Buber provides the basis for the aesthetic view here "applied" to sport. Accordingly, an aesthetic experience is construed to entail an I-Thou, or sympathetic subject-subject relation between oneself and one's medium, no pretense of knowing or possessing, a purposive but non-utilitarian act, a universal sensibility outside ordinary temporal constraints, an expression of pure possibility or spontaneity, and a constitution of wholeness and harmony. Fisher concludes in view of this that sport provides an extraordinarily rich source for aesthetic experience, most particularly in the form of the actions or movements of individuals, bounded actions or events within a game, and the whole game itself.

Gaskin, Geoffrey and Masterson, Don W. "The Work of Art in Sport".
In this essay, both sport and art are said to primarily entail the resolution of problems intrinsic to unique media in search of an aesthetic ideal. Both are also thought wholes which exceed the sum of their parts, and similarly disposed with respect to self-fulfillment, beauty, form, composition, rhythm, color, harmony, audience-performer relationship, and content. This leads Gaskin and Masterson to the conclusion that certain sports performances may be considered works of art, and so that sport qualifies as a medium in which works of art are occasionally produced.

Kaelin, Eugene F. "The Well-Played Game: Notes Toward an Aesthetics of Sport".
It is the intent of this essay to present a phenomenological reading of the essence of sporting aesthetics--to grasp the distinctly sporting and the distinctly aesthetic in the nature of several sports as viewed by the sensitive spectator. Kaelin explains the increasing popularity of football and the declining enthusiasm for baseball on aesthetic grounds, as distinct from the fashionable explanation which points to the ostensibly more violent character of football

than baseball. This latter explanation is dismissed on the basis of there being other more violent, yet less popular sports. By this account, violence is not itself of value in sport; it is the control of violence toward the dramatic achievement of a contested end which sustains our interest in it. Kaelin attributes the growing dissatisfaction with baseball to an increase in uncontrolled violence in it, and baseball's relatively poor continuity of action, dramatic unity, and so aesthetic appeal. That is, baseball lacks the aesthetic development of many meaningful events which variously build up, release, and bring to culmination tensions which are ultimately created by the opposition of substantially equal performers. Conversely, football exhibits a responsible control of violence and a superior dramatic unity. According to Kaelin, its action is more continuous and tightly structured, and its climax more genuinely culminating than is the action typical of baseball. That this is shown conclusively is not altogether clear, but Kaelin's conception of a well-played game, which grows out of this, is clearly articulated and compelling. Effectively, the claim goes that the aesthetic ideal of sport, the well-played game, is realized wherein the victor narrowly surpasses a worthy opponent, and wherein the controlled violence which leads to this conclusion edifies all contestants. This ideal is then likened to the creative activity of the arts by comparing competitive sport with a well established form of art, dance. The two are most alike in their both being discrete forms of movement media; they are both regarded as ends in themselves, and so as extraordinary; they both create an abstract effect and do so through the same general medium; the particular goals of both are artificial and conventional, as distinct from natural; the aim of both is to perform a physical act with utmost "efficiency"; in both cases the performers as such and the performance cannot be separated; in both cases the success of performance depends principally on "aesthetic" criteria; and in both a qualitative, aesthetic aspect, called form, is very much prominent. They are most unlike in that dance is not bound to stringent, objective rules as is sport; and the significance of dance is internal, while in sport the significance of performance is often conceived in external, quantitative terms--a conception which commonly operates to the detriment of the qualitative and aesthetic aspects of the experience. Kaelin reconciles the competitive motif in sport with its aesthetic dimension by arguing that sport is made an aesthetic event by the opposition of wills which seek victory, and that winning or losing itself is aesthetically irrelevant.

Keenan, Francis W. "The Athletic Contest as a 'Tragic'
Form of Art".

In this, Keenan interprets Aristotle's model of dramatic
tragedy, as worked out in the Poetics, in terms of its
meaning for the athletic contest. Athletic contests are
conceived as potentially dramatic events in which dramatic tensions are created by athletes attempting to perform excellently under conditions which constrain or limit
this attempt in some respect. These tensions are likened
to those characteristic of the arts in that, they are in both
sporting and artistic instances qualitative or aesthetic expressions of a becoming process which is of greater importance than quantitative result. By this view, then,
aesthetic measures are the most appropriate criteria for
judging sporting, no less than artistic excellence. Also
like the arts generally, the athletic contest creates an illusion of facility and raises human limits of insight and
expectancy. And like dramatic tragedy more particularly,
the athletic contest envisions beauty in the pain and suffering of conflict and competition in man's struggle with the
inequities and paradoxes of life, in man's attempt to overcome the hostile energies of the world to which he must in
the end yield, and in man's display of courage in the face
of this adversity. These common attributes of the dramatic tragedy and athletic contest are taken to explain the
tragic elements (plot, character, thought, diction, melody,
and spectacle) in the athlete's and the spectator's perspectives of the athletic contest. These perspectives equate
the imitation of action and life, and the evocation of pity
and fear inherent in the dramatic tragedy to those also apparent in the athletic contest.

Kuntz, Paul G. "Aesthetics Applies to Sports as Well as
to the Arts".

This essay is devoted to an examination of the terms in
which sport may qualify as an instance of artistic performance to be judged by aesthetic standards, or to an examination of the terms in which sport can have great art in it.
Cited as common features of sport and art are the similarly spontaneous, intense, and playful character of each,
the constraint to excellence proper to both, the highly emotional experience and impression of beauty characteristic
of both, the common intimacy of the audience-athlete and
audience-artist relationships, the symbolic significance of
the two (in culturo-historical, as well as in aesthetic
terms), and the status of both as products of leisure.

Kuntz, Paul G. "The Aesthetics of Sport".

Following the insight of Camus, Kuntz likens sport to the theater and ascribes unusually high value to it. Emphasized are the similarities of sporting and artistic performance--similarities based principally on a general conception of performance as the doing of an activity largely for the pleasure of another individual or group of individuals. The most notable of these similarities include: both sporting and artistic forms of performance arise in a special, contrived world, an idealization of the everyday, governed by freely chosen rules and values and occurring in exclusive and isolated times and places; both are productive of a beauty and excellence vicariously available to the spectator; and both are a vital part of human life occurring quite apart from work. Kuntz holds as well that sport ought to more fully cultivate its likeness to the arts.

Kupfer, Joseph. "Purpose and Beauty in Sport".

This essay challenges two fashionable notions about sport: 1) sport is inherently purposeful, and the purpose of sport is to win by out-scoring one's opponent(s), in which case the play of sport becomes a mere means to achieving victory. And, 2) unlike competitive sport, in which the scoring issues naturally from the playing, and which requires opposition and so is incapable of aesthetic development; non-competitive sport, in which the scoring is a forced abstraction from performance, does not require opposition--that is to say, performance in such sports serves no end or purpose beyond itself (the end cannot be identified apart from the manner of achieving it)--and is as such capable of aesthetic development. These notions, however, are based on the false view that sport is externally purposeful, and so are themselves false. Kupfer holds instead that: 1) competitive sport is not determined by external purpose, and 2) competition adds to, rather than detracts from the aesthetic qualities in sport. With respect to the former claim, it is held that sporting activity is not externally differentiated by scoring, but internally differentiated by what is required to score, by the manner of play whose issue is scoring. Scoring is, then, a sign of excellence, and competitive sport is engaged in for its own sake. By this view, scoring and winning are conclusions of play, and are essentially internal to it. They become external to it only in terms of their consequences (such as financial benefit, etc.). As such, and with respect to the second claim, the antagonism between part and whole is overcome in competitive sport no less than in non-competitive sport and art. Competitive interaction,

therefore, contributes to the aesthetic, as it heightens
and makes more extraordinary the drama of the activity.

Maheu, René. "Sport and Culture".
In this essay, Maheu compares sport and the arts (culture)
in both their present and their normative, or proper forms.
He argues that the present status of this relationship is
virtually non-existent, for few works of art are based on
sport, or have sport as their subject; different socio-
economic classes are typically attracted to the two enter-
prises (higher in the case of the arts, lower in the case of
sport); sport is based principally on bodily matters, the
arts on intellectual ones; and, the beauty begotten by sport
is immanent in the act which creates it, and so ephemeral,
or without a preserving notation, while that of the arts is
through signs which endure and bring a mastery over time
and space. Despite this, however, sport has much in common with the arts, and even now fulfills a cultural function
for many persons. Principal among these likenesses are
that both sport and art emanate from the same source,
leisure, and fulfill identical functions, dignifying leisure;
play is common to both; sympathetic participation of the
audience is common to both; both objectify, or express
emotion; both create and are surrounded by myths, or epic
sagas; both create beauty, or an impression of appealing
harmony; both allow for individual interpretations, or
stylistic variations, within established contexts; and both
are vehicles for the implicit expression of ethical values.

Reid, Louis A. "Sport, the Aesthetic and Art".
In this, Reid shows the similarities and differences among
the arts and sport. He argues that the dominating motive
of the arts is to produce a form for aesthetic contemplation,
and that the dominating motive of sport is not this, but to
play the game for the primary end or purpose of the game,
which is to secure victory in the contest. Though sport is
like the arts in many superficial ways, and even incorpo-
rates artistic elements on occasion, it is of a fundamentally different genus altogether. For, the aesthetic qualities
of sport are secondarily important in varying degree to its
primary purpose, while such qualities are primarily significant to art. "Style" in sport, then, commonly thought
sport's aesthetic element, unlike its place in the arts, is
assessed under competitive conditions; and so is not called
artistic without qualification.

Roberts, Terence J. "Sport and the Sense of Beauty".
This essay examines sport as an object of aesthetic appreciation irrespective of its status as art or not art.

Through an interpretation of Santayana's subjectivistic aesthetic, in particular, his treatment of beauty, form, and expression, Roberts demonstrates that sporting events can be understood in aesthetic terms. Most importantly discussed in this context are the apperceived ideal (a formal aesthetic feature composed of lines, movements, proportions) and expression (a nonformal aesthetic feature composed of ideas or emotions thought or felt in association with the perceived object or event) as they serve to explain our aesthetic response to sporting events. An apperceived ideal is the composite photograph of our several prior experiences of the object of which the apperceived ideal is the type--a photograph which tends toward pleasure and forms the basis of our aesthetic expectations. The notion of expression explains how our impression of economy and fitness (practical fitness and utility), that of partisan, practical advantage, and the exemplification of high moral standards, courage, dedication, and the like contribute to our aesthetic appreciation of sporting events.

Thomas, Carolyn E. "The Perfect Moment: An Aesthetic Perspective of the Sport Experience".

Thomas here examines the common features of the sporting and the aesthetic experience, and shows the terms in which sport itself may be considered an aesthetic experience. Principal among these features are: the common intent and desire to achieve some internal or external standard of excellence; the voluntary character of the involvement in both; the spatio-temporal characteristics of both; the non-utilitarian and conventional nature of both; their Dionysian affectivity, subjectivity, and spontaneity; their common use of technique; the unique and unified character of both; the common authenticity of the performer's intent; the high expertise of the performer common to both; the genuine integration of the intellectual and physical attributes of the performer in both; and the complete, poetic immersion of the performer in both. Drawing largely from the views of Sartre and Buber, Thomas concludes that the experiential sport aesthetic, or perfect moment, is an instance of general aesthetic experience, most particularly as that experience is found in the arts.

Thomas, Carolyn E. "Toward an Experiential Sport Aesthetic".

The intent of this essay is to suggest that the development of a worthy sport aesthetic must emphasize the process, or experience of artistic creation and expression in sport, as distinct from having an emphasis on sport as an art object. Thomas argues that the aesthetic object, sport, is

significant only insofar as it facilitates the experience of
sport. A regard for the objective features of sport as primarily significant is thereby considered an undue objectification of an essentially subjective, individual, affective,
and lived experience. The aesthetic moment in sport is
then likened to such moments in the arts. These moments
share a common authenticity, they both entail "competition" against a standard of qualitative excellence, the
spatio-temporal characteristics of the two are similar,
both persist outside of everydayness as being intrinsic and
extraordinary, both require a prerequisite technical mastery, and both provide a basis for self-realization.

White, David A. "'Great Moments in Sport:' The One and
the Many".
It is the intent of this essay to show the ready intimacy
between the popular language found in casual descriptions
of sport (most particularly with respect to excellence, the
role of the audience, and temporal characteristics in great
sporting moments) and the theoretically problematic dimensions of a classical sort also present in these activities. The principal goal is to sketch the experience of a
great moment from the perspective of the participating
athlete, as excellence, the role of the audience, and the
moment's peculiar temporality bear on such experience.
The most apparent conditions required for a great athletic
moment are:

> -the excellent performance of an athlete relative to
> the level at which the performance occurs, and
> asymmetric to the moment for those against whom
> the greatness is achieved
> -the conjunction of athletic excellence with the ap-
> probation of the audience (producing an order of
> self-fulfillment for the athlete and audience by
> allowing for the realization of the inherent and
> mutual urge to excel physically, thereby effecting a
> unity between athlete and audience in this respect)
> --for the purpose of an athletic action intended for
> excellence is to actualize a humanly physical possi-
> bility as if it were an actual possibility for all indi-
> viduals--this realization is "one" by virtue of the
> mutual awareness of physical excellence, and
> "many" in that each member of the community
> actually experiences this realization, or moment
> differently

-and, the coalescence of an athlete's athletic past,
present, and future during the actual event of the
great moment--the temporal characteristic of great
moments.

Ziff, Paul. "A Fine Forehand".
Ziff holds that there are no significant problems that can
sensibly be characterized as problems in the aesthetics of
sport; that is to say, there are no aesthetic features which
are novel to sport, and so no features of sport which indi-
viduate it aesthetically. One wonders, however, if this
same charge, at least as drawn on these grounds, cannot
be effectively levelled at the "other", particular arts. If
so, this would apparently lead to the dissolution of aesthetics altogether. By Ziff's account, significant philosophic
problems about sport are limited instead to matters of a
logical, linguistic, or epistemic character. Though some
sports explicitly display aesthetic aspects (such as gymnastics, ski jumping, figure skating, and diving), most do
not, and of those which do, form (as their aesthetic element) in them is itself a grading factor, and so itself an-
cillary. The aesthetic appeal of even these sports, let
alone the others, is, therefore, a mere byproduct, or epi-
phenomenon of technical aspects.

The socio-political status of physical education and sport

Keenan, Francis W. "Justice and Sport".
Keenan argues from Rawls' general principle of justice--
that all social values (liberty and opportunity, income and
wealth, and the bases of self-respect) are to be distributed
equally unless an unequal distribution of any, or all, of
these values is to everyone's advantage--to the view that
social values must benefit the least well off members of
society. By this notion, if we are to remove or at least to
minimize objectionable outcomes of sporting activities, the
context of rules and other conditions in which these activities occur must satisfy this principle. To violate such
rules is to undermine the most sacred trust of free people,
the duty to honor social contracts. A sense of self-respect
and communal spirit develops in sport when games are
played fairly according to the rules, when both sides are
rather evenly matched, and when the players sense that
they are playing well. A just organization of the institution
of sport demands practices which allow each individual,
regardless of gender or other such circumstance, to develop a sense of personal worth and self-respect by sharing
in the interests common to the sport community.

Lenk, Hans. "Alienation, Manipulation, or Emancipation of the Athlete ?"

Lenk here opposes the fashionable neo-Marxist notions that sport by its nature manipulates the athlete toward an affirmation of the established politico-economic order, that it does not instigate or champion political interests in the general social realm, but suppresses them, that the "achievement principle" in sport operates as an indirect, but nonetheless superimposed concept of social repression, and that sporting achievement is a form of alienated labor, and so the athlete as such one alienated from his activity and self. Lenk claims instead that a searching analysis of Marx' own discussions of alienation reveals that sporting achievement cannot be interpreted as compulsory work, de-humanizing, routine labor, or alienated labor. According to this view, sporting activity is properly conceived as a medium in which emancipation and humanization occur, a medium in which critical thinking and enlightenment are fashioned, and a medium in which the alienation and manipulation of man is overcome.

Osterhoudt, Robert G. "On Keating on the Competitive Motif in Athletics and Playful Activity".

This essay concentrates not so much on the nature of competition, athletics, and playful activity as construed by Keating in his "The Ethics of Competition and Its Relation to Some Moral Problems in Athletics" (an abstract of which appears in the section of this chapter devoted to the ethical status of physical education and sport), as on the implications of these views for a synoptic conception of man, the social substance, and the common good. Osterhoudt argues that in order to be fully and adequately understood the competitive motif must be examined in its relation to the social order and the public interest, and not, therefore, be viewed apart from these connections. Keating's distinction of athletics and playful activity is then interpreted as a discrimination between two radically different ways of regarding activities which, however similar in phenomenal appearance, are necessarily discrete in essence, or in terms of the goals or ends intended by their participants. These ways provide the germ of two characteristically different and opposing views of man, the social substance, and the common good. Of these ways, that which underlies playful activity is preferred to the one governing athletics, as it allows for the coalescence of self-interest and public interest, and thereby establishes a harmony among persons which is unknown when these two forms of interest are separated (as in the view which underlies athletics). As an essentially cooperative venture,

playful activity entails the genuinely sympathetic regard
for other persons which we seek actively for ourselves,
and which is not apparent in the spirit of exclusivity which
dominates athletics. In this latter, persons are regarded
as objects to be overcome, and are, therefore, employed
primarily as means for our own gratification. Osterhoudt
concludes that such a disposition is potentially destructive
of the whole of humanity, let alone the social order and
sport itself.

Sadler, William A. "A Contextual Approach to an Understanding of Competition: A Response to Keating's Philosophy
of Athletics".
    In this response to Keating's "The Ethics of Competition
and Its Relation to Some Moral Problems in Athletics",
Sadler opposes Keating's notion and defense of competition
on the dual grounds that they are ultimately detrimental to
the realization of a full humanness in that they promote a
regard for others as material objects and so interfere with
having a regard for others as persons, and that they fail to
understand competition in its full cultural context. Concerning this latter, a cross-cultural examination of competition reveals that it (as conceived by Keating) is not a
universal phenomenon, but one found only in cultures of a
particular sort instead. In this, Sadler shows four types
of social order which differ widely as to dominant values
and so also with respect to views of competition:

        -a being society is past-oriented, submissive to na-
         ture, fatalistic, and having no notion of competition
         of the Keatingesque sort
        -a becoming society is present-oriented, cooper-
         ative with nature, and having a notion of competi-
         tion as occurring within a condition of moderation
         and cooperation
        -a doing society is future-oriented, controlling of
         nature, practical, productive, utilitarian, and
         having a favorable view of competition
        -and, a having society is future-oriented, acquisitive
         of nature, consumptive, and having such a favor-
         able view of competition as to develop a spectator-
         ial, as well as participatory interest in it.

According to Sadler, then, Keating's conception of competition rests in transition between the regards which are
had for it by doing and having societies, and it fails to account for alternative views of competition as it occurs in
other cultural contexts. The essay concludes by suggesting the compatibility of play and competition in a so-termed

sharing culture. In such a culture, play and competition come together creating a circumstance in which the development of the self and the culture occur at once, out of the same impulse, and so toward the same ends. Play and sport thereby promote the development of a more fully human world.

The unity of these various insights, and the conclusion to which all in the end point, concerns the fulfillment of humanity in, and the high axiologic status of physical education and sport. Each suggests the basic character of this fulfillment in ethical, aesthetic, or sociopolitical terms.

The philosophy of physical education and sport has been discussed here in terms of its historical development, as well as in terms of its extant literature's treatment of the major concepts and issues which make it up. This direct accounting of concepts and issues is only one of several ways that the philosophy of physical education and sport has been, and so may be studied, however. It may also be studied by drawing implications from the major systems of philosophic thought (e.g., naturalism, realism, idealism), from the views of major philosophic figures (e.g., Plato, Aristotle, Kant), or from the views of the major historico-philosophic periods (e.g., ancient, medieval, modern) to concepts and issues of important and peculiar concern to physical education and sport. A treatment of the first of these other ways follows in Chapter IV. Discussions of the last two have been reserved for Chapter V.

CHAPTER IV

THE MAJOR PHILOSOPHIC SYSTEMS AND THEIR IMPLICATIONS FOR PHYSICAL EDUCATION AND SPORT

Introduction

An understanding of, and appreciation for philosophy generally, the philosophy of physical education and sport more particularly, is further enhanced by a treatment of the major philosophic systems, and their implications for physical education and sport. Such systems consist in an assembly of philosophic concepts (as well as the criteria for their establishment and treatment) which authentically accounts for the whole of reality, and provides a basis for considering new issues with respect to this whole. They represent the major alternative world views, and are as such the most systematic and comprehensive treatments of reality generally, physical education and sport more particularly. The compendious character of these systems rather demands that they extend over at least several figures and periods.

A grand number and variety of such attempts have punctuated the history of philosophic reflection. Most of these efforts, however, are of a more parochial or less authentic kind than the systems to which reference is made here. The most celebrated of such efforts include: singularly metaphysical (e.g., creationism, evolutionism), epistemic (e.g., empiricism, rationalism), axiologic (e.g., personalism, stoicism), or departmental (e.g., rational humanism) doctrines; views of individual figures (e.g., Platonism, Aristotelianism, Kantianism) or their hybrid forms (e.g., neo-Pythagoreanism, aritomism, neo-Hegelianism); notions characteristic of a philosophic function or operation (e.g., eclecticism, analytic philosophy) or a philosophic period (e.g., scholasticism, Alexandrian philosophy); religious (e.g., Judaism, Hinduism, Buddhism, Christianity, Islam) or political (e.g., communism, democracy, fascism) ideologies; or very general tendencies of thought which variously attach themselves to philosophic systems (e.g., essentialism, perennialism, progressivism, reconstructionism). Of those which remain, eight are sufficiently all-embracing, prominent, and genuine to invite the further attentions of this inquiry. They are, in general order of their historical development, naturalism, idealism, realism, pragmatism, existentialism, philosophical anthropology, linguistic analysis, and phenomenology.

Though clearly and distinctly differentiated by fundamental commitment, these systems are not mutually exclusive in every respect.

There are great similarities as well as differences among them. Neither do they collectively exhaust the philosophic literature--they are the most significant systems according to the criteria adduced above, but they are not the only systems. Nor has any one of them fully dominated any major historico-philosophic period, or been typically adopted in pure form by major philosophic figures. Many great philosophers are adherents of certain, compatible aspects of several systems. The discussion here is consequently limited to the most fundamental and commonly held features of each system. An examination of even important idiosyncratic interpretations of these systems is, therefore, left to Chapter V. Even at this, it is not possible in every case to be entirely true to the views of every major exponent of a system, since the diversity of judgment even among those of common basic allegiance is commonly great. On these grounds, then, the the discussions concerning major philosophic systems and their implications for physical education and sport have been separated in large from those devoted to major philosophic periods and figures and their implications for physical education and sport.

On first glance, some of the views expressed in the form of these systems gives a peculiar, even an uncompelling appearance. A serious and careful reflection on the matters they treat reveals their genius, bequeaths to us an appreciation of their deep significance, and hopefully exhorts us to a personal inquiry of a similar character, however. A reflection of this sort shows the great difficulty with which such systems are established, and the high importance of their conclusions. It allows us insight into that for which each accounts, and that for which others account better, or explain more consistently, systematically, and plausibly. Even at this, however, these systems cannot be fully understood in the absence of stipulating their historico-philosophic underpinnings; that is, in the absence of designating the sequence and type of event which led to them. These underpinnings are the subject of Chapter V.

Sometimes included in discussions of major philosophic systems and their implications for physical education and sport are accounts of systematic philosophic views concerning physical education and sport predominantly held by a selected group of persons. Typical of such accounts is Donn E. Bair's "An Identification of Some Philosophical Beliefs Held by Influential Professional Leaders in American Physical Education". By survey checklist Bair identifies and interprets the philosophic beliefs of leading American physical educators as tending either toward eclecticism, naturalism, or spiritualism. Such studies are more so sociologic than philosophic projects, however, and will not be further considered here in virtue of this.

An examination of the eight systems now follows. They are discussed in the general order of their historical development, and in terms of their general character and major adherents, their meta-physics, epistemology, and axiology, their philosophy of education, physical education and sport, and their strengths and weaknesses. Treatments of the metaphysics, epistemology, and axiology of existentialism, philosophical anthropology, linguistic analysis, and phenomenology are incorporated into the general characterizations of these systems, since these have not very much developed in the form of such distinctions. Distinctions of this sort are displayed with some prominence in naturalism, idealism, realism, and pragmatism, however, and so are given separate mention in the discussions of these.

Naturalism

General characterization and major adherents. Naturalism holds that Nature and reality are identical, or one; that all is explained in terms of its participation in Nature, or by reference to the terms in which it is natural. By this view, Nature is primary, and all that falls under its purview (which is all that is) is derivative of, or dependent on it. Nature is the self-evident truth, and all that is flows from, and is as such a part or an expression of it--it is the fundamental interpretive principle of reality. The major adherents of naturalism have been Thales, Anaximander, Anaximenes, Empedocles, Anaxagoras, Leucippus, Democritus, and Epicurus of the ancient period; Thomas Hobbes and Jean Jacques Rousseau of the modern era; Karl Marx and Herbert Spencer of the nineteenth century; and Samuel Alexander, Alfred North Whitehead, and George Santayana of the twentieth century.

Naturalistic metaphysics. Naturalism tends to be monistic, conceiving of Nature as a single, all-embracing entity--an entity which constitutes the human and divine dimensions of reality no less than the natural. Nature itself, however, has been variously construed, as a single or several inert substance(s) moving in space (materialism), as a propelling universal energy (energism), as the form or the laws, not the material, of Nature (positivism), or as the process, neither the material nor the laws, of natural continuity (process philosophy). This progression is from naive to progressively more refined, or critical forms of thought. As naturalism becomes more critical it also becomes less mechanistic and deterministic, and tends more fully toward realistic and pragmatic inclinations. In whatever form, however, naturalism is principally a metaphysical doctrine. Its epistemology and axiology are strongly derivative of, and less distinctive than its metaphysics. It is a metaphysically dominated system of thought.

Naturalistic epistemology. Owing to the strict sciences having Nature as their object of inquiry, these sciences are regarded by naturalism as the means by which dependable knowledge is obtained. And induction, as the major logical or methodologic process of scientific disciplines is considered the primary means by which knowledge is a acquired. This epistemic allegiance to science further reveals the confidence in Nature, as the source of all knowledge, which is the keystone of the naturalistic epistemology.

Naturalistic axiology. The naturalistic axiology holds that values are inherent in Nature, that they are resident in Nature as its qualitative aspect, and that Nature is, therefore, the purposeful guide of all action. The naturalistic axiology is in virtue of this metaphysically objective. According to this account, man best achieves happiness and purges himself of pain and suffering by cultivating fully his membership in Nature, by fostering his basically natural character, by acting in accord with Nature. The summum bonum of naturalism is the most sublime form of pleasure, usually called peace or contentment, construed as a being at harmony with Nature. It is this pleasure which consequently provides the basis for moral, aesthetic, and sociopolitical judgment.

Naturalistic philosophy of education, physical education and sport. The naturalistic view of education, physical education and sport tends toward essentialistic, or absolutistic, as distinct from progressivistic, or relativistic, forms of judgment. It commands that education be conducted in accord with natural expectation, and fulfill the natural inclination to learn. Formal education is necessary in order to systematically expose and attune man to the terms of his membership in the natural order, thereby efficiently and productively preserving him through a prolonged (relative to other animals) infancy, as well as preparing him for adult life. This education is acquired primarily through through a dutiful exposure to Nature, or through sensation, and so by induction. The sciences and their experimental methods are thereby thought most important, and as insuring the success of the educational venture. As the receptacle of the senses, the body, or biological constitution is of great importance in this process; such that, establishing a "rugged animalism" becomes a major educational and sporting objective for naturalism. The purposes of this view are accomplished by making the educational and sporting experiences pleasurable in the highest sense; that is, by engaging the spontaneous self-activity of the individual participant. The educational curriculum, which includes such as physical education and sport, is nature-centered and consequently consists in a propitious balance of uncontrived intellectual and physical activities. Artificial and undemanding forms of activity are set aside in favor of activities more thoroughly endowed with Nature.

Strengths and weaknesses of naturalism. The relative presuppositionlessness, and so apparent simplicity of naturalism provides the root both of its greatest strength and its most salient weakness. With respect to the former, it takes on a certain aesthetic appeal, and, in the case of the latter, it tends to oversimplify an inherently and strikingly complex world. In particular, it tends to leave the likes of subjective events and social intricacies as such, which are not wholly accessible to strictly scientific inquiry, insufficiently well explained. Like all philosophic systems naturalism best accounts for that on which it focuses most ambitiously--in this case the natural order--and explains "other" matters less well.

Idealism

General characterization and major adherents. According to idealism, Idea (or Mind, Soul, Spirit, or Thought) and reality are conterminous --the whole of things is explained in terms of Idea. It is a world view in which all things are thought derivative, or elaborations of Idea. Idea is the self-evident truth, and all that is is a part or an expression of it--it is the fundamental interpretive principle of reality. The major adherents of idealism have been Pythagoras, Parmenides, Zeno the Eleatic, Anaxagoras, Socrates, Plato, Aristotle, Zeno the Stoic, Philo, and Plotinus of the ancient period; St. Augustine, John Scotus Erigena, St. Anselm, and Meister Eckhart of the medieval era; Nicolas of Cusa, Giordano Bruno, René Descartes, Blaise Pascal, Nicolas Malebranche, Gottfried W. Leibniz, Benedict Spinoza, John Locke, George Berkeley, and Immanuel Kant of the modern period; Johann Gottlieb Fichte, Friedrich W. J. Schelling, Friedrich Schleiermacher, Georg W. F. Hegel, Arthur Schopenhauer, Hermann Lotze, Gustav T. Fechner, Wilhelm Wundt, Wilhelm Windelband, and Rudolf Eucken of the nineteenth century; and Thomas Hill Green, Bernard Bosanquet, Francis H. Bradley, John Ellis McTaggart, Josiah Royce, Charles Renouvier, Émile Boutroux, Alfred Fouillée, Benedetto Croce, and Giovanni Gentile of the twentieth century.

Idealistic metaphysics. Though many idealistic-tending views are dualistically or pluralistically inclined, idealism is, in its unsullied forms, monistic. As such, it conceives of Idea as a single, all-embracing entity. Idea itself, however, has been variously conceived as an impersonal pure thought, or consciousness (impersonalistic idealism) or as a personal self-consciousness (personalistic idealism). And, differing views concerning the relation of Idea and nature have given rise to the distinction between subjective, or Absolute idealism, according to which there is nothing in nature which is not purely and exclusively Idea, and objective idealism, which construes nature as an impure aspect, or expression of Idea, and so as something other than purely and exclusively Idea, but nonetheless remaining of Idea. This latter thinks itself a valid synthesis of two notions, subjective idealism and naturalism, which are in themselves extreme, and so incomplete. Idealism does not, therefore, deny the existence of the so-termed "external world", but construes and accounts for that world in terms of Idea. Idea, or Spirit, which constitutes the natural, human, and divine dimensions of reality, is consequently taken to explain both the unity of these dimensions and the existence of particular "things". A single Spirit is, therefore, understood to permeate all individuated forms. Idealistic views thereby typically consist in a qualitative monism and a quantitative pluralism. Moreover, evil as such is conceived either as non-existent, or as an impure and transient inclination of nature--it is not an enduring expression of Spirit. And, free will is exercised within the limits of inherent determinations. Like naturalism, idealism is a metaphysically dominated system of thought with epistemic and axiologic appendages.

Idealistic epistemology. The virtual conflation of knowledge and reality in idealism makes for an intimate metaphysico-epistemic relation. According to the idealistic epistemology, consciousness as such, in the form of knowing, is the most direct and indubitable fact of existence and of concrete experience--it is the source of all reality and knowledge. Induction is taken to provide the content, and deduction the form of this knowledge. The two mutually refine one another and ultimately account for the participation of the particular in the universal. Sense perceptual experience thereby provides the primitive data for the higher, or interpretive acts of intelligence, and is as such considered the occasion of these acts. The apparent order of reality and knowledge is conterminous with the eternal, systematic order of Idea. Insofar as so-termed disorder and imperfection make an appearance in the world, they take on the form of a not yet fully realized spirituality, but as nonetheless progressing in the direction of a spiritual fulfillment.

Idealistic axiology. The idealistic axiology is metaphysically objective in that moral, aesthetic, and socio-political value is thought inherently contained in Idea. It is, therefore, the primary axiologic duty of humanity to pursue a full harmony with, to cultivate its likeness to, to act in accord with Idea and the values which reside in it as its axiologic part. According to idealism, it is significantly these self-conscious moral, aesthetic, and socio-political, as well as intellectual, possibilities which distinguish the spirituality of the human circumstance from the spirituality of other aspects of reality. And since man is primarily obligated to fulfill his uniqueness, he is primarily obligated to a cultivation of these possibilities. His life is good, his creative activity beautiful, his socio-political institutions just in virtue of the quality and fullness of his response to these possibilities.

Idealistic philosophy of education, physical education and sport. Like the naturalistic view, the idealistic philosophy of education, physical education and sport tends toward absolutistic forms of judgment. Moreover, it advocates a finely distinguished division of responsibility among social institutions. By this view, education is to take on only certain carefully delimited, vital, and largely formal intellectual, moral, aesthetic, and socio-political obligations. That is, it is to give instruction in, and so to fashion and extend a refined understanding of, and appreciation for the nature and significance of reality in its various, integral forms. An apprehension of this nature and significance is considered a spiritual necessity--a compelling search for Idea. It is the ideal of ideas which is consequently understood to illumine all "other" order of responsible ideal with which education has become affiliated, such as emotive catharsis, socialization, and vocationalism. Thus, physical education and sport, no less than other features of the curriculum and life, must be principally devoted to summoning an enlightened insight into the essential character of reality as spiritual, albeit through the guise of their special medium, and so primarily concerning the "physical" attributes of this character. Predominantly physical types of activity are, therefore, highly regarded both in terms of their perfecting bio-psychological faculties, and in terms of their being themselves media for the expression of sublime orders of consciousness.

The idealistic philosophy of education, physical education and sport advocates the cultivation of one's "likeness" to Idea, an upbuilding of oneself in the image of Idea, an advance toward intellectual and creative perfection. The constraint to this advance is substantial, and is thought the major source of purpose in the world. It is an advance to which all persons by their nature are called. And it is the task of such as education, physical education and sport to effect such a calling, and to carry out its terms. The idealistic curriculum is, therefore, idea-centered, or spiritually constituted, consisting in a common core of relatively fixed knowledges and concomitant skills. In this curriculum, fundamental knowledges are taught directly and basic values by the example of great persons, methodology and the sciences are subordinate to content and the humanities, lecture and discussion teaching techniques are considered most appropriate, the teacher is thought centrally important, as chairing the community of ideas, systematically outlining alternatives, and inspiring his students by force of argument and personal example, and the character of experience is typically arduous. Principal among the essay literature directly examining the implications of idealism for physical education and sport is Robert G. Osterhoudt's "Toward an Idealistic Conception of Physical Education and Sport". In this are discussed the general philosophic commitments of idealism, the implications of these commitments for an all-embracing view of education, physical education and sport, and the alleged strengths and weaknesses of such commitments and implications. Demonstrated are the merits of an idealistic conception of physical education and sport, and the misdirected nature of misunderstandings concerning a conception of this sort.

Strengths and weaknesses of idealism. Idealism has its beginning and its end in the most immediate and indubitable feature of experience, in fundamental forms of awareness, or ideas. Better than other systems it accounts for the basic character of ideas, and the contribution

of ideas to experience. Its basis consequently evokes a certain intuitive approbation. The system also advances an ambitiously synoptic
account of reality, and so brings under its purview an unusually vast
range of events--in fact, all accessible events. Its vision is wide and
its order of skepticism and intolerance sharply limited. This com-
prehensiveness is sometimes attacked, however, as arbitrary, contrived, dogmatic, and so ingenuine; the view being that an explanation
of as large a whole as idealism envisions exceeds the rightful bounds
of knowledge. Another commonly levelled accusation has idealism being too complex, too difficult to understand, and thereby encouraging
too numerous misinterpretations. The simplicity and so popular
appeal of a system--describing such complexities as philosophic systems do--is not so much at issue, however, as the persuasive force
of its argument. Idealism, then, like other systems of philosophic
thought, best accounts for its fundamental ordering principle, in this
case idea, and accounts less well for other matters, such as objectivity as such.

Realism

General characterization and major adherents. Realism has as its
fundamental interpretive principle of reality the notions that an objective order persists independently of consciousness, and that this self-
evident and primary order is nonetheless known as it is in itself by
consciousness. That is, the independence of the material and the per-
ceptual-cognitive worlds, together with the capacity of the latter to
know the former as such, form the basis of realistic doctrine. Objectivity as such is, therefore, very substantially as it appears to consciousness. According to this view, reality is constituted by such
objectivity and by such a consciousness of it--all is explained by reference to this objectivity and consciousness. The major adherents of
realism have been Aristotle and Zeno the Stoic of the ancient period;
St. Anselm, Peter Abelard, St. Thomas Aquinas, John Duns Scotus,
and William of Occam of the medieval period; Tommaso Campanella,
René Descartes, Benedict Spinoza, John Locke, and Immanuel Kant of
the modern era; Johann F. Herbart of the nineteenth century; and
George E. Moore, Bertrand Russell, Samuel Alexander, Alfred North
Whitehead, George Santayana, and William James of the twentieth century.

Realistic metaphysics. The realistic metaphysics is diverse and
thereby difficult to characterize in general terms. It tends, however,
either toward holding that the terms of objectivity are directly and unproblematically known (naive realism) or indirectly and problematically known (critical realism). It inclines primarily, though not in
every instance, toward pluralistic, deterministic, and mechanistic
interpretations. As such, it emphasizes the order and precision of
objectivity and natural law, and holds that humanity and intelligence

themselves are grounded in objective or bodily existence and are, therefore, derivative of it. Realistic theology ranges from atheistic to devoutly theistic persuasions--there seems to be little distinctive of it.

Realistic epistemology. The indistinct character of realistic metaphysics is partially a consequence of the general doctrine's epistemic emphasis. Unlike naturalism and idealism, realism is an epistemologically dominated system of thought. The major problem of realistic epistemology concerns the terms in which knowledge of the objective order is obtained; that is, the relation of consciousness and objectivity. This relation is typically conceived either as entailing no mediation, in which case objectivity and consciousness are said to come together directly, or to be one in the mind (epistemological monism which requires a presentative theory of knowledge); or as entailing a mediating device or energy having its source in objectivity, in which case objects of consciousness are regarded as concretely and qualitatively distinct from material objects, and so as indirect apprehensions of objectivity (epistemological dualism which requires a representative theory of knowledge).

Realistic axiology. The realistic axiology conceives of values either as simple moral, aesthetic, and socio-political attributes of the objective world which when authentically experienced are accurately experienced (logical objectivism or metaphysical objectivism); or as simple moral, aesthetic, and socio-political attributes of possible judgment in the objective world which depend for their value on the dispositions of those experiencing them (subjectivism). Like its metaphysics, the axiology of realism is neither as distinctive nor as important as its epistemology. Its major exhortation is to fashion and refine the inclination to act in genuine accord with these attributes, which are in some sense inexorably grounded in objectivity, or the physical order.

Realistic philosophy of education, physical education and sport. The realistic philosophy of education, physical education and sport, like both the naturalistic and idealistic views, tends toward absolutistic forms of judgment. By realistic account, education ought to be conducted in accord with the demands of the physical order, which is the cultural heritage and prevailing social circumstance. Since the physical order, or objectivity, is the primary bearer of the stuff of reality, knowledge, and value, the curriculum is dominated by the order, precision, and objectivity of mathematics and the sciences--it is object-centered. And since sensation is the primary means by which objectivity and consciousness "touch", realistic education advocates a methodology of active and rigorous exposure to, and involvement in the physical order, which is regarded as the most basic of civilizing agents and as the source of all theoretical and practical activity. As in other essentialistic-tending views of education, realism regards the teacher as centrally important, and so as holding to whatever authority is required to assure the success of the process. It also holds that physically demonstrable objectives (such as, health, strength, endurance, and the like) are foremostly important in physical education and sport.

Strengths and weaknesses of realism. The independence of objectivity and consciousness and the high proficiency of the latter in apprehending the former, provides realism with a possible perspective from which the physical order can be understood in itself, that is as it is as such, unaffected by thought. Realism explains the basic character of this order as such better than alternative systems. And insofar as this order can be said to persist apart from consciousness, the terms in which it is known is also well explained by it. Its concrete tendencies also allow it to escape the necessity of explaining the problematic relationship of finitude and infinitude. The independence of the two realms does give rise, however, to a dualistic inclination and to the problems typically accompanying such an inclination. Accounts of the relationship between these two realms are not altogether free of exotic and unpersuasive turns. Realism does not explain well intellectual complexities, or what could be called the contributions of thought to experience and knowledge. Its pluralistic disposition makes it further open to the charge that its insights are too fully separated, that they are fragmented and without a compelling unity. It does, therefore, neither provide the all-embracing enlightenment properly provided by philosophic systems, nor does it consequently take on the aesthetic appeal which surrounds such enlightenment. And as a philosophy of education, physical education and sport, it makes the most evidently humanistic interests subservient to others.

Pragmatism

General characterization and major adherents. The fundamental interpretive principle of reality for pragmatism is man's practical experience. Pragmatism holds that such experience is the measure of the knowable universe, and so that knowledge otherwise construed is no knowledge at all. It is no knowledge at all in virtue of its violating the principle of verifiability and determinateness. By this view, the certitude required of knowledge can be a product, and only a product of practical, human consequences. It is a practical experience-centered world view. The major adherents of pragmatism have been Heraclitus, Protagoras, Gorgias, Isocrates, Socrates, and Pyrrho of the ancient period; Francis Bacon and David Hume of the modern era; Auguste Comte, Jeremy Bentham, and John Stuart Mill of the nineteenth century; and Charles Sanders Peirce, William James, and John Dewey of the twentieth century.

Pragmatic metaphysics. The pragmatic metaphysics much resembles the most critical forms of naturalistic metaphysics, according to which reality is construed as the process or foreground of individual and social life. This process is by its nature dynamic, indeterminate, relative, and plural. Moreover, humanity is conceived as continuous with this process, not as distinct from it; the mind is regarded as a naturally evolved attendant of the body; and man is thought neither an absolutely active cause, or free will in the world, nor absolutely determined by the world, but capable of activity which assists in the determination of consequences without affecting them qualitatively.

Pragmatic epistemology. Pragmatism is most emphatically a practical experience-centered theory of knowledge. Like realism, and unlike naturalism and idealism, then, pragmatism is an epistemologically dominated system of thought, whose metaphysics and axiology are relatively indistinct and in any case largely derivations of epistemic doctrine. Unlike the other systematic epistemologies thus far discussed, the pragmatic view emphasizes the particular, individual, and unique character of experience and knowledge. It regards coherent units of experience, which constitute the basis of reality, as consisting in individuated facts, and not in sweepingly general propositions. Knowledge is, therefore, conceived as a successful organization of particular facts, the pattern for which is provided by the results of a scientific examination of experiential hypotheses. The criterion of truth is thereby fastened to the consequences of doing and acting, and is attached to present units of experience. What is known by this account is an hypothesis operating satisfactorily, or the successful resolution of a course of action in an experiment. Knowledge can thereby be said to originate in experimental circumstance, and is acquired in interactive sense-perceptual relation between oneself and one's milieu. It is acquired neither in passive relationships with the world, nor by pre-established principles of reason. It is the objective and publicly observable character of such interaction which defines experience as the medium of such interaction. And it is this experience, or interaction which provides hypotheses for experimental action, and which in the end gives purpose or significance to the use of particular facts. Pragmatism's primary interest in such facts is nonetheless an interest in their use. It is in this sense instrumentalistic, and a philosophic expression of the operational genius of modern science. Its process entails a direct and active involvement in an activity, the definition of a problem with respect to this involvement, the observation of events pertinent to such a problem, the formulation of hypotheses from such observation, and the experimental testing of these hypotheses.

Pragmatic axiology. The pragmatic axiology construes value as providing for the effective function of present, as well as foreseeable future, individual and social event. Like experience itself, of which value is a feature, it resides in the interaction of selves and their environments, principally their social environments, and serves as the foundation for social self-realization. Values are, therefore, participants in the continuity of ever-changing human experience, and they are values in virtue of their satisfying present desires, as well as yet unrealized possibilities implicit in these desires, relative to the resolution of problems. Since the world itself is indeterminate with respect to values, pragmatism exhorts humanity to an active, courageous, and responsible interaction with the events in the world, so as to come upon his own values, which goes as coming upon the fulfillment of individual and social desires. The pragmatic axiology is, therefore, neither strictly optimistic nor pessimistic, but melioristic instead. That is, it withholds absolute judgment concerning the merit of life, preferring to hold that the merit of life is a function of one's response to it. According to this view, values are realized by intending to act and by acting so as to resolve the indeterminacy of problematic events, or so as to make a provisional resolution of such events. The subjective and objective constraints to morality, aestheticality, and socio-politicality are reconciled by gathering them into a situational synthesis. Aesthetic values are further construed as consisting in an operational continuity, or a functional ebb and flow of experiential uncertainty (indeterminateness) and its resolution (determinateness), which is equivalent to the beauty and pleasure of life generally. And the socio-political fabric, which is a very major consideration for pragmatism, is interpreted as an organic process persisting in coextensive interdependence with individuals. Individuals are thereby admonished both to a preservation of socio-political institutions themselves, as well as to a preservation of individual freedoms shared by all within, or directly influenced by such institutions. Moreover, pragmatism tends toward a preference for democratic forms of institution and for freedom.

Pragmatic philosophy of education, physical education and sport. Unlike naturalistic, idealistic, and realistic views of education, physical education and sport, the pragmatic notion tends toward relativistic forms of judgment. And like idealism in particular, it grants education a central place among socio-political institutions, as uniquely performing the necessary social function of systematically preserving and extending the heritage of man. By this account, the complexities of individual and social life require a controlled and cosmopolitan treatment of the world in the form of an educational treatment of it. The pragmatic view of eduction, physical education and sport exhibits a discernible penchant for democracy, freedom, individuality and the unique, and informality and the indeterminate. And it identifies the objectives of education as specific to the resolution of certain ever-changing, or emergent problems. It emphasizes problem-solving experiences, or experience in effective experiencing. It is primarily concerned with utilitarian consequences that are to serve the ultimate purpose of individual and social efficiency--with the satisfaction of human needs in concrete experience. The nature of these objectives and commitments is consonant with, in fact, an expression of the basic character of concrete human experience itself. The sciences and social action provide the core of curricular content, and the experimental method is the dominant means of treating this content. Through such content and method is fashioned an understanding of the continuity of past, present, and foreseeable future event, a recognition of the present as the most significant stage in this continuity, and an appreciation of the contributions made by such understanding and recognition to an effective handling of the indeterminate situation. Life itself, as being not distinct from education but the contrary, is construed as an experiment made intelligible by the interactions of education. Moreover, in this experience- and utility-centered view of progressivistic learning, the teacher is considered the principal planner and leader of activities, but does not occupy the strong central position advocated by such as idealism and realism. Among the most important essays providing a direct account of the implications of pragmatism for physical education and sport are Earle F. Zeigler's "The Implications of Experimentalism for Physical, Health and Recreation Education" and his "The Pragmatic (Experimentalistic) Ethic as It Relates to Sport and Physical Education". In the former, Zeigler shows the terms in which a conception of physical education and sport is issued by the general philosophic position of pragmatism, experimentalism, or pragmatic naturalism. Demonstrated are the basic metaphysical, epistemic, axiologic, and educational allegiances of this position, as centering around the nature and significance of practical human experience, and the implications of these allegiances for physical education and sport. Emphasized in physical education and sport, when conducted under a pragmatic guide, are such as individual-social action, problem-solving experiences, freedom and democracy, and natural and total fitness. And in the latter piece, Zeigler concentrates primarily on the implications of the pragmatic ethics for physical education and sport, showing the fundamental significance of socio-cultural experience, change, plurality, relativity, science, democracy, freedom, practicality, utility, and problem-solving in such activities. He concludes that pragmatism offers the most humane and best approach to resolving the problem of new values generally, and those indigenous to education, physical education and sport more particularly.

Strengths and weaknesses of pragmatism. Owing to pragmatism's emphasis on the merit of living present experience fully, it tends to provide wise counsel for effective action in everyday circumstance. It explains well the vitality and flow of human experience as a succession of experimentally determined, instrumental events. And it awakens to the importance of direct experience, informality, and freedom in life generally and in such as education, physical education and sport more particularly. It accomplishes this, however, at the possible expense of explaining events which do not meet its strict principle of verification. Pragmatism, then, does not account well for such as natural, intellectual, physical, subjective, cultural, or linguistic concerns, at least as these concerns persist independently of practical experience. Of course, pragmatism holds that, insofar as there are such concerns, they cannot be conceived apart from practical experience. Similar difficulties are evident in the commonly raised objection to pragmatism's universal application of experimental means to phenomena which do not inevitably appear as problems; in what is sometimes taken as pragmatism's undue emphasis on individuation and so plurality by which insufficient account of the common and unifying features of human experience is made; and in pragmatism's situational standard of value which fails to provide an independent principle of good and beauty, and so, some have claimed, an adequate principle of such at all. Perhaps most telling, however, is the related objection to pragmatism's denial of a "universal" consciousness which its notion of experience (as a certain admixture of determinate and indeterminate elements occurring in historical continuity) apparently presupposes.

Existentialism

General characterization and major adherents. Existentialism, or existential philosophy (existenzphilosophie), argues that the whole of explainable events in exhausted by reference to the character of the uniquely human subject; which is to say that, this character is the primary "stuff" of reality. According to this view, the distinctive nature of human existence, as being unique individual, or personal subjectivity, forms the fundamental interpretive principle of reality. It is a human subjectivity-centered system--a reawakening of man to himself. Commonly distinguished, in some cases as separated opposites which come together in some way and in others as unreconciled antitheses, are the central focus of the system, human existence, being, or existential status, and that which this focus in some sense opposes, an essence or formal nature which is more properly the province of the other-than-human. From this, and what is further implied by it, comes the now celebrated to infamous notion that existence precedes essence. Existentialism takes the uniquely human mode of existence as self-evident and indivisible, and so as being at the foundation of all things. It is, in virtue of this, variously dominated by axiologic considerations, or, it might be said, by orthodox axiologic concerns "raised" to the level of metaphysical, in particular to the level of ontologic insight. In any case, existentialism holds that metaphysics consists primarily in such concerns. Existentialism's distaste for the orthodox philosophy, or metaphysics as remote from life and thereby a betrayal of it, while not a distinctive quality of the system, is nonetheless among its more legion features. In this sense, it represents a protest against, in the form of an extension and reform of established cultural forms and the philosophic systems which explain and undergird them.

According to existentialism, human life is continuous with the observable existence of the spatio-temporal world, while nonetheless being distinct from the existence of empirical objects. It holds that the existence, or facticity, of self and objects are distinct; that they exist as they are in themselves. This is to say that, human and objective forms of existence are characteristically different. They differ most significantly and fundamentally with respect to the human capacity to freely choose and to assume responsibility for such choice, and the absence of this capacity in objects. This freedom of genuine choice is at once both exhilarating, in that it provides opportunity for joyful and individualizing experience unknown to other beings and things, as well as terrifying, in that it carries with it a solitary and ominous responsibility equally unknown to other beings and things. Under the sway of existential thought, human life is typically conceived as a troublesome and futile plight which goes on in a largely hostile world. And men are taught to forthrightly confront this world, to exercise their free choice in it, and to thereby sustain themselves in the inevitably absurd relation in which they stand to it. They must actively challenge the terms of their existence in order to live authentically. They must be bold and heroic in the face of this adversity, which goes as being bold and heroic in the face of a negation of being, a nothingness. This negation invokes the moods of alienation, solitude, anxiety, dread, anguish, guilt, death, and despair which dominate the existential mode.

Knowledge of this mode, and so knowledge generally, is disclosed immediately to the unique human subjective consciousness by being itself. And insofar as choice is genuine and free in this mode, it is not determined by the laws of nature or by the maxims governing community life as such, but by the character of unique human subjective consciousness itself. In fact, it is the making of such choices and the assumption of personal responsibility for them which both distinguishes humanity and endows the world with value. Prior to such acts of choosing, there is only existence, or pure facticity--it is through, and only through these acts that the essential nature and significance of the human circumstance are disclosed. The existential axiology does not, therefore, precede such acts, as if it were an inherent feature of the world awaiting discovery, but is instead a consequence of them. Man is thrown into, he simply finds himself in, a world of this sort, and it is from such a world that he must make a beginning of himself, and ultimately fulfill himself as a unique human subjective consciousness. Life is itself conceived as a development toward being what one is--it is a search for authentic existence, and so an attempt to triumph over the collective "imperatives" of nature and society which constitute the principal origins of inauthenticity.

Among the more significant controversies in recent existential thought has been the dispute between theistic and atheistic tendencies in it. Both tendencies have been developed in the wider context of fundamentally existential principles, however, and would, therefore, seem incidental to the notion of existentialism itself. The major adherents of existentialism have been Sören Kierkegaard of the nineteenth century; and Martin Heidegger, Karl Jaspers, Jean-Paul Sartre, Gabriel Marcel, Albert Camus, Nicolas Berdyaev, Martin Buber, Rudolph Bultmann, Karl Barth, Paul Tillich, and Reinhold Niebuhr of the twentieth century.

Existentialistic philosophy of education, physical education and sport. Though some instructive things have been said about existentialistic interpretations of education, physical education and sport, existentialism has not taken as full account of these as the systems of longer standing tradition earlier discussed. Enough is nonetheless known of it to observe its progressivistic-relativistic tendencies and what is generally entailed by such tendencies in its case. According to this view, education, physical education and sport must be conducted so as to promote the authentic self-fulfillment of unique human subjective individuality. Education, physical education and sport must expose and attune man to the terms of his existence, awaken man to himself so to speak. Existentialiam advocates a human subjectivity-centered educational experience. It emphasizes direct involvement (one becomes by doing), freedom and independently personal choice, a study of the humanities (with their concern for distinctly human matters) more so than the sciences (and their concern for largely objective matters), and a use of dialogue or dialectic methodology. And the teacher is regarded as a free and quasi-central agent who must hold to, and express a personal concern for individual students, and arouse them to an awareness of their being their own moral and aesthetic centers, to an awareness of their own basically subjective nature. Moreover, since the body is revered as integral to the self, the likes of physical education and sport enjoy a high place in the existential curriculum and social order. Perhaps the most important essay providing a direct account of the implications of existentialism for physical education and sport is Howard S. Slusher's "The Existential Function of Physical Education". In this is demonstrated the primary obligation of physical education, no less than education generally, as providing the individual with the necessary knowledge, skill, and sentiment to discover utterly personal existence. More particularly, the essay considers the contributions of physical education to the individual through such existential modes as doubt (a momentary anxiety over the terms of one's existence), faith (an ultimate concern over the terms of one's existence), existence itself (the uncertainty and infinite possibility of life), and awareness (the symbolic expression of one's own existence).

Strengths and weaknesses of existentialism. Like other systems, existentialism best explains that on which it focuses most basically; in this case, unique human subjectivity. And it explains less well such as natural, spiritual, physical, and social intricacies. Though it has on occasion objected to systematic orderings of idea, and to widely general types of philosophic thought as well, it has nonetheless itself necessarily developed in the form of such orderings and types. It differs from the traditional systems, which it has sometimes criticized in these ways, principally in virtue of what it takes to be at the ground of reality, which has an influence on tendencies to systematize and generalize, but is not synonymous with these tendencies. The major weakness of existential thought, however, has to do with the cleavages and antagonisms it envisions between the subjective individual, nature, and the social order; and consequently with the difficulties it inherits in explaining the continuity of these phenomena. Its cosmology, epistemology, and politics are not comparatively well developed in view of this. Nor is it fully apparent that the foundations of existentialism are as free of presupposition, and so as self-evidently true as commonly thought.

Philosophical anthropology

General characterization and major adherents. Philosophical anthropology is primarily concerned with explaining the essential character of humanity as species, or as cultural participant. This is distinguished from existential thought in that it emphasizes the intersubjective, as distinct from the uniquely subjective, dimensions of human life. As such, it is principally interested in the cultural characteristics of humanity, and is, therefore, also known as lebensphilosphie. Its fundamental interpretive principle of reality is genuine human life as such life has developed in cultural forms. In any case, such life is not much distinguished from the cultural forms in which it develops according to this view. Philosophical anthropology is consequently dominated by the philosophy of history, and is thereby also much taken up with ontologic, epistemic, and axiologic matters. According to this human culture-centered world view, culture itself is construed as the collective product of man's creative faculties, and so as that which most fully and satisfactorily reveals the basic nature and significance of the human circumstance. Its view of human life is thereby vitalistic, or crucially pertaining to an authentically creative force. It understands humanity as the historical flow of its creative activity, and so as confined to the sense-perceptible world, though nonetheless remaining substantially distinct from material objects. And it is axiologically committed to the enhancement of the creative faculties and experiences of the human species. The major adherents of philosophical anthropology have been Karl Marx and Friedrich Nietzsche of the nineteenth century; and Henri Bergson, Max Scheler, Helmut Plessner, Ernst Cassirer, and Susanne K. Langer of the twentieth century.

Philosophical anthropologic philosophy of education, physical education and sport. Like existentialism, philosophical anthropology has not dealt as completely as the more fully established systems with education, physical education and sport. Also like existentialism, the view tends toward progressivistic-relativistic forms of judgment. It advocates a human culture-centered notion of education, physical education and sport, and as such emphasizes a study of, and a concern for intersubjective, creative, and humanistic matters. It is committed most fundamentally to the development of an authentic cultural humanity. And, since it holds to an organismic, or unified notion of self, it shows an unusually high regard for the body and its activities; and reserves a high place for physical education and sport in the educational curriculum and social order generally in virtue of this.

Strengths and weaknesses of philosophical anthropology. Philosophical anthropology explains well the character and development of human culturality. It explains the natural, spiritual, physical, social, and subjective orders less well. And like existentialism, its attack of traditional philosophy as unduly speculative and systematic falls also and necessarily back onto itself in some measure.

Linguistic analysis

General characterization and major adherents. Like other forms of analytic philosophy, most notably logical atomism and logical positivism, linguistic analysis conceives of reality as a logico-linguistic order. The nature and function of language, as well as the relationship of language to that which it represents or signifies, dominate the system. These epistemic emphases distinguish verbal or mathematical, ordinary or symbolic concepts expressed precisely in language and thereby thought common sensical and meaningful, from such concepts imprecisely expressed and thought nonsensical or meaningless. It also determines the criteria by which such judgments are made. According to this view, philosophical perplexity, ambiguity, and confusion arise from subtle misuses of language, and can be exploded only by linguistic clarification. The system limits philosophic reflection to methodologic (logical, linguistic, and mathematical) forms of consciousness. By this account, truth resides only in the directly observable, and thereby verifiable and clearly precise, interrelationships among terms or propositions of logical, linguistic, or mathematical certainty. Orthodox metaphysical and axiologic claims are consequently thought speculative and systematic in spurious extreme, and so nonsensical--they are thought an improper use of precise language about matters of fact in the world. Linguistic analysis holds that an astute understanding and use of precise language elucidates the basic character of reality in as full a measure as such elucidation is possible. The major adherents of linguistic analysis have been Ernst Mach, Richard Avenarius, Hans Vaihinger, Henri Poincare, Ludwig Wittgenstein, G. E. Moore, Bertrand Russell, Alfred North Whitehead,

Moritz Schlick, Rudolph Carnap, A. J. Ayer, and Gilbert Ryle, all of the twentieth century.

Linguistic analytic philosophy of education, physical education and sport. Among the concerns incapable in significant measure of the sort of precision required by linguistic analysis, are such as education, physical education and sport. The metaphysical and axiologic status of these phenomena, at least as traditionally conceived, are thought particularly inaccessible. The remaining, largely epistemic emphases of the system limit its reflections on such as education, physical education and sport to definitive linguistic descriptions thereof, or aspects thereof. The wide extent of these limits has not much encouraged reflections on the basic nature and significance of education, physical education and sport, except to clarify the meaning of linguistic terms pertaining to them. The most prominent pieces suggesting such a clarification tend toward progressivistic-relativistic forms of judgment. They are Robert J. Fogelin's "Sport: The Diversity of the Concept", Larry Fox' "A Linguistic Analysis of the Concept 'Health' in Sport", Peter Spencer-Kraus' "The Application of 'Linguistic Phenomenology' to the Philosophy of Physical Education and Sport", and Earle F. Zeigler's "An Analysis of the Claim that 'Physical Education' Has Become a 'Family Resemblance' Term". Fogelin's essay shows that the concept of sport, as revealed by "its" language, is constituted as a diverse system of overlapping notions, and cannot be known as a collection of so-termed necessary and sufficient conditions. The most prominent of these notions is that of a contest and that of an exhibition of physical prowess. Fox ferrets out the possible circumstances under which the term 'health' is used with respect to sport, and critically examines the fashionable assumption that participation in sport leads to the attainment and sustenance of health. According to Fox, this latter is not an assumption well disposed, as vague and ambiguous meanings of the term 'health' underlie it. In an attempt to clarify these meanings, he distinguishes the positive notion of health (as optimum organic, mental, and social well-being) from the privative (as absence of disease, illness, and infirmity). The positive concept occurs by degrees and has no firm criteria for judging it. Sport, most particularly in the form of training, contributes to this only if it is directly responsible for such. The privative concept fashions more absolute distinctions. Unless sport participation has a direct effect on restoring an organ to condition, however, it has not assisted in securing good health, even of this sort. In fact, sport injury often transforms a person from a privative state of health to a state of unhealthiness. Spencer-Kraus' study applies ordinary language analysis to a discussion of some of the most important and persistent problems in physical education and sport: the role of women, dance, professional education, methods of instruction, the healthy body, values, and amateurism-professionalism. This technique entails achieving a consensus regarding the unambiguous use of terms by reflective dialogue among a jury of authoritative investigators,

for the purpose of resolving linguistic, and so also practical confus-
ions and difficulties over them. And Zeigler's work sets out the different meanings currently being applied to the term 'physical education' in the English language. The distinctions proposed are based
principally on Wittgenstein's notion of "family resemblances", whereby the terms in which a linguistic device is used in language, and not
its so-termed "essential" features, are stipulated, and whereby every
such use has something, though not everything, in common with other
uses. An examination of the term under these conditions reveals six
major meanings: subject matter (e.g., gymnastics), activity carried
on by teachers and institutions, process of being physically educated
(or learning), result, discipline or field of inquiry, and profession.

Strengths and weaknesses of linguistic analysis. Linguistic analysis
explains well the basic character of logico-linguistic events, and its
precision in examining such events--events which are given to such a ·
high order of precision--is admirable. It tends, however, to leave so
much of life, which is of an inclination apart from this, unexamined as
such. It leaves entire perspectives of meaning and significance which
have rightly perplexed and concerned humanity from its self-conscious
beginnings, and which cry out for philosophic insight, philosophically
uninspected. The most prominent of these perspectives are among
those which explain and guide such integral features of existence as
nature, humanity, divinity, morality, socio-political life, and the aesthetic use of language in poetry, literature, drama, theater, and
opera, as well as the implications of these features for religion, history, education, physical education and sport. Neither is it apparent
that language itself is as unencumbered of presupposition, and so as
self-evidently clear and precise a medium as commonly thought.

Phenomenology

General characterization and major adherents. Phenomenology is
basically devoted to securing descriptive interpretations of pure phenomena, of things or events known as immediate experiences. It
shows both the distinctive structure, or imminent meaning of sense
impressions, as well as the significance of this meaning in the form
of lived experiences. According to this view, sense impressions, or
immediate experiences, are not empty, but having themselves essential characteristics, and giving experience in general its fundamental
cast. Phenomenology takes as its fundamental interpretive principle
of reality what immediately confronts it; that is, pure subjective con-
sciousness--consciousness, or immediate experience free from basic
presuppositions as to the existential or metaphysical status of "things".
It neither concerns itself with the genesis of this consciousness, as the
traditional philosophy and psychology commonly do, nor with the relationship of such consciousness to the so-termed objectivity from
which it is tacitly distinct. The pure subjective consciousness takes

what it finds itself experiencing as given--as a subjective world of interpreted impressions, or universal essences, which are, despite their subjective residence, intersubjectively valid--and fashions that experience as an intentional world, or a world which intends or thinks objects (intentional objects). By this account, all essences, which are the true nature of all actual and potential things and events, are without presupposition, and so are free of the unduly speculative hindrances of objective science and traditional philosophy. In this way, phenomenology thinks itself superior to such science and philosophy, and to have revealed the true nature and significance of existence insofar as this can be revealed. As such, it undertakes a scrutiny of all knowledge--suggesting its limits, means, and substantial content --and is, therefore, dominated by epistemic concerns. The major adherents of phenomenology have been Franz Brentano, Alexius Meinong, Edmund Husserl, and Maurice Merleau-Ponty, all of the twentieth century.

Phenomenologic philosophy of education, physical education and sport. Like other philosophic products of the nineteenth and twentieth centuries, save pragmatism, phenomenology has not dealt as fully with education, physical education and sport as the systems of longer established tradition. And since it devotes most, though not all, of its energies to methodological concerns, neither has it been as instructive in substantive terms as these systems. It has nonetheless considered education, physical education and sport as no less intentional objects than other fundamental forms of human event, and as consisting in the distinctive sorts of experience which merit interpretation. Its essentialistic-absolutistic tendencies with respect to these phenomena move in what it regards as other than orthodox metaphysical, epistemic, and axiologic ways, however, and it is more so inclined to a descriptive interpretation of them than to providing a guide to their conduct. Its notion of lived experience has nonetheless provided reflection on physical education and sport with among its richest insights. The implications of this notion for physical education and sport are perhaps most directly stated in Seymour Kleinman's "The Significance of Human Movement: A Phenomenlogical Approach". In this effort, Kleinman distinguishes the scientific view of movement as being a knowledge about the body, from a phenomenological perception as taking the form of an awareness of the self. To the end of further articulating this awareness, the terms in which movement contributes to the realization of self are discussed. In this, Kleinman argues against a conception of the body which has it a mere obstacle to be overcome, or means to ends without it, in which case movement has neither human meaning nor significance; and in favor of a notion of the body and movement which develops and nurtures a peculiarly human awareness of, and openness to self. Sports and games seem intent on encouraging the former, or scientific concept and less formal movements, or lived experiences committed to the latter, or phenomenological inclination. Kleinman concludes that physical education is more properly taken up with lived experiences of phenomenological form than with sports and games.

Strengths and weaknesses of phenomenology. Like the other systems, phenomenology accounts well for that on which it focues primarily, human subjective consciousness or intentionality, and less well for natural, spiritual, physical, social, individual, cultural, and linguistic concerns as such. Moreover, owing to its highly strict conditions for knowledge, it tends to leave unexamined much of life which requires philosophic insight. And though its disdain for the orthodox philosophy as unduly full of unreflective assumptions runs deep, it is not as free of this charge itself as commonly supposed.

CHAPTER V

THE MAJOR PHILOSOPHIC PERIODS AND FIGURES AND THEIR IMPLICATIONS FOR PHYSICAL EDUCATION AND SPORT

Introduction

No account of philosophic thought generally, nor one of philosophic thought concerning physical education and sport more particularly, not even an introductory such account, can be complete without a discussion of the thought of concrete philosophic periods and figures. Such a discussion here takes the form of illustrating the development of philosophic ideas and problems among the great thinkers and across the major periods of thought, and of showing the implications of these ideas and problems for physical education and sport. This history of philosophy demonstrates the character of prior circumstance, and conveys a certain illumination of philosophic possibilities and the present condition in view of this circumstance. Present event is sharply influenced in any case by prior occurrence, and cannot be fully understood apart from such occurrence. A fully satisfactory understanding of past events brings the relief of our heritage into contemporary focus, and assists in the determination, or in the making of an informed response to current affairs. Moreover, an understanding of this sort invests us with a visionary perspective which enlarges all others, gives us a sense of continuity with respect to our various efforts, confers on us a consciousness of our unity and an appreciation for the genius and importance of human achievement, and shows us the reign of our human possibilities. New things are learned well, fully appropriated, only insofar as they are given the perspective of history. In this, philosophy generally and the philosophy of physical education and sport more particularly are no exceptions--they virtually presuppose a thorough historical orientation. It is rather such an historical rendering which brings philosophy in its various forms to "completion" --not only to show what it is, but to demonstrate its development as well. The following accounts attempt to make a beginning in such a demonstration. What is collected here, and in histories of philosophic reflection generally, is neither a mere congeries of unexamined opinion, nor an aggregation of isolated ideas. What is collected here are the most insightful and astute accounts of the basic nature and significance of reality in its various forms--accounts which have the most intimate and well drawn connections between them; even, it might be claimed, accounts which provide our development with an impression of continuity. Contained in these accounts are the most penetrating and profound resolutions to the most fundamental issues of existence-- the enduring insight of man's highest and noblest reach.

The treatments of major philosophic concepts and systems and their implications for physical education and sport have been separated from this examination of major periods and figures because the latter is not exhausted, nor is it even very effectively characterized by reference to the former. The sequence of concrete idea, personality, and circumstance is what is missing from the talk about concepts and systems, and is what now needs to be filled in. As a filling in, then, the ensuing discussion is not separate from earlier examinations, but is a completion of these examinations. Moreover, though much of this discussion may give the appearance of having little or no viable and direct relation to such as education, physical education and sport--in fact, some of the figures considered nowhere make explicit mention of these activities--it is throughout addressing the basic character of all things, education, physical education and sport among them. Treatments of education, physical education and sport are thereby made variously explicit and implicit. Even in the case of implicit treatments, however, an immense and instructive resource for explicit reflection is provided. And it is precisely this sort of resource, and only this sort of resource, which in any case prepares adequate foundation for explicit discourse on particular matters such as education, physical education and sport. Only in full view of such foundations can activities of this variety be seen in the larger context of human event, and so be understood and appreciated in a fully satisfactory way at all. Another caution may also be helpful here. On first and superficial glance, many of the following notions may seem unduly exotic and unworthy of earnest study. An adequate comprehension of them in the early stages of one's philosophic development, however, depends more significantly on a charitable and sympathetic immersion in them, than on a premature dismissal or uncompromising criticism of them. Only in this way can progress be made through and beyond them. Also importantly noticed about these discussions is their confining their attentions to the salient trends in the ancient, medieval, modern, nineteenth century, and twentieth century periods, as these trends are expressed in the thought of their major philosophic figures; and to historico-philosophic, as distinct from historico-cultural developments, though an altogether satisfactory account of the history of philosophic ideas depends greatly on an understanding of the history of cultural events themselves. This latter is the subject of historical inquiry as such in any case, and so needs be left either the concern of historical tracts, or the concern of discourse whose explicit aim it is to show the intimate connections between history and philosophy. The intent here is to concentrate on philosophic insights, and the discussion has been delimited on that basis. What follows consequently is an overview account of the history of philosophy, as revealed by the thought of its major periods and figures, and of the terms in which the developments of this history strongly suggest or explicitly propose implications for physical education and sport.

Ancient philosophy

To the time of the Greeks (and significantly in other ancient cultures during and after the Greek pre-eminence), the intellectual life of ancient civilization had been largely dominated by various systems of mythological religiosity. These systems depended more fully on submission to a mysterious fate than on an independent rational inquiry into the fundamental nature and significance of the world. Perhaps the most notable of these systems are embodied in the works of Hesiod (fl. 8th century B.C.). The Greeks of the sixth century B.C. were the first to think constructively and systematically about philosophical problems per se. Even at this, however, Greek philosophy itself developed in a curious blend of mythological religion and self-conscious reason--a blend which it never fully relinquished. Insofar as the Greek philosophy is memorable, however, and there is no philosophy any more memorable than it; it is memorable in virtue of the fullness of attention that it gives to human life and experience as such. The entire point of Greek philosophy is that it has humanity at its center; for it, humanity as such is an issue in a way in which it had not before been an issue. Religion had prepared the way for ancient philosophy in general, and for Greek philosophy in particular, and this philosophy would again come under the domination of religion at its end; but the best and most distinctive of this philosophy comes from a rigorously critical treatment of the traditional mythology, and not from an apologetic restatement of it. And the best and most distinctive of this philosophy is Greek. This is so much the case that the history of ancient philosophy can be thought virtually synonymous with the history of Greek thought. This thought leaves the highest ancient insights, and establishes the foundations on which virtually all philosophic reflection to follow is based. The discussion of ancient philosophy offered here is worked out in the following divisions: the Milesians, the Pythagoreans, Heraclitus, the Eleactics, the qualitative atomists, the quantitative atomists, the sophists, Socrates, Plato, Aristotle, epicureanism, stoicism, skepticism, and eclecticism, Philo, and Neo-Platonism.

The Milesians: Thales, Anaximander, Anaximenes. The history of genuinely philosophic reflection begins with the Milesians' rational accounts of the essential character of the objective world. According to these accounts, the objective world is best and most plausibly explained by reference to natural, as distinct from mythological events. The force and extent of their commitment to direct observation and the appeal of reason marked a significant departure from prior tendency. The Milesians explained the whole of reality (the objective world for them) in terms of a single concrete, or natural substance in which motion, or change, was considered inherent. The dual matters of substance and change as first talked about by the Milesians would dominate ancient philosophic discourse at least until the sophists, and remains yet an issue of some philosophic interest. The earliest of

these figures, Thales (624-c. 554, 548 B.C.), thought water the basis
of all reality. His student, Anaximander (611-c.547, 546 B.C.),
held, with Thales, that the fundamental principle of reality is concrete; but, against Thales, that it is indeterminate substance. Anaximander called this substance, the Boundless or Infinite, and explained
all determinations (including water) as features or manifestations of
it, and so as less basic than it. The mere fact that these determinations possess opposites suggests that they are not of an utterly basic
order according to Anaximander. The Infinite itself is conceived by
him as undifferentiated, natural or concrete, and changeless; as the
eternally recurring source and denouement of all things. It is from
the Infinite that all things cyclically come, and to which all things cyclically return. Anaximenes (588-524 B.C.), a student of Anaximander, argued, with both Thales and Anaximander, that the first
principle of reality is concrete; but, with Thales and against Anaximander, that it is determinate. For him, the primary substance
underlying all reality is air, vapor, or mist. His notions of rarefac-
tion and condensation, themselves inherent in vapor as transformations of it, are taken to explain change in terms of motion. The view
of education, physical education and sport implied by the Milesian
conception of the world tends in the direction of naive naturalism.

The Pythagoreans: Pythagoras. Pythagoras (c.572, 570-c.500, 497
B.C.) founded and was the principal exponent of one of the earliest
and most influential philosophic doctrines, what became known as
Pythagoreanism. This doctrine was less concerned with the composition of reality's most basic substance and the terms in which this substance undergoes observable transformations (philosophy's most important issue for the Milesians), than with the formal relations among
the parts of such a substance. He was convinced that the order and
uniformity of the world can be explained only by reference to the quantitative relations among things. By this view, things are regarded as
copies of numbers and as knowable, both in their own form and in external relation with other forms, only by a system of numbers. In an
idealistic-tending fashion, Pythagoras conflates the laws of mathematics and those of nature. Man is thereby obligated, in axiologic
and in educational terms, to act in accord with these laws, and to pursue his likeness to them.

Heraclitus. The philosophy of Heraclitus (c.536-c.470 B.C.) is principally devoted to the problem of change, most particularly to a critical treatment of the Milesians' resolution to it. With Anaximenes
most importantly, Heraclitus holds that change is not best conceived
as a vacillation between opposites, but as a transformation of tendencies inherent in reality (like the transformations apparent in fire and
vapor). He considered incorrect, however, the Milesian notion of a
concrete, natural, or material first principle. He concluded instead
that change itself, as the form of continual transformation, is the

most fundamental of principles, and that nothing is, therefore, permanent in any basic sense--nothing that is except the rational principle by which change itself is ordered, the logos. Reality is thereby
construed as an harmoniously ordered succession of tranformations.
And man is constrained to conduct himself, in general as well as in
educational terms, in accord with his needs as they take on the form
of the logos. The foundations of pragmatism's "principle of flux",
and what these say of such as education, physical education and sport,
are consequently apparent in Heraclitus' thought.

The Eleatics: Parmenides, Zeno. The Eleatic thesis is just the opposite of Heraclitus'. It argues that reality is fundamentally permanent,
or substantial. Xenophanes (c.570-c.480 B.C.) foresees the Eleatic
argument in highly speculative, theological terms, but it is Parmenides (c.515-c.450 B.C.) who works it out in full and elegant detail.
From an appeal to the principle of sufficient reason, Parmenides argues that from being only being may come, that something cannot
come from nothing, and that nothing may, therefore, become something else, or be transformed, but always necessarily remains what it
is. It follows from this that in order for there to be something at all,
there can be only one indivisible, eternal being. The true nature of
the world is thereby understood as permanent; the impression of the
world as changing is understood as illusory. By this idealistic-tending view, thought and being are considered equivalent, for only thought
(and not sense) apprehends the unity of the world, as distinct from its
plurality. Zeno (c.490-c.430 B.C.), a student of Parmenides, demonstrates the Eleatic thesis by showing the inscrutability of Heraclitus'
position. Zeno's ingenius paradoxes of space and motion attempt to
show the impossibility of change along Parmenidean lines. Melissus
of Samos (fl. 5th century B.C.) is similarly remembered as offering
an insightful proof of the Eleatic doctrine. This doctrine does not
give as central a place to the movement phenomena of principal concern to the present inquiry as the others thus far reviewed. The medium of these phenomena itself, if not their substantial contributions to
being, is considered chimerical.

The qualitative atomists: Empedocles, Anaxagoras. The qualitative
atomists aimed at a conciliation of what they took to be the unduly
strict and extreme theses of absolute change (Heraclitus' view) and absolute permanence (the Eleatic view). They held, with the Eleatics,
that the doctrine of absolute change as such is untenable; and yet,
somewhat with Heraclitus, that an account of at least relative change
is nonetheless required. According to this view, a fully satisfactory
explanation of the world must take account of its real tendencies both
to permanence and to change. The qualitative atomists argued that
the world is permanent in its being composed of numerous qualitative
elements, and it is changing insofar as the relations among these elements are in continuous flux. Empedocles (c.495-c.435 B.C.) was of
the naturalistic-tending view that the four qualitative elements, earth,

air, fire, and water, are sufficient to account for the substantial composition of the world, and that change is best explained by the attraction and separation of elements according to the respective principles of Love and Hate. Anaxagoras (c.500-c.428 B.C.) held to an idealistic-tending notion which postulates the existence of an infinite number of qualitative substances, set into motion by an impersonal, intelligent principle, or nous--by a purposeful, omniscient, and omnipotent intelligence.

The quantitative atomists: Leucippus, Democritus. Leucippus (fl. 5th century B.C.) and his student, Democritus (c.460-c.370 B.C.), were the most accomplished of the quantitative atomists. Like Empedocles and Anaxagoras, they, too, construed the world as a mosaic of changeless, eternal particles, or atoms; but unlike their predecessors of qualitative persuasion, they think unnecessary the ascription of qualities to them, and they think inferior the notion that these atoms are moved from without. They argue instead that motion is inherent in, and continuous with the quantitatively discrete atoms themselves-- that these atoms move through the void (or non-being) by immanent force. According to this naturalistic-tending view, reality generally (including, of course, such as the mind, sensation, and the gods) is conceived as an aggregate of particles of various form, weight, size, arrangement, and direction. With respect to epistemic, axiologic, and educational matters, the position expresses a principal allegiance to reason (and the pleasures of exercising the rational faculties) as distinct from sense (which merely provides a foundation for reason).

The sophists: Protagoras, Gorgias, Isocrates. The sophists are most widely remembered for their skeptical revolt against what they regarded as the unduly speculative systems of metaphysical reflection which went before them. For a brief period, they are successful in turning the focus of philosophic thought from metaphysical to epistemic and axiologic concerns. They were convinced that the metaphysical speculations of the past had not resolved, and could not have resolved the issues they had treated. The sophists were taken up instead with a a critical examination of the mind, or intellect, so as to show the limits of the mind's capacity to obtain truth. This change in the direction of philosophic inquiry brought to the center of philosophic thought an issue which had been previously assumed. The new challenge was dominated by a spirit of freedom and individualism in which the knowing subject becomes the focus of philosophy. The deeply skeptical mood which characterizes the sophist movement limits knowledge to subjective truth, or opinion. According to this mood, only individual subjective perceptions can be known--only the perceptions, not what is perceived, or what "underlies" these perceptions can be known. This leads to the characteristically sophist idea that things are what they appear to be for each subject in each circumstance. Since all knowledge thereby rests on the disparate claims of particular knowers, no objective truth is thought possible. By this pragmatic-tending view, man is the measure of all things in the sense in which his opinion as such is incontrovertible. There are quite simply no objective criteria by which it may be judged--any person's opinion is just as good as any other's, for there is no "true" one. This radically relativistic and subjectivistic conception of humanity and knowledge spilled also over into the ethics and politics of the sophists (insofar as it can be called an ethics and/or politics), according to which social and political institutions are formed in the image of, and respond to the needs of man, as distinct from man fashioning himself in accord with the demands of an institutional hierarchy. Protagoras (c.480-c.410 B.C.) was the leading figure in this movement which also claimed the allegiance of Gorgias (c.480-c.375 B.C.) and Isocrates (436-338 B.C.) most importantly. The most constructive contribution of the sophists to the development of philosophic thought has to do with their views on education. Though they are principally remembered, largely from Plato's unsympathetic accounts of them, as the creators of clever and persuasive, but invalid arguments, they were nonetheless the first to give serious attention to a philosophic account of education. They proposed a functional curriculum which emphasized the study of language and logic, which stressed the virtues of an independent mind, and which recognized the character and merits of dialectic discourse.

Socrates. Socrates (469-399 B.C.), who left no literature himself, is known largely through Plato's early dialogues. The general program of Socrates, his ingenious execution of it, and his immense courage in the face of what went against it, mark him as one of the most remarkable and important figures in the history of philosophic reflection. He attempted to bring order to an age of philosophic chaos, an age created largely by the excessive skepticism and subjectivism of the sophists. He wanted to reaffirm the foundations of knowledge, morality, and the state which the sophists had in significant measure devastated. Like the sophists, however, he was of the pragmatic-tending view that philosophy is properly limited to matters of a distinctly human, epistemic, and moral sort, and that it cannot effectively carry out the kind of metaphysical system-building so fashionable among his predecessors. Socrates thought of philosophy (as well as education) not so much as a collection of doctrines, but as an activity of fundamental self- and general human examination; and so, as basically practical, or methodologic, rather than speculative. Unlike the sophists, however, Socrates was convinced that universal, or general judgments about human life, knowledge, and value are possible, and that it is precisely such judgments, and the restored sense of confidence in human reason which underlies them, which provide a basis on which the practical dilemmas of the time could be resolved. The method by which Socrates comes to such judgments (variously called Socratic irony, or the elenchus) is also owed, in its original formulation, to the sophists. The method in general, as well as in its educational uses, begins with an examination of a popular opinion, proceeds through an ingenious

series of dialectic moves, and ends in an insightful rejection or reformulation of that opinion. By this method, Socrates inductively forms
provisional characterizations which are, in turn, taken through the
refinements which result both from a looking back at the basic assumptions on which they are founded, and from an observation of the
examples which rightly apply to such assumptions and what logically
follows from these assumptions. The results of these reflections show
that man can know more than the merely particular, accidental, and
idiosyncratic; and that, insofar as humanity has a ground for its moral
and socio-political judgments, it has these reflections, and only these
reflections, for such a ground. In fact, according to Socrates, right
reason, or knowledge of good and bad, is both necessary and sufficient
to right action, or virtue--the continuity of knowledge and action is
thereby complete in Socrates, the one entailing the other. And virtue
is itself and, in turn, taken as guided by a rational impulse to make
life pleasant and painless. This rational impulse is, therefore, itself
rooted in man's inherent inclination for happiness. And socio-politically, happiness depends on a coalescence of individual and public goods,
and so of morality and legality. Even with all of this, however,
Socrates cannot be said to have left a comprehensively worked out system of philosophy. Such a working out he left to his students. Plato
was, of course, the ablest of these, though other prominent disciples
are well remembered for the founding of the Megarian school of philosophy (which combined the Socratic epistemology and ethics with
Eleatic metaphysics), the Cyrenaic school of philosophy (which taught
that the cultivation of pleasure is ethically primary), and the Cynic
school of philosophy (which taught that the renunciation of pleasure is
ethically primary).

Plato. Though the influence of Socrates and the pre-Socratics on the
history of philosophy had been remarkable, it remained for Plato (427-
347 B.C.), a student of Socrates and one of the most richly talented
thinkers in the history of human civilization, to work out the first (and
what has also proved to be one of the most accomplished) genuinely
comprehensive system of philosophy. While the Platonic program pro-
ceeded largely on the methodologic grounds established by Socrates, it
was in the end of a far less skeptical inclination than its progenitor.
This is to say that Plato sought a solution to the problem of metaphysical reality, a solution thought unobtainable by Socrates and the sophists.
Plato even held that a solution to the problems of knowledge, ethics,
aesthetics, and politics depends necessarily on a solution to this problem. His system reformed Greek philosophy both in terms of its sum-
ming, and in most cases improving on the efforts of its predecessors,
and in terms of its launching an entirely new era in the history of
philosophic thought--an era not yet fully at an end.

In idealistic-tending fashion, Plato argued that reality is fundamentally rational; and so, that the structure of reality (insofar as reality is knowable, and the notion of reality itself significantly entails the

criterion of knowability) corresponds to that of knowledge. This is so, for Plato, because only rational, or genuine knowledge is capable of comprehending itself--only such knowledge is self-conscious, or capable of authenticating itself. Conversely, sense-derived knowledge, or mere opinion, cannot support itself by such an appeal; and it thereby goes as the source of ingenuine knowledge, or a mere knowledge of disparate, particular impressions--impressions which the sophists had thought the only possible basis of knowledge. According to Plato, then, genuine knowledge is conceived as knowledge of the universal, or permanent, and is accessible only to reason. The senses merely clarify or arouse what reason already knows; namely, the essential nature, or forms of things. That is to say, these forms are necessarily presupposed by our experience--our experience cannot be explained apart from them. Plato explains the origin of knowledge in terms of the transmigration of immortal souls. By this view, knowledge is not acquired anew by individual beings, but rather, actively and systematically recollected, or recalled by such beings. Knowledge is acquired prior to the moral life of man, as the existence of his soul is antecedent to his mortal, or individual existence, and is the immortal vehicle of knowledge. Knowledge thereby takes the form of ideas (or forms) and is equivalent to recognizing the reason in things. Though these ideas are qualitatively separated from sense-perceptual objects, they are nonetheless intimately related to such objects; in that, they are paradigms of, or references for these objects. Unlike sense impressions which are ephemeral and particular, these ideas are gathered into an eternal and systematic unity known as the form of the Good, or the Absolute. The Absolute is the source of all less general forms, and representative of the cosmic purpose. Sense-perceptual objects themselves are considered independent exemplifications of forms. They are said to participate in the forms in the sense of their being copies of them. The relationship between these two independent realms, the realm of forms (or being) and the realm of matter (or non-being), is governed by what Plato calls the world-soul, or Demiurge. According to Plato, then, true knowledge, justice, and beauty are products of the ideal realm, and the measure in which they are experienced as less-than-perfect is a function of materiality's contaminating influence on the realm of pure reason. The body is itself regarded as a corporeal impediment to knowledge--an obstacle to be overcome in reason's search for pure intellectuality. False belief consists in the misconjunction, or imprecise correspondence, of a sense-perception and its rational remembrance. Only opinion invested with reason can be called true knowledge, justice, and beauty. Man, by this account, is the measure of all things in virtue of his being the agent of such truth, and not because he is the unique, subjective holder of opinion as the sophists had claimed.

Plato's ethical and political thought holds that the good of the individual and the good of the state are effectively equivalent. For him, the state forms itself in accord with the character of man's soul, and so in accord "as well" with the character of the Good. As reason, will (or spirit), and appetite divide the soul; rulers, warriors, and merchant-artisans divide the state. Plato proposes an organic conception of private and public interests, according to which a political order properly disposed insures individual happiness by insuring that reason controls sense. Justice is conceived as the doing of what one is best suited to do, so as to best serve the good of the state, and thereby one's own best interests as well. Such service and such interests come only to those who cultivate their rational, or immortal aspects foremost, to those who work through and beyond their sensuous, or material and mutable attributes; in short, to those who allow the highest orders of consciousness to prevail over the lower. Plato's aesthetics thinks the arts taken up with the making of mere imitations of the world of sense, a world which is itself a mere imitation of the true essences, or forms of things. As such, the arts are regarded as mere copies of yet other copies, and so as twice removed from pure ideas, and so as raising false and potentially pernicious affections, and being largely unworthy of human attention.

The educational philosophy of Plato follows well the basic commitments of his general metaphysical, epistemic, and axiologic program. Learning is construed as a matter of reminiscence which makes its way by means of Socratic dialectic. Plato's Academy was devoted to a monastic presentation of the great ideas of Pythagorean mathematics, the arts, gymnastics, and philosophy. It emphasized learning of and through concepts and symbols, as distinct from learning of and through experience as such. It emphasized pure, as distinct from applied knowledge--knowledge of properties which distinguish classes of objects (or general ideas), as distinct from spontaneous observation and experiment. Moreover, educational institutions are also expected to determine the social class of students, by determining their inclinations and abilities, and the socio-political functions they must be consequently expected to perform. Plato's dualism, together with the view of materiality and the body which it carries, leads to the view that the body is of value principally in virtue of its sustaining and enhancing the cognitive faculties. For Plato, then, the major importance of such as physical education and sport has to do with their pedagogical (and to a lesser, but nonetheless important extent their military) possibilities.

The most instructive studies dealing with the implications of Platonic thought for physical education and sport are L. Joseph Cahn's "Contribution of Plato to Thought on Physical Education, Health, and Recreation," John R. Fairs' "The Influence of Plato and Platonism on the Development of Physical Education in Western Culture," and Seymour Kleinman's "Will the Real Plato Please Stand Up?" The purpose of Cahn's study is to collate the widely distributed passages of Plato's work concerning physical education, health, and recreation, so as to suggest the unity of these passages. He concludes that Plato's treatment of physical education, health, and recreation grows out of a more general metaphysical doctrine, and more general views concerning the good man, the good life, and the good society. Plato's views on the subjects of physical education, health, and recreation can be effectively reduced to his considering them an integral and vital part of life, though their principal significance is confined to their acting as a corollary or prerequisite to intellectual pursuits. Fairs' study attempts a comparative analysis of two opposing systems of Greek thought concerning the body, and the subsequent effects of these systems on the development of physical education in Western culture. Each of these systems came out of, in the form of being parts of, metaphysical discourses. The first is a reflection of the Periclean anthropology and education, and argues for a balanced and integrated program of physical and intellectual education so as to fulfill the basically human strife for an equanimity and balance between its spiritual and material parts. The second comes from what Fairs calls the anti-physical anti-naturalism of Platonic anthropology and education, according to which the physical serves the intellectual. Fairs concludes that this metaphysical dualism symbolizes the betrayal of the body in Western culture, and is the most decisive event in the history of Western physical education. And Kleinman's study defends Plato against those who accuse him of holding to an ambivalent view of the body. Kleinman argues that Plato was a substantially consistent metaphysical dualist who devotes himself to an account of the intimate relationship between the higher mind and the lower body. He concludes the proclamations of organismic unity (the position embraced by many of Plato's alleged antagonists) alone fail to adequately explain the distinction between mind and body, and the dualistic tendencies which are the product of this distinction.

Aristotle. Few thinkers, perhaps none, can rank with Plato's most celebrated and accomplished student, Aristotle (384-322 B.C.). Aristotle attempted to re-work the great system of his teacher in what he regarded as more consistent, impersonal, scientific, and realistic-tending terms. He argued that merely because there is something different than particular things (namely, the eternal forms which go to explain these things) is itself insufficient reason to suppose them separate from those things. For Aristotle, then, forms are not apart from, but inherent in things--forms are immanent, not transcendent. This, together and with Aristotle's highly favorable regard for the so-termed natural sciences, leads him to a much more sympathetic view of nature and the material than had been put up by Plato. For Aristotle, matter is not the inert, passive stuff of non-being, but is itself a dynamic being in which form invariably appears. Individual things, or substances are constituted only by the inseparable combination of form and matter, according to this account. In this combination, form remains the most important, as for Plato. This is so because it is the essential quality of a substance--the quality which is shared by all things ot the same type, the quality which distinguishes these things from things of another type, the quality which makes these things what they are. There are a great many substances according to Aristotle. These arrange themselves in a hierarchy from indeterminate matter at the bottom, to pure form, or God, at the top. Even at this, however, the material world is not considered a mere "imitation" of the ideational (as for Plato), but is itself endowed with idea, form, or purpose. This world is, therefore, taken as the only real world, and so as the object of all scientific and philosophic inquiry. Experience is regarded as the source of all knowledge and the means of scientific demonstration. Genuine knowledge, however, depends on an understanding of the necessary causes (material, formal, efficient, and final) of experiential events--experience alone does not constitute knowledge, though it is a necessary condition of knowledge. Knowledge entails bringing streams of experiential consciousness under the influence of logic, and thereby raising them to higher orders of thought. Unlike in the Platonic program, then, in this one thought and the material come genuinely together--the continuity between them is more plausibly drawn. Also unlike Plato's position, Aristotle's shows that things work for an end naturally, and so not from pure intention. The real and necessary order and purpose of the world is, therefore, apparent in nature for Aristotle.

Aristotle explains change as the movement of substances from potential to actual, and from actual to potential states as these substances become more or less thoroughly endowed with form. By this account, matter is conceived as the principle of potentiality, or particularity, and form as the principle of actuality, or universality. Form is the mover, matter that which is moved. According to Aristotle, the whole of this view further presupposes the existence of an Unmoved Mover, or Uncaused Cause, or God, which acts as the principle of movement, or causation, but which does not itself move, or is not itself caused. Thus, only in the case of the changeless Mover, or pure form, is form distinct from the change and motion inherent in matter. For the changeless Mover is the pure actuality, or thought thinking itself, toward which all things strive.

Aristotle was the first to recognize the need for developing an explicit method for obtaining knowledge and dealing with the formal relations of ideas. He recognized the need for a science of logic as a prior condition of philosophy. Using mathematics as a model, and armed with the view that the goal of such a science is complete demonstration, or knowledge, Aristotle formulated a mosaic of principles by which the particular is derived from the universal. He fashioned a syllogistic-deductive system in which inductive operations are used as a preparation for deductive ones. Only such a system of scientific demonstration, according to Aristotle, and so not the Platonic doctrine of recollection, brings one to true knowledge. As a part of his work on logic, Aristotle also uncovered the predicates, or basic categories, which apply to all things: substance, quality, quantity, relation, space, time, position, state, activity, and passivity.

Aristotle's metaphysics may be described as vitalistic; that is, its animating principle is spiritual, as distinct from material. This fundamental tendency also spills noticeably over into his physics, biology, psychology, ethics, and politics. In his ethics and politics, he holds that the highest good is moved toward as a substance culti- vates that which is essential to it, that by which it is distinguished from all else. With respect to man, as the end of nature, it is his rational capabilities which make such a distinction. The pursuit of virtue, and so happiness, or eudaemonia, is thereby dominated by an enrichment of the rational faculty, or the rational activity of soul. This enrichment carries with it both the "perfection" of reason as such, and the fashioning of a well-ordered soul, or a soul in which a proper and balanced relation between reason, feeling, and desire is achieved. In fact, this latter is entailed by the former according to Aristotle. The matter of a proper and balanced relation among the activities of the soul is further defined as a moderation, or mean, be- tween extremes of excess and deficiency with respect to any voluntary sentiment, action, or intent. Right rule is what the virtuous, or good man does in regard to this moderation. Like the organicism of Pla- tonic socio-political thought, the Aristotelian politics promotes the collapse of the individual good into the common good. The socio- political order, by this account, must be designed for the good of each and every person participating in it, for the good of all is necessarily involved in the good of each. Also with Plato, Aristotle argues that man's socio-political involvement is essential to his fulfillment--that man's continuous association with virtuous law and institution lies at the root of his happiness and his pursuit of the good life.

Art, for Aristotle, as for Plato, is fundamentally imitative. Though, for Aristotle, it does not imitate the "form of the beautiful", but distinctly human character, emotion, and action. Nor, by Aristotle's view, do the arts have the generally unfavorable effects Plato supposes. They, instead, fulfill the simple pleasures, realize a useful order of emotional catharsis, and perform an important di- dactic function as well. Unlike for Plato, then, who tended toward an absolutistic interpretation of the arts, Aristotle holds that beauty is a function of the observer's response to a work of art--it is relative to the aesthetic sensibilities of a cultivated man.

Aristotle's general devotion to the basic spirit of the empirical sciences is prominent in his educational thought as well. His Lyceum, or Peripatetic School, emphasized this spirit in such as language, mathematics, astronomy, the arts, and gymnastics. Since education is most importantly of universal essences, however, according to Aristotle; logic, as the methodologic basis of such essences, is the most important subject in the curriculum. The end of education is,

therefore, having most to do with realizing one's own essential nature
--with fulfilling one's fundamentally rational character, or with dialectically actualizing the rational potential of each person. This is
done both through formal study, and through ongoing associations with
virtuous persons and institutions. Moreover, because Aristotle held
that the body is our material, or lower aspect, and the mind our formal, or higher one, and because he recognized that lower order capacities need to be developed prior to higher ones in order to provide a
satisfactory foundation for them; he advocated experiences in physical
education and sport both as a preparation for, and as an accompani-
ment to predominantly intellectual forms of education. The major
study on the implications of Aristotle's thought for physical education
and sport is Jean E. Chryssafis' "Aristotle on Physical Education".
This essay examines Aristotle's views concerning the role of physical
education in forming good citizens and a just socio-political order.
Education, in general, is the proper means by which such citizens and
orders are obtained in any case. Aristotle also held that education
must be uniform for all persons so as to assure that the goal of the individual and the social order is diligently and singularly sought. And
that, the body, or that aspect of man dominated by desire, appears (
(or is recognized) in life before the mind, or that aspect of man dominated by thought or reason, and so must be the first object of education,
albeit an object the education of which is ultimately directed to intellectual ends. This view of education and physical education allows for a
unity of experience, conceived as having a distinct beginning, middle,
and end; allows for the education of an integral humanity, an education
which aims at a methodical cultivation of all human qualities, according to an established order, and allows the educational process to follow the order of nature, that is, allows education to move from a
treatment of those qualities which nature causes to appear first and
which are lowest, to those qualities which appear latest and are highest. The Aristotelian education and physical education is thereby one
which provides for the natural, harmonious, and symmetric development of body and mind--provides for the development of men of vigorous action and high intellect.

The scope, genius, and influence of Aristotle's thought can
hardly be overstated. He has rightly enjoyed one of the highest places
in the history of human reflection. His thought and Plato's so much
dominated Greek philosophy, however, that it underwent a serious decline after their deaths. Greek philosophy after Aristotle was largely
devoted either to a restatement of, or a commentary on the doctrines
of the two past giants, or to a reflection on highly practical matters.
It became a skeptical consolation of life, emphasized ethical and political concerns, and never again so much as approached the creative
genius of either Plato or Aristotle.

<u>Epicureanism, stoicism, skepticism, and eclecticism</u>. Despite claims to the contrary, the major interpreters of Epicureanism, stoicism, skepticism, and eclecticism, like most of their noteworthy predecessors, developed a metaphysical basis for their largely ethico-political theories. They intended, however, to dispense as fully as possible with what were regarded as the insufficiently practical problems of metaphysics. It was significantly this tendency, in fact, which led them progressively farther from the enlightenment of such as Plato and Aristotle. Epicurus (341-270 B.C.), the founder and principal figure in the school of thought which bears his name, proposed a naturalistic-tending view reminiscent of Democritus' quantitative atomism. Into the rigid mechanism of Democritus' materialism, however, Epicurus introduces a measure of contingency which allows for the possibility of human freedom. He was also committed to a strict empiricism which demonstrated that knowledge is based primarily on clear sense perceptions, and that concepts of a more general order are abstracted from these perceptions. His most lasting contribution to the history of philosophy, however, is found in his hedonistic ethics. According to this view, man's happiness, in the form of pleasure, is the highest good and the primary issue of philosophy, or the issue in which philosophy culminates. The pleasure which constitutes Epicurean happiness entails an elimination of pain by achieving good health (through proper exercise and diet) and an informed tranquility (through the study of philosophy), and by reducing one's needs (through an ascetic tranquility) and fears (by making friends of all men). Pleasure, then, is construed in terms of the serenity of the soul and the health of the body. More specifically, the reference is to basically intellectual pleasures, as distinct from those of a mere bodily sort. Like its other aspects, the Epicurean politics too stands in substantial contrast to the organic views of Plato and Aristotle. It reverts in significant measure to the individualistic conception provided by the sophists. As such, it argues that social and political institutions arise out of an impulse to protect the self-interest of all. Its view of justice is utilitarian, as distinct from working out of any rational necessity.

Stoicism, founded by Zeno (336-264 B.C.), is principally remembered for its popularized accounts of the ethico-political views of Socrates, Plato, and Aristotle. Like the views it reformulated, the Stoa, or school of stoicism, opposed the naturalistic and hedonistic fashions of Epicureanism. It did, however, share with the Epicureans their empiricist tendencies, arguing that all knowledge comes through the perception of particulars. For the Stoics, the cosmos is governed by a dynamic, rationally intelligent principle, or logos or God, somewhat as for Heraclitus. The world is consequently well ordered and inherently good. Even so, only particular objects have "real" existence by this variously idealistic- and realistic-tending view. Universal, or general ideas are considered subjective abstractions of independently existing objects. Though governed by the logos, the world has its origin in the original divine fire, and is, in virtue of this, active as soul and as passive as matter, as well as determined absolutely. Man, who is constituted as body and soul, is free only in terms of his possessing reason. The basic and most important challenge of philosophy for stoicism (as for Epicureanism) is to decide what is to be ethically done with this reason. The Stoics held (against the Epicureans) that man ought to rid himself of his passions, which effectively goes as becoming virtuous by organizing oneself in accord with right reason. The fundamental appeal was to subordinate oneself to universal ends, such as duty, and to willfully accept the course of the world with grace and without passion, or apathia--to live the virtuous and happy life which is equivalent to living in accord with the logos. By this account, all things in the well ordered universe naturally function together in a rational pursuit of the common good, and so natural law and rational law coincide in a universal commonwealth. All seek a common social benevolence and justice as dictated by reason. Cicero (106-43 B.C.) is perhaps most notable among the Stoics as the creator of a distinctly stoic social and political philosophy, and as an advocate of the stoic ideal of universal education, or a humanistic education for all men.

Skepticism, or Pyrrhonism, founded by Pyrrho (365-270 B.C.), and further developed most importantly by Carneades (213-129 B.C.) and Sextus Empiricus (160-210 A.D.), unfolded in substantially the same periods as Epicureanism and stoicism, and gave a critical response to them. In a pragmatic-tending fashion, the Sceptics argue that human reason cannot penetrate to the ultimate character of reality. Against the Epicurean and stoic criterion of truth, skepticism holds that sensation shows only how things appear and not how they are in themselves; and that there is no non-sensual criterion(a) against which the validity of sensation can be determined. Nor is it the case that sense experience is invariably consistent. What follows from this is that nothing can be known with the certainty required of true knowledge, and so that true knowledge is itself impossible. One thing cannot be conclusively demonstrated or justified by another, nor is there anything which is self-evidently true, for there is nothing on which all agree. Only a rational probability of occurrence remains as a determinant of right action. A suspension of absolute judgment which reaches this deeply produces a resignation to the impossibility of certitude, and a tranquility of the soul which accompanies such a resignation. Skepticism had the general effect of reducing the dogmatic differences, and strengthening the likenesses among the period's contending schools of philosophic thought.

Eclecticism grew out of this emphasis on likeness and similarity. It took the form of common sense pronouncements which had been upbuilt by gathering the attractive features of other systems together into an amalgram. The Roman thinkers, owing largely to their practical interests and inclinations, were particularly drawn to this position.

The great reliance of these thinkers on Greek scholarship most especially, contributed much to the eclectic urge and detracted much from
the possibility of an original and creative Roman philosophy itself.
Cicero and Seneca (3-65 A.D.) are perhaps the most illustrious of this
persuasion, though Quintilian (c.35-c.95 A.D.) is too remembered for
his philosophic reflections on education. The principal features of
Quintilian's work include arguments favoring massed as against tutorial instruction, instruction in moral precepts, early instruction in
foreign languages, and a widely liberal education so as to produce the
desired end of education, the skilled orator.

Philo. The association of Greek philosophy with Eastern religion,
most importantly Judaism, led Greek thought in its end, as in its origins, to a collapse into religion. The cosmopolitan Egyptian city of
Alexandria provided the conditions most conducive to this development.
It was here, in what we have come to know as the waning centuries of
classical antiquity, that Jewish-Greek, as well as neo-Pythagorean
and neo-Platonic religico-philosophic thought flourished most widely.
The concept of God as a transcendent being and all of the consequences
of that view, together with the preference for world-denial, were common features of these programs. The Jewish-Greek tendencies culmi-
nate in the philosophy, or theosophy, of Philo (30 B.C.-50 A.D.).
Philo attempted to demonstrate, more so by allegorical representation
than by reasoned argument, that Pythagoras, Plato, Aristotle, and the
Stoics had all put out the same wisdom, though, of course, in somewhat different forms. And that, this wisdom is basically the same as
that given in the Scriptures of Judaism. For Philo, the fundamental
interpretive principle of reality is God, or absolute transcendent, one,
immutable, ineffable, eternal, incorporeal creator. God is known by
no means, but only immediately by revelation. And since God, the
Logos, or world-soul is the creator of all things and without imperfection, evil owes its place in the world to material encumbrance. The
ethical and socio-political charge of this program is to live in accord
with the commands of the soul (the principle of good) and to deny the
requirements of the material body (the principle of evil). This is done
by a form of religious contemplation, or asceticism, which fashions
an active turning away from the body. The implications of such a view
for physical education and sport are obviously and decisively unfavorable.

Neo-Platonism: Plotinus. The neo-Pythagorean movement, which
had developed from Plato's interpretation of Pythagoras' thought, was
most influential during the first and second centuries A.D. This movement gave way in the second and third centuries A.D., however, to
neo-Platonism, in which the final stage of ancient philosophy unfolds.
The most important figures in this latter movement were Ammonius
Saccas (175-242 A.D.), Origen (185-254 A.D.), a student of Ammonius
Saccas, Plotinus (204-269 A.D.), also a student of Ammonius Saccas,
and Porphyry (232-304 A.D.), a student of Plotinus. Of these, the

most representative, profound, and influential was Plotinus, who is considered the last major philosophic figure of the ancient world. His view is made up of an admixture of Platonic thought and mystic experience. And it is ultimately devoted to the fulfillment of his life and the lives of other devoted and consistent neo-Platonists. His idealistic-tending mysticism defends as primary a form of knowledge which comes to one as a presence, or an immediate apprehension of the system of ideas as a whole which is reality. This intuitive presence, ecstasy, or union, which is superior to the mediate knowledge of science, comes only to those who have shared in its experience. There is in it a conspicuous absence of sense and reason, a lapse in differentiated consciousness--all things are recognized as a unity. This unity, or God, the Good, or the One, is construed as the transcendent source of all reality, and so as prior to all multiplicity and beyond thought and substance, or ineffable. Nothing may be predicated of this Supreme Consciousness, else He be limited by such a predication, and so thrown into imperfection. Only a negative theology, or an exposition of what He is not, is rationally possible. Perhaps the most important consequence of this is that God cannot be said to have created the world, because the differentiations and negations of consciousness and will which one finds therein would go as limitations of Him. Plotinus holds instead that the world can be explained only as emanations of God, or as the result of an inevitable overflow of His infinitude, or actuality. A tripartite hierarchy of metaphysical principle is given in order to explain the world and its transcendent relationship to the One. The first hypostasis, emanation, or multiplicity in this hierarchy is pure thought, understanding, or mind (the Ideas, or nous). The nous reflects directly back on the One, is beyond time, and falls into the second hypostasis, called soul. In this, the world of appearances reflects directly back on the images of Ideas and functions in a temporal realm. This second stage falls into the third, termed matter, body, or corporeality, which is the farthest removed from God, is absolutely passive and impotent, and is the source of all privation and the principle of evil. The immanent world, on this account, is a mere copy of the model of existence inherent in the One. Particular instances of alleged truth, justice, and beauty are, therefore, determined by comparison to absolute exemplars, as in significant measure for Plato. Plotinus explains the derivation of a lower order in the hierarchy from a higher by arguing that a thing naturally produces another thing, which, though in some degree distinct from its cause, is nonetheless dependent on that cause, and is in a paradigmatic sense similar to it. Such effects are inferior to their causes and continuously seeking a reunification with them. Plotinus' ethics is principally devoted to an account of how one comes to mystic experience, ecstasy, or a return to God. It concludes that only by a complete purgation of the external, only by a complete turning inward, a turning away from the contaminating influence of the body, is such a return, a flight of the one to the One, possible. With Plotinus the final major act in the drama of ancient philosophy is concluded, and the great reflections of the ancients give way to a new discourse, to medieval philosophy.

Medieval philosophy

The centuries in which the vitality of the ancient world in general and Greek philosophy in particular, were in decline marked also the development of the Christian religion. The intellectual life of the medieval millennium, and significantly the medieval millennium in general, would be dominated by the philosophic perplexities of the new religion. The transition period between ancient and medieval periods is commonly known as the patristic period. This period begins with the time of Christ and ends with the death of St. Augustine in 430. It is more so a period in which theology takes over philosophy, than one in which philosophy itself flourishes. Philosophy is more so run over with dogmatic proclamations of Christian faith, than it is devoted to an independent inquiry into the fundamental nature and significance of reality. Philosophy became not a great deal other than a rational elaboration of Christianity--it was used in the explanation and support of what was already held to be true on theologic authority. The basic tenets of Christianity were formed during this period, and insofar as these tenets were influenced by philosophic persuasions, they were influenced most importantly by neo-Platonism. Philosophically, the period is of interest because in it are found the basic inclinations which run throughout medieval thought. The most significant of these inclinations has to do with justifying the new faith to reason. This is a task first taken up in earnest by the Gnostics and the Apologists in the second century. Both schools sought a conciliation between reason and faith, science and religion. The wildly speculative initiatives of the Gnostics ended in an ineffective mythological personification of metaphysical principles. The Apologists held that, though the source of truth is supernatural, it is nonetheless rational, and so rationally comprehensible by divinely inspired minds. They argued that the apparent reason and order in the world presuppose the existence of a transcendent and immutable First Cause, which has itself willfully emitted, or begotten, the Logos with which the First Cause is one. This Logos doctrine, or doctrine of the trinity, later canonized as the Nicene Creed, postulates the terms in which divine reason instantiates itself in the incarnate person of Christ, and in this postulation explains the relationship of Christianity's transcendent God and the immanent world. Under the considerable influence of neo-Platonism, the Apologists were also of the view that the highest good resides in a resignation from the world of sense, and as aspiration to the supernatural world, or God. Evil is construed as the human tendency to freely act other than toward such an aspiration. The Apologists made a particularly great deal of the need to communicate these truths to all persons, and the need to move all persons to an acceptance of them. The major figures in this movement were Justin Martyr (c.100-166), Tertullian (160-240), and Origen. The developments of the patristic period, dominated as they were by neo-Platonism and apologetics, provide the foundations on which medieval thought itself is built. The discussion of medieval philosophy which follows is set out in the following divisions: Augustine, Erigena, Anselm, Abelard, Thomas Aquinas, Duns Scotus and Occam, and Mysticism.

Augustine. St. Augustine (354-430) was the most authentic, constructive, and influential of the early Christian philosophers. His thought represents the culmination of patristic tendencies, and it remains the dominant influence on Christian philosophy for centuries. Augustine was most heavily influenced by neo-Platonism, most emphatically by Plotinus. In effect, his system is a neo-Platonic interpretation of Christian theology. According to this account, the most worthy knowledge is of God and of self. Knowledge of all else is of value only insofar as it enhances these understandings. The primary importance of revelation in coming to such knowledge is apparent in Augustine's view that reason only determines the authenticity or inauthenticity of revelation (it is revelation which reason acts on, and not the reverse), and that this judgment is affirmed by faith. This leads to the conclusion that one understands only so that he may believe, and believe dutifully under the guidance of reason--Augustine's credo ut intelligam. The source of revelation is, of course, God, or Absolute Spirit, construed as omnipotent, and thereby also omniscient, omnibenevolent, transcendent, absolutely free and self-sufficient, and willing and doing at once without means. He is the source and creator of all things. From nothing He has created, and He sustains, continuously in every moment and through every expanse, the most perfect world possible. Augustine accepts the Trinity on faith alone, as a revelation of indisputable merit.

Much as had Plato, Augustine conceives man as a rational soul inhabitating a body. The soul itself is considered a rational substance constituting the principle of life. The body is essentially different than, and separate from this substance, though it is given life by it, and lives in it. The soul, as the contrary of body, is unextended, immutable, and immortal. Since no thing lacks itself in any measure, and since the soul is itself eternal, it cannot die, though it does not exist prior to the body as for Plato. It nonetheless persists into eternity from the moment of its creation. It inhabits every part of the body at once and completely, and effects bodily changes without itself changing. Even with this, what gives the impression of an unfavorable view of the body, however, Augustine stops short of the neo-Platonist inclination to think it the principle of evil itself. What allows Augustine this prospect is the differences he has with both Plato and the neo-Platonists on the general issue of evil. For him, evil is indispensable to goodness, and so in the most significant sense continuous with it, as distinct from qualitatively opposed to it. From the perspective of divinity, then, if not from superficial human perspectives, this is the best of all possible worlds. Still at this, the ethical ideal of man is to achieve a union of the soul with God, to obtain an eternal

blessedness in God, or the true life of pure form. This life is obtained by exercise of the supreme virtue, love. The record of this exercise constitutes history according to Augustine. This record reveals
that the world unfolds in accord with the nature and purpose of God,
and it does this through a perpetual conflict between the earthly kingdom, which is dominated by love of self and contempt of God, and the
heavenly kingdom, which is dominated by love of God and contempt of
self.

Augustine's attack on skepticism is particularly memorable and
telling. It shows that in the act of doubting itself one comes on a proposition the very doubt of which affirms it. This proposition is the
cogito ergo sum, the I think, therefore I am. Augustine holds that the
act of doubting presupposes an agent of doubt, and that man cannot,
therefore, plausibly doubt that he doubts, and so that he thinks, and so
that he exists. This is the first part of a discussion which attempts
to re-establish confidence in human understanding. The second part
talks about the validity and reliability of sense knowledge. In this part
is found Augustine's treatment of sensation as an active awareness of
the soul, and his distinction between the five exterior senses which
cannot be mistaken, and the interior senses of organizing external
data according to concepts of shape, size, motion, etc., about which
one can be misled. He thus both accounts for perceptual error and resists the fall to skepticism concerning contingent truths. The matter
of necessary truth is reserved for divine illumination, however.
Augustine solves the general problem of truth in much the same way as
Plato; that is, by arguing that truth is neither a purely subjective nor
a purely objective phenomenon. Truth appears as divine revelation
and in the attendant correspondence of an objective world with an independent awareness of that world.

The process of systematic doubt which so marks Augustine's
epistemology is also at the center of his philosophy of education. In
this process, one deliberately casts doubt on all that one is inclined to
believe. The end of this process is the cogito, and it is from this end
that the lot of contingent truth emanates. The philosophy of education
is further distinguished by Augustine's view that all speech is for
teaching or learning, because it is the basic function of words to call
things to mind of which words are mere signs. And though nothing can
be taught or learned without such speech, words, or signs, it is the
awareness of the thing that the sign represents which is actually learned or taught, and which is most fundamental and important. Only the
meanings of signs constitute knowledge, not the signs themselves. It
is things which give meaning to words, not words to things. One is,
therefore, taught by means of words which are either known or not
known. In both of these cases, however, the student cannot be said to
have learned anything, in the sense in which he can be said to have
"acquired" knowledge. This is Plato's educational paradox which
stems from his metaphysical position, and which Augustine inherits

from him. According to this paradox, one teaches only by stimulating recollection of what is already known, one learns only by making such a recollection. These recollections come to one either through an interior light of reason which allows insight into necessary truths, or through an exterior light which reveals insight into contingent truths. And since only God holds necessary truths, which are after all the basis of all contingent truths, only God is in full possession of the internal light of reason and the basic means of recollection, and so only God is teacher, or **magistro**, in the full sense. Owing to this, and to the deeply pagan character of most of this period's formal education, Augustine resolutely condemned such eduation.

Little of philosophic significance was achieved from the end of the patristic period to the ninth century reflections of Erigena. Perhaps only Porphyry and Boethius (480-525) warrant mention as exceptions to this early medieval hiatus. During this period, the speculative impulse so apparent in Augustine and the best ancient philosophy was covered over by appeals to religious authority, and to those philosophic ideas which supported this authority (principally the ideas of Plato, Aristotle, and Augustine). What remains in this treatment of medieval philosophy is a discussion of Erigena's work, of the flowering of scholasticism in the twelfth and thirteenth centuries, and of the decline of scholasticism in the fourteenth and fifteenth centuries. Throughout what is left of the medieval period, the major philosophic issue remains the relation of faith (in which the will is dominant) and reason (in which the intellect is dominant). The distinctions inherent in this relation are applied most importantly to the problem of the Christian Trinity, and to the problem of universals (or, substantive classes of things).

Erigena. The fourth century lacuna in early medieval philosophy comes to an end with the pantheistic thought of John Scotus Erigena (810-c.877). Erigena's reformulation of neo-Platonic and Augustinian notions of reality conceives of God as the transcendent, omniscient, omnipotent, omnibenevolent, and ineffable creator and sustainer of all things. From Him all things flow, in Him all things exist, and to Him all things return. Reality is nothing other than God evidencing Himself to the world, nothing other than a reflection of the Divine Light. Erigena's division of nature distinguishes things that are not created but create (God), things that are both created and create (ideas), things that are created but do not create (objects), and things which are neither created nor create (God in His rest). Principal among his other major ideas are his imputing evil to man's willful fall from God, his exhorting man to lose himself in the Divine Darkness by rising above sense and reason through mystic exaltation in order to behold God and to dwell in His life, and his heretical rejection of the orthodox Christian notion of individual immortality and eternal punishment. Erigena was the earliest of the schoolmen to assimilate a Christian conception of reality into a universal system of thought. He was also the last until the eleventh century when the full impact of nominalism revealed itself, most importantly in the work of Roscelin (c.1045-c.1120), an advocate of nominalism, and Anselm, an opponent of the nominalist heresy.

Anselm. St. Anselm (1033-1109) is widely remembered as one of the most characteristic of the schoolmen (most particularly in terms of his relative allegiances to faith and reason), and for his opposition to the nominalistic heresy of Roscelin (according to which universals are not themselves "real", but mere names which refer to "real" particulars), for his restatement of Augustine's cosmological argument for the existence of God, and most importantly for his original formulation of the ontological argument for the existence of God. This latter contribution makes use of Plato's realistic conception of universals as having an existence independent of particular objects, but as nonetheless making nothing other than appearances in such objects. Anselm begins this argument by assuming the perfection of God, and he ends it by showing that the existence of God is entailed by His perfection. Otherwise, God would lack the perfection of existence. That is, from the view that God is that than which none greater can be conceived, or absolute perfection, comes the deductive conclusion of His necessary existence. God cannot, therefore, be conceived not to exist according to Anselm. Gaunilon (fl. 11th century) pointed up the apparent fallacy in Anselm's argument by demonstrating that one can conceive of perfections which are not in actual fact part of the metaphysical whole. He suggests a perfect island as an example of this. Thus, as for Kant later, Gaunilon argued that existence cannot be necessarily predicated of a concept, not even the concept of perfection, or God. Another of the most significant figures of this period arguing against the nominalistic view of universals and in favor of the realistic interpretation of them is William of Champeaux (1070-1121), who holds that each universal category is completely present in every instance of the category. This strict realism, together with the strict nominalism of Roscelin, led Abelard, a student of both Roscelin and William, to a moderation of the two positions.

Abelard. Though Peter Abelard (1079-1142) wished to oppose the solutions to the problem of universals of both Roscelin and William, he did not himself give an altogether concise interpretation of the problem. He apparently held that universals are given only to significant words, which are, in turn, predicated of many things because of their likeness in these things. Things, therefore, agree with respect to the universals predicated of them, but these universals are not themselves things, nor are they in things. This nominalistic-tending view consequently argues that only individual substances exist of themselves, but that these substances possess within common qualities of which universals may be predicated. Abelard was convinced that this "resolution" overcomes both the ascription of contradictory qualities to identical substances apparent in the realism of William, and the existential dilemma (most importantly with respect to the Trinity) raised by the nominalism of Roscelin. Abelard's contributions to the philosophy of education are also legion. In both thought and practice, Abelard was one of the most brilliant teachers of his time. He is best remembered in this respect for his innovative method of intellectual discourse. This method, later adopted by high scholasticism and known in that circumstance as the scholastic method, was called dicta pro et contra. In it, both affirmative and negative arguments concerning theological issues in which there was great interest, but also typically great disagreement, were given. The relative merits of these arguments were then left to the independent and informed judgment of individual students and teachers. This preserved a certain integrity of mind which it was Abelard's great concern to preserve. The work of Peter Lombard (c.1100-c.1160), a student of Abelard, rigorously followed and applied Abelard's method, and became the medieval model for all succeeding attempts of the kind--attempts called sentences.

Also profitably talked about here are the important developments in Eastern, most particularly in Arabian philosophy during the medieval period. Armed with the teachings of Mohammed and a familiarity of Plato and Aristotle most prominently, the Islamic East fashioned a philosophic account of its religious faith--a rational defense of Islam --which in outline very much resembled Western scholasticism. This account tended toward a rationalistic and deductive view of reality, and on occasion fell into mythological interpretations of nature. It reached its Eastern apogee in the metaphysical work of Avicenna (980-1037), who was most influenced by Plato, and who argued from fact to necessary being, or God. According to Avicenna, God's quiddity, or essence, is uniquely necessary to His existence: He is thereby uncaused, though the cause of all else. And it reached its highest level in the West with the thought of the great Islamic commentator on Aristotle, Averroës (1126-1198). Like Aristotle, Averroës defends the reliability of causality, and so of the sciences which are established by it. He holds that science is the knowledge of causes by which even the existence of God is probable. His system is devoted principally to securing demonstrative, scientific, or necessary knowledge of such causes, and so not merely to the gathering of contingent explanations. The notions of corporeal and spiritual immortality are accepted on religious authority alone, however. Arabian philosophy, most emphatically that of Aristotelian persuasion, also greatly influenced the Jewish philosophers of the medieval period. The most notable of these was Moses Maimonides (1135-1204), who carried out a Judaic scholasticism not unlike the Christian and Islamic forms. That is, Maimonides attempted the same sort of conciliation between divine revelation, considered the primary source of knowledge, and rational dictate, regarded as of derivative importance, as it was the Christian and Islamic custom to attempt. Most significant of Maimonides' views are his conception of God as absolute existence (the I am who am), and his argument for spiritual (and not bodily) immortality.

The culminating stages of Christian scholasticism are much assisted by the rise of the great European universities and the enthusiasm for high scholarship which comes with them, by the establishment of the mendicant orders (principally the Dominicans and the Franciscans), which incline toward accomplished intellectual activity, and which greatly influence the universities in this respect, and by the rediscovery of the exiled thought of Plato, Aristotle, and Augustine, largely through new associations with Arabian philosophy. Though scholasticism is moving to its highest triumphs in the twelfth and thirteenth centuries, most significantly in the synthetic genius of Thomas Aquinas, there are also some influential antischolastic tendencies apparent in this time, some of which show themselves more fully in the later decline of scholasticism. The most notable of these include appeals to emphasize more practical expressions of faith (expressions less contaminated by reason and scholarship) as in mysticism, and heretical appeals to pantheism which challenge the transcendence of God.

Thomas Aquinas. The richly talented Dominican teacher of
St. Thomas Aquinas (1225-1274), Albertus Magnus, or Albert the Great (1193-1280), was the first ecclesiastic to carefully set the system of Aristotle to scholastic themes. It remained for Thomas, however, to work this system out in full articulate, systematic, and comprehensive fashion. Thomas' system represents the highest reach of scholasticism, and it is perhaps the best developed philosophic account of orthodox Christianity yet achieved. At bottom, the system attempts to demonstrate the rationality of the universe as a revelation of God. Accordingly, such trappings of Christian gogma as the Trinity and original sin are to be accepted on faith alone--they are revealed, and so beyond reason, and so not a proper object of philosophic inquiry, though they are in no sense nor measure contrary to reason. For Thomas, philosophy, in which the intellect is dominant, moves from facts, or known effects, to God, or unknown cause; and theology, in which the will is dominant, from God to facts. A philosophic apprehension of God is, therefore, inferred from His creation, a posteriori. Such an apprehension is gained through an observation of His effects in the world (the five ways of Thomas), effects which cannot be explained except by appeal to Him (the cosmological argument for the existence of God). Insofar as God's existence is not self-evident and so outside the purview of demonstration, it may be demonstrated only by those things which are more known to man, if not less known and perfect in themselves. Thomas' epistemology, like Aristotle's, holds that all knowledge has its basis in the particularity of sense perception, but that genuine knowledge consists in the universality of conceptual science. Sensation is not what we know, but that by which we know. And in the realist-nominalist dispute concerning universals, Thomas sides

with the realist thesis, arguing that universals are the essences of things and that they have no existence apart from their being in particular objects.

Thomas also adopts Aristotle's principle of individuation as matter, or potentiality, and his view of essence as form, or actuality. Nature is then explained as the union of form and matter. Angels and human souls are pure spiritual, or formal beings, which have their individuality within themselves. And God is pure actuality, His being and essence are eternally undifferentiated, or one, He is His own existence, and His knowledge is one and at once, or intuitive as distinct from discursive, or rational. According to this view, truth goes as the correspondence of the world to God's ideas, which are the first and the cause of all things, material and spiritual. The world is constituted by bodies, which are below man, human souls, which are at the level of man, and intellectual substances, which are above man. Man as such is construed as the autonomous unity (or substance) of a soul aspect and a bodily aspect--as a composite being, or a conjunction of intelligence and sensibility. The cleavage between intelligence and sensibility is so radical on Thomas' account that a linking principle, called the agent intellect, is required. It is by means of this principle that man raises sense impressions to intellectual knowledge. This dualistic view allows Thomas to say that the incorporeal soul can live unembodied, and that it is, by divine grace, immortal from the moment of its finite beginning.

For Thomas, an intuitive knowledge, vision, or love of God is the highest good. Man fulfills his true self; that is, approaches his own perfection by standing in viable relation to this knowledge. This return to God is achieved by cultivating one's uniquely human aspect, the rational aspect. By acting in accord with this aspect, and so the divine purpose, one realizes his goodness and experiences greatest happiness. Such an acting is tantamount to living the contemplative life, or the life lived for the love of God, as distinct from the practical life, or the life dominated by the love of man. Accordingly, man is the cause of evil only in the sense in which, or insofar as, he fails to move in the direction of his perfection. In such an instance the will is said to have been the unsatisfactory guide of reason. Moreover, in order both to preserve the omniscience of God, and to escape the clutches of necessary pre-destination (which would, if not escaped, relieve man of his free moral choice), Thomas argues that God must have knowledge of future contingencies (like one's salvation or damnation) without pre-ordaining them. Moral acts, then, are those guided by the intention of deliberated and free reason, toward a particular end, and in particular circumstances. The politics of Thomas grows easily out of his ethics, as well as the ethics and politics of Aristotle. It proceeds on the organic notion that the socio-political domain is not primarily an aggregate of individuals, but itself an ordered multitude, or community of virtuous souls, held together by a Christian vision of

God. Thomas favors a monarchial form of government, as adequately avoiding the extremes of totalitarianism and anarchy, and as best serving the common good. This monarchy is obligated to conduct itself in accord with the unfolding of divine law, and so effect an ordering of law whereby the divine instructs and fashions the natural in its own image. In this, man comes to share the divine light of reason in the form of the natural law, and the socio-political order becomes itself a divine realm of sorts--the socio-political fabric is invested with divinity, one might say. It is further the case, by Thomas' account, that the common good is assured only wherein the internal unity of the state is secure from external transgression, and that it is only the unity of a virtuous multitude which obtains such a security. The monarch is thereby entrusted with the protection of this unity, and so with the preservation of the common good.

Thomas, like many other prominent thirteenth century thinkers such as Raymond Lilly (1235-1315), clung to the scholastic belief in the capacity of reason to demonstrate the certitude of virtually all things. This belief, however, was fast giving way to an eroding confidence in reason as a worthy auxiliary to faith. Most important among thirteenth century opponents of scholasticism were St. Bonaventura (1221-1274), a Franciscan mystic-ascetic of neo-Platonist leaning, Roger Bacon (1214-1294), a Franciscan logician, mathematician, and scientist, and the late medieval champions of pantheism. The final blows to the scholastic urge were delivered in the fourteenth century, however, in the form of Duns Scotus' moderate realism, Occam's nominalist triumph, and Eckhart's mysticism.

Duns Scotus and Occam. The great dialectician and Franciscan opponent of Thomas, John Duns Scotus (c.1226, 1274-1308), called "the subtle doctor", held that human knowledge is defective in certain crucial respects. He imputes the imperfection of such knowledge to the Fall from grace. With Thomas, Duns Scotus argues that, though there is no dispute between the truths of faith and those of reason, only faith can sustain the fundamental truths of Christian ideology. Duns Scotus much more dramatically restricts the scope of reason than Thomas, however. This more skeptical line suggests a separation between the practical concerns of theology which operate under the dictates of faith and in a divinely revealed dogma, and the theoretical concerns of philosophy which operate in accord with rational precept--the doctrine of twofold truth. Accordingly, Duns Scotus thinks himself the liberator of both philosophy and theology. Moreover, his realistic concept of universals argues that acts of thought correspond to a concrete reality, and that universals exist prior to their instantiation in the world (in the mind of God), in objects in the world as their essence, and after such objects as remembrances in the minds of men. This concept accounts both for the universality of thought, as well as for the principle of individuation inherent in matter. The highest universal, and so the highest object of metaphysics, for Duns Scotus, is being, for being can be predicated of all things. God alone possesses, or is pure being, pure form, or pure actuality, is unlimited, eternal, and independent. Like Thomas, Duns Scotus is convinced that the only possible demonstration of God's existence is from His effects, a posteriori. From these effects, he infers the possibility of God's existence, and urges from this, that if God did not exist His existence would be impossible, and that God, therefore, necessarily exists. Though this argument apparently rests on an equivocal notion of possibility, Duns Scotus nonetheless concludes that it is not possible for God not to exist, as the very idea of God itself would be self-contradictory and so impossible in such a circumstance. And, since the free will of God is thought the source of all moral principles, His existence also makes morality possible.

The skeptical tendencies of Duns Scotus prepared the way for a yet more "radical" departure from the orthodox Christian position. This departure is much opposed to Thomas, and, to a lesser but nonetheless important extent, to Duns Scotus as well. It is nominalistic, convinced that there are no theologic truths accessible to reason, and led by William of Occam (c.1280-1347), a Franciscan student of Duns Scotus called "the invincible doctor". According to Occam, the only source of true, demonstrable knowledge is experience. All knowledge which cannot be traced to a beginning in experience is known on faith alone. The existence of God cannot, therefore, be demonstrated either a priori or a posteriori--it is wholly unintelligible to reason, and so known only by faith. The separation of philosophy and theology is thereby made complete, and with this completion the scholastic impulse is buried. Occam held that only particular substances and qualities exist, and that only an appeal to such substances and qualities is, therefore, needed in giving an account of the whole of reality. This movement in the direction of ontological simplicity concludes in the view that all science, all knowledge, consists in organized bodies of propositions about particular things. Universals, therefore, exist only as objects of knowledge, or acts of intellect, abstracted from particular things. They are neither inherent in things, nor are they held in the mind of God. This nominalistic concept of universals, and the metaphysical presuppositions which underlie it rest on the hypothesis that principles or entities are not to be multiplied without necessity. In the case of Occam's own system, this comes to claiming that there is insufficient reason for leaping to the realistic inclination which makes things of ideas--Occam's Razor.

Mysticism: Eckhart. A certain tendency to mysticism spread itself throughout the medieval period. The widely skeptical mood of the fourteenth century encouraged a fuller expression of this tendency than it had earlier got. The movement was unsatisfied with purely intellectual accounts of God and religion, and sought instead a method for obtaining personal experience of God. The most prominent fourteenth century exponent of this position was the Dominican heretic,

Meister Eckhart (1260-1327). In accord with his neo-Platonist proclivity, Eckhart conceives God as an eternal, immutable, ineffable,
limitless, spiritual substance in which all things are united, and which
becomes manifest only in the Trinity. For him, all things are in God
and God in all things. And it is the most basic need and obligation of
man to obtain an intuitive contemplation of, and thereby unification
with God--to obtain through grace a reunified being with God, a selfless amalgamation of the one to the One. With Occam and mysticism,
then, comes the dissolution of scholasticism, and the dissolution of
what made medieval thought what it was. The period, in general, was
not favorably disposed to bodily events, and so neither to such as
physical education and sport. The changing trends which are already
apparent in the thirteenth and fourteenth centuries, however, will be
accelerated and variously reformulated in the modern period, and this
reformulation will bring with it a more approving disposition concerning the body and physical education and sport.

Modern philosophy

The new philosophic era emerged as an opposing response to
medievalism. It was characterized by a classic interest in free and
independent inquiry, by a preference for secular, as distinct from
religious authority, and by an advancing individualism, a renewed
confidence in reason, and a more fully developed attention to the human. The liberation of philosophy from theology was continued and
greatly advanced through this period. The period's debt to classical
antiquity cannot be easily overemphasized. Plato and Aristotle, in
particular, were major influences on early modern thought. Marsilio
Ficino (1433-1499) is best remembered as the most accomplished of
the Renaissance Platonists. Aristotle remained an important authority
for Christian theology, and greatly influenced the movement from
supernatural to natural religion (as most notably in the work of
Herbert of Cherbury, 1583-1648), the movement toward modern science through philosophic reflections on nature (as most notably in the
occult-like accounts of Bernardino Telesio, 1508-1588), the scientific
tendency to appeal to natural, as distinct from divine law, the educational inclination to humanize itself and to harmonize its intellectual
and its physical parts, and the development of a new politics emphasizing the sovereignty of socio-political orders (as most notably in the
work of Niccolo Machiavelli, 1469-1527). And as has been typically
the case since the beginning of genuinely philosophic reflection, traces
of mysticism, as in Jacob Boehme (1575-1624), and skepticism, as in
Pierre Bayle (1647-1706), also run through the period. The discussion of modern philosophy given here is worked out in the following
divisions: Nicolas, Bruno, and Campanella, Bacon and Hobbes, the
rationalists, the empiricists, Rousseau, and Kant.

<u>Nicolas, Bruno, and Campanella</u>. Nicolas of Cusa (1401-1464) gives the fifteenth century its only original system. The idealistic-tending character of his thought represents a unique admixture of, and provides a transitive link between medieval and modern philosophy. Nicolas rejects the fashionable skeptical enticements of the period, and embraces instead a mystic conception of God. By this view, God is infinite, inaccessible to reason, and knowable only by mystic intuition. The world is then construed as distinct from God, but nonetheless a copy of Him. The first authentically modern philosophy comes from the Dominicans, Giordano Bruno (1548-1600) and Tommaso Campanella (1568-1639), however. Like Nicolas, Bruno opts for an idealistic-tending, mystic world view, according to which God is the rationally unobtainable unity of all things. Unlike Nicolas, however, Bruno's God is immanent, and so the active principle of the infinite universe. In Campanella is found a realistic-tending position which variously argues that all knowledge is based on sensation, that nature is a revelation of God, and that the best form of socio-political organization is socialistic, the best form of socio-political power is governed by knowledge, and the best form of education is universal and compulsory.

<u>Bacon and Hobbes</u>. The genius of empirical science gave the seventeenth century its greatest disputations and its most overwhelming preoccupation. The new science discredited some of the ancient insights, propelled modern thought beyond the authority of the past, and generally demanded that deductive principles concerning the world consult the evidence produced by empirical experimentation. Francis Bacon (1561-1626) was the first of the great scientific humanists--the first to give philosophic expression to the new age of science. He held that scientific advancements make for the most significant sorts of humanistic contribution, and that a responsible and viable promotion of the common good depends on the participation of all persons in the empirical form of scientific awareness. Bacon attempts to replace the deductive logic of Aristotle as the ideal of science, knowledge, morality, and society with a formal system of inductive logic extrapolated from operations of experimental observation. His empiricistic program looks to erect a new method, instrument, or organ by which a reconstruction of the whole of human knowledge can be achieved. This method is used to explain the world (but for the divine revelations of heavenly mystery known only by faith) as a mosaic of natural, or material causes and effects. According to this pragmatic-tending view, philosophy is thought the highest of all knowledges, for it serves by force of reason to combine all experimental insights, and to see their most general significance. John Amos Comenius (1593-1670) was the most celebrated and accomplished educational interpreter of Baconianism, and the first major, modern philosopher of education. He is best remembered for his ingenious use of nature and inductionism in the educational process, his insistence on rich sense

experience in a balanced intellectual and physical education, and his doctrine of pansophism, or universal education (all knowledge to all men).

Few thinkers of this time are as characteristically modern as Thomas Hobbes (1588-1679). Like Bacon, Hobbes emphasized the empirical source of knowledge, the practical utility of science and philosophy, and the radical distinction between the reason and experience of science and the faith of theology. Hobbes' materialistic naturalism explains the world in terms of the motion of material causes and effects. Unlike Bacon, however, Hobbes' epistemology demonstrates the important role of deduction, as well as that of induction, in scientific demonstration. Hobbes is also well remembered for his unique concept of mind, known since as epiphenomenalism, according to which the mind is considered a mosaic of cognitive events, or processes themselves construed as appearances, or effects of motions. Perhaps Hobbes' most significant and enduring contribution to the history of philosophic thought is contained in his social and poltiical philosophy, however. In this aspect of his thought, Hobbes suggests that it is "right" and reasonable for men to do whatever they must to preserve themselves. In a state of nature, then, men would be led to a perpetual and generalized conflict of all against all. The commodities requisite to preservation would of necessity be warred over. In such a circumstance, each attempts to possess all power in order to assure its not being used against him, thereby denying him the preservation he most desires. According to Hobbes, there is the greatest need for a sovereign to rescue such an "order" from its self-destructive tendencies. For, in the state of nature there is no peace, security, justice, right, wrong, or property, and so one's preservation is not so much assured as it is an object of endless attack. The natural "right" to do harm to others must, therefore, be relinquished in the interest of obtaining peace, justice, right conduct, and so one's preservation. One must be content only with so much liberty as one is prepared to allow others. Man thereby voluntarily enters a social contract which binds him by duty to a commonwealth. This commonwealth must be so formed as to compel all men equally to honor their avowed obligations to it. For Hobbes, this entails a commonwealth in which absolute power is invested in one man, or assembly of men. In this man or assembly, the wills of all men become one. This one is Hobbes' Leviathan from which the supreme power of the sovereign is derived. The sovereign consequently represents the subjects who have granted him authority, and he holds their loyalty only so long as he assures peace, security, justice, and right conduct. Much could likely be made of this notion with respect to the socio-political dimensions of education, physical education and sport.

The rationalists: Descartes, Leibniz, and Spinoza. No issue runs more pervasively through, nor has such a profound impact on modern philosophy as the issue concerning the origin and nature of knowledge.

The transitional figures, Nicolas, Bruno, and Campanella, yet relied principally on theological explanations of this, and Bacon and Hobbes gave largely scientific accounts of it. The major disputants with respect to this issue per se are the seventeenth century Continental rationalists and the eighteenth century British empiricists, however. The rationalists were the intellectual descendants of Plato, Aristotle, and the medieval realists, while the empiricists inherited the philosophic lineage of the medieval nominalists. Both groups agreed that nothing can be known independelty of experience, but they differed widely concerning the origin of knowledge and its model, or nature.

René Descartes (1596-1650) was the first of the three great rationalist thinkers of this period. In his system, which shows both idealistic and realistic tendencies, Descartes erects mathematics as the model of all knowledge, and hopes to obtain mathematical certainty even in philosophic matters. He argues that knowledge must be based on that which cannot be doubted--it must be an absolutely certain, self-contained, and formal system of thought. This is Descartes' celebrated methodologic skepticism which concludes that the gamut of human knowledge must be reconstructed on such an indubitable foundation. The major metaphysical difficulty Descartes faced had to do with the reconciliation of a mechanistic, passive, or determined natural order, and a free and active divine order--the reconciliation of nature, man, and God. The final resolution has science and theology each operating in a separate realm, and neither influencing the events of the other.

By the principle of systematic doubt, which accepts only that which there is no occasion or reason to doubt (namely, simple, self-evident propositions and what follows progressively from such propositions), Descartes first calls the testimony of the senses, which have on occasion deceived us, into serious question; then the authority of others, the existence of the external world, and even the truths of mathematics are challenged. This process is followed out until he comes on a notion that by its nature cannot be doubted. Much as for Augustine, that notion is bound up in the matter of doubt itself. Descartes argues that doubting itself entails thinking, which, in turn, entails being. The presence of the activity of doubting, therefore, gives rise to the proposition that, I think, therefore I am--the cogito ergo sum. It is from the certainty of the cogito that Descartes draws other so-termed clear and distinct ideas, like the existence of an external world, to which our ideas correspond, and by which they are awakened, the existence of man as comprised of extended and unextended substance, the veracity of well considered sense perceptions, and the existence of God and His goodness by which man achieves a knowledge of the world.

Descartes' dualistic concept of man resembles Plato's and Augustine's. It holds that man is comprised of mind, or intellectual substance, or _res cogitans_, and body, or material substance, or _res extensans_. By this view, the body, which is extended and unthinking, is merely something that man has; the mind, however, which is un-extended and thinking, is what man essentially is, what makes him peculiarly human. The primary status of the mind in human nature and activity then forms the basis of Descartes' ethics as a search for the mind's freedom from material influences. The radical propor-tions of this mind-body dualism led Descartes to the most extreme imaginable lengths in trying to show how the mind and body get to-gether as they evidently do. The solution he ultimately gives, the in-famous "pineal gland hypothesis", is a form of interactionism, ac-cording to which the mind and body "simply" act on each other in the pineal gland.

Moreover, Descartes is also convinced that the extension of knowledge--its development from the cogito--depends on establishing the existence of God as a non-deceiver, else our knowledge be the possible consequence of an evil demon's handicraft. Proceeding from an innately held clear and distinct idea of God as eternal, omniscient, omnipotent, omnibenevolent, and the creator and sustainer of all things, Descartes advances three major arguments for the existence of God. One is a causal proof which establishes the existence of God by the principle of sufficient reason--an effect cannot contain more than its cause. Another, related proof, suggests that the existence of God is presupposed by the existence of man--only God could have created such a thinking being. And the third is a form of the ontologi-cal argument--the conception of God itself entails His existence.

In the end, Descartes was convinced that he had achieved the re-constrution of human knowledge that had been promised in the begin-ning. And though few features of his system did anything other than affirm the orthodox Christian world view, the system nonetheless ele-vated the terms of this view to knowledge, in his judgment. He thought that by reason he had discovered the a priori ideas held innately in the mind which explain the whole of things.

It was the radically dualistic aspects of Descartes' philosophy--aspects which prevented a satisfactory link between the material bod-ies of science and the free minds of spiritualistic theology--together with his largely unresolved relation between man and God, that vari-ously inspired and provoked a rich volume of response for centuries to follow. In fact, much of modern philosophy is taken up with com-mentaries on, or critiques of his system. The Jansenists, who trans-lated his system into educational terms, were perhaps his greatest admirers. They were variously committed to eliminating the innate depravity of learners by demanding of them the memorization of pon-derous numbers of clear and distinct ideas, to the use of vernacular language in promoting clear communication, and to the reduction of complex ideas to their simplest possible logical and mathematical

forms. The learned voices against him, most particularly on the
matter of dualistic tendency and the pineal linking principle, however,
were both more numerous and more persuasive. Occasionalism, as
most notably expressed in the thought of Arnold Geulincx (1624-1669),
argued that Descartes' mind-body relation is better formulated either
as a continuous divine interference, or as a pre-established harmony.
Blaise Pascal (1623-1662) defended Descartes' dualism, but thought a
knowledge of ultimates unobtainable. And Nicolas Malebranche (1638-
1715) gave an idealistic-tending response which claimed that, though
we are aware by revelation of the existence of a material world, we
cannot know it as a world of extended things. It is a world which is
constituted we know not how, a terra incognita. By this account, we
know only a world of ideas, an intelligible world in ideal space.
Descartes' mind-body dualism is, therefore, overcome by arguing
that only ideas of bodies, and not bodies themselves, affect minds and
are known.

One of the most instructive rationalistic critiques of Cartesianism comes from one of the most accomplished rationalists of the time,
the celebrated German mathematician and philosophic essayist,
Gottfried Wilhelm Leibniz (1646-1716). In idealistic-tending fashion,
Leibniz hoped to discover the true organon, or ideal language, what
turned out to be the infinitesimal calculus, of reason for the sciences,
and to reconcile modern science, philosophy, and Christian theology
through this discovery. He regarded Descartes' methodological skepticism as incapable of yielding any knowledge whatever, recognizing
instead that a definitive system of thought necessarily rests on plausible assumptions, or first principles. One must take something as
given in order to make a beginning at all. Leibniz constructs his system, then, on the principle of contradiction (which considers false all
that may be contradicted), the principle of sufficient reason (which
postulates that all that has come into existence has been caused, and
so that some reason explains all existence), the cogito, the existence
of the external world, and the existence of God. He was also critical
of Descartes' circular dependence on the existence of God and his lack
of adequate criteria for clear and distinct ideas. For Leibniz, the
universe is an harmonious whole governed by universal and necessary
principles of a logical and mathematical sort. The world is so constituted that it can be explained by the application of these innate principles to our experience. This experience does not create these principles, it furnishes the occasion in which they are demonstrated.
Leibniz' devotion to reason as the ultimate instrument of knowledge--
as that capable of discovering all that our finite perspectives will al-
low--is virtually complete.

Leibniz was convinced that, since bodies gain and lose motion,
and since the continuity of nature is always preserved, there must be
a ground of motion, or something more fundamental than motion which
explains its varying presence. This something Leibniz terms force,

or the constant tendency of a body to move. According to this view, all substances are expressions of force. And units of force, various- ly called essential forms, formal atoms, or monads, are constituted as the union of souls, or active, unitary, psychic substances, and matter, or passive, differentiated, corporeal substances. An infinite number of these units formally comprise the world, and though no one of them is extended, groups of them are, as in the case of a point's relationship to a line. They are eternal (that is, neither created, nor, except by miracle, can they be destroyed), and so also immater- ial and unextended. Leibniz thus fashions a dynamic, or energetic, as distinct from a geometric, or static, view of the world--he takes account of both the substance and the motion in it. He also succeeds in overcoming Descartes' circular reliance on the existence of God, though himself offering forms of the ontological and cosmological proofs for His existence.

Though every monad is a self-contained microcosm of the entire universe, each also represents the universe in a unique way. Monads are, therefore, alike only in the most widely general terms. And they arrange themselves in a hierarchy according to clearness. The lowest monads are dominated by obscurity and confusion, while the highest, the monad of monads, the perfect monad, or God, is con- strued as pure activity. Man is distinguished by his possession of a dominant, psychic monad which is capable of obtaining knowledge of necessary, or a priori truths. The animals share sense perceptual, empirical, or a posteriori knowledge with man, and plants and in- organic bodies are comprised of largely comatose monads. Sensa- tions are distinguished from understandings in that they are made up of more obscure psychic atoms than understandings--the continuity of sensation and understanding is thereby preserved. Leibniz explains knowledge, ethics, and history by claiming that every monad, except God, of course, evolves by inner necessity to realize itself. These monads have no windows, and they are thereby free in the sense in which they are not externally determined. Each thereby contains with- in itself the terms of its own past, present, and future, and each moves inherently to a fulfillment of its own basic character.

Like Descartes, however, Leibniz too was a dualist, thus con- ceiving of mind and body as independently existing substances. Leibniz' resolution of the implacable dualistic problem of the mind- body relation differs widely from Descartes' interactionism, however. It is more like Geulincx' parallelism instead. He argues that, though these two substances give the appearance of influencing one another, they do in concrete fact not. They act in a harmony pre-established by God, and in accord with the principle of universal perfection in- herent in God. Also following from this principle is the view that the greatest possible perfection is attained in the world. The parallelism of Leibniz concludes that the body is the material expression of the mind. Also contained in this parallelism is Leibniz' promised solutions to the problem of mechanism and teleology.

Principal among Leibniz' disciples were Christian Wolff (1679-1754) and Alexander Gottlieb Baumgarten (1714-1762). Both contributed much to the early development of German philosophy. Wolff is mainly remembered for his systematization of, and commentaries on Leibniz, as well as for his eclectic, common sense attempt to reconcile the rationalistic and empiricistic theses of this time--an attempt which would later have a significant impact on Kant's early work. And Baumgarten is remembered largely for his pioneering reflections on aesthetics.

The third of the three remarkable Continental rationalists of the seventeenth century coming in for discussion here is the highly admirable and brilliant Dutch, Jewish thinker, Baruch (Benedict) de Spinoza (1632-1677). Like both Descartes and Leibniz, Spinoza hoped to uncover the true natrue of the understanding through rational discourse, or what he calls clear and distinct thinking--to obtain a complete, eternal, universal knowledge of things by appeal to reason. Unlike either Descartes or Leibniz, however, Spinoza's profound love of truth and ascetic disposition led him to stake his happiness and his basis for living on the successful completion of a mathematically precise system. For Spinoza, we can come to knowledge, and happiness as well, only if we come to an understanding of what is absolutely and eternally certain, or logically necessary. Based on the necessary consequences of a logical principle which is fundamental and given, Spinoza spins out an elaborate and ingenious determinism. In Spinoza, as in Descartes and Leibniz, then, the rational system is taken to reflect the nature of reality, and experience merely provides the primitive data for this system. Spinoza argues that we possess an idea, based on logically necessary precepts (such as the principle of non-contradiction most significantly), which, though otherwise indefensible, is nonetheless itself necessarily true. And it is from this principle that other, equally certain ideas are deduced. This idea is substance, or that whose conception, or sustained existence requires nothing other than itself--it is cause of and for itself, or causa sui, God. What follows from the notion of substance as such is that all "else" is derivative of it, or Him, for there can be no substance outside of God --whatever is, is in God. God thereby entails existence, and is infinite, independent, indivisible, free, and the immanent, active principle, or underlying structure of the world. Thought and extension cannot, therefore, be considered separate substances, as Descartes and Leibniz had taught, but must be two (from an infinite number of) attributes, or aspects, of God. While independent in themselves, they are consequently processes of the same thing expressed in two different ways. The dualism, theism, and respective interactionism and parallelism of Descartes and Leibniz thereby pass over into the monism, pantheism, and double aspect theory of Spinoza.

According to this view, which has both idealistic and realistic tendencies in it, the world is not the aggregate of finite things, but God viewed through the attribute of extension. Individual minds and bodies cannot, however, be considered direct effects of God, for finite things may be efficiently caused only by other finite things. They are instead temporal modes of substance which correspond to one another—the doctrine of modes. In this way, the order and connection of objects are the same as the order and connection of ideas. This is to say that, the idea of an object and the object are one in God, but that, the two are viewed through the modes of different attributes. A modification of thought, therefore, entails a modification of extension —the mind perceives all bodily states, and bodily occurrences are inexorably accompanied by corresponding intellectual events. The human body is conceived as the most complex of actually existing extensions, and the human mind is construed as the idea of body. The mind and body are inseparable in this sense. The mind is passive insofar as it is affected by bodies, but active insofar as it acts in accord with logical precept. Under the terms of this view, man is considered a mode of substance possessing the attributes of thought and extension— man is knowledge of his body. A knowledge of self is thereby made dependent on—it is, in fact, constituted by—the variety of ways in which the body may be influenced, and this variety is, therefore, in turn a function of the body's complexity. Man is consequently distinguished from other finite modes of substance by the greater complexity of his body, and so by the correlative, quantitative superiority of his intelligence. As for Leibniz, Spinoza holds that our knowledge is defective only insofar as we claim to have contingent perceptions, when, as the analysis to this point has revealed, all exists necessarily in this, the best and only possible world. This claim suggests itself through the confusion of sense experience by the passions. Only the coherence of reason with reason truly enlightens. Spinoza's ethics and politics act out the basic purpose of reality revealed in his metaphysico-epistemic thought. Accordingly, the highest good is bound up with the rational necessity of knowing and loving God. For only through such a knowledge and love does one come to the sorts of understandings, the necessary understandings, which qualify as true knowledge, and so coextensively to happiness. Men governed fully by reason are, therefore, also inherently moral and socio-politically responsive. That is, such men allow everything to work through its natural inclination to preserve and fulfill itself, and they desire nothing for themselves which they are not also prepared to desire for all men. From this treatment of the rationalists, we now turn to a discussion of those who made the most vigorous and effective response to them, the eighteenth century British empiricists.

The empiricists: Locke, Berkeley, Hume. The earliest of these figures, John Locke (1632-1704), has become one of the most influential epistemic, social and political, and educational thinkers of the modern period. His basic gambit was to make a thorough examination of philosophy's most fundamental and important issue, the origin and nature of knowledge; and, in the course of this examination, to make a response to the alleged conflict in Hobbes' variously rationalistic (reason as the proper model for knowledge) and empiristic (sense-perception as the source of knowledge) sentiments, as well as to Descartes' rationalism. He argued that the scope of human knowledge is both more problematically determined and more limited than the rationalists had claimed. He also held, against the rationalists, that the natural sciences provide a more suitable model for knowledge than mathematics. By his view, the sciences and philosophy need to be liberated from the alienation of mathematics by showing the correspondence of ideas to observable data. In this program of liberation is found one of the first and one of the most telling challenges to rationalism.

Locke begins with the notion that we think and that we possess ideas corresponding to distinct objects in an independent world of such objects as given. From this, he gives an account of how these ideas come into the mind. The two possibilities are that they either come into the mind by experience, or they are innate. They cannot be innate, however, for we are unable to point to any ideas that we bring into the world with us, and the notion of unconscious ideas is barren because it fails to demonstrate what is native to the mind and what is not. All knowledge must, therefore, come from experience. An appeal to empirical knowledge, therefore, accounts for the whole of reality insofar as that whole can be accounted for--empirical knowledge is the only sort possible for man. In its original state, then, the mind is an empty closet, or an empty tablet, a tabula rasa, or slate without ideas. Only through experience are sensations, or passively received simple ideas of the external senses, and reflections, or actively received complex ideas of the internal senses, impressed on it. Only through experience is the mind filled with these two kinds of ideas. The mind, therefore, thinks in the sense in which it abstracts, compares, remembers, generalizes, combines, and repeats ideas, but it does neither bring those ideas into the world with it (these ideas are not its ideas), nor does it subsequently generate them. There are, on his view, no ideas which haven't an empirical source. Even his clear and distinct ideas of substance, power, motion, causality, space, time, and existence are taken to come originally from simple ideas.

While both idealistic and realistic tendencies can be found in Locke's thought, his program inclines more fully toward the dualistic materialism of the realist, than toward the monistic spiritualism of the idealist. He holds that we are conscious of having ideas produced by things which are distinct from the ideas they produce. Our direct consciousness is of sensations, however, and not things. Bodies, therefore, cause us to have the ideas that we do, but they are not themselves what we have a direct consciousness of. The power that objects have to produce ideas in us is called qualities. According to

Locke, some of these qualities reside in the objects themselves--such qualities as extension, solidity, figure, motion, rest, and number--and are called primary qualities. Others are nothing other than the sensations they produce in us--such qualities as color, sound, and taste--and are called secondary qualities. Even though the perception of these qualities is the first step toward knowledge, it is not knowledge itself, however. Knowledge itself requires the operation of additional faculties. The highest of these faculties, the faculty on which true knowledge most depends, is abstraction. Abstraction is the faculty of mind held only by man, and so the faculty by which man is distinguished from the animals--the quality by which man is man.

Though highly critical of rationalism in many respects, Locke himself falls frequently into rationalistic sorts of appeals. The most important of these have to do with the self-evident existence of God, self, and extended and unextended substances (bodies and minds respectively) in which qualities inhere. And, like Descartes, he is left with an interactionist view of the mind-body relation--a view with no stipulated linking principle which is characterized instead as an undemonstrable truth. He is even prepared to admit, with the rationalists, that, since the propositions of natural science concern matters of fact, or ideas about the external world, they are less certain than those of mathematics which concern the formal relations of ideas. What one desires in philosophy, however, is, among other things, knowledge of the external world; and in this, empirical observation surpasses formal systems of thought. According to Locke, then, we can have ideas, which satisfy the strict conditions of knowledge, of only three kinds of matters of fact: God, by rational demonstration of a causal and teleological sort, our finite selves, by intuition, and bodies, by sensation. And, we can neither deduce the essential natures of these substances (having to settle for knowledge of only some of their attributes), nor can we have anything other than probable knowledge of anything else. Absolute certitude, of the sort rationalism thought possible, with respect to the most general nature and significance of things, is, therefore, considered unobtainable.

As there are no innate metaphysico-epistemic truths, neither according to Locke are there any such moral or socio-political verities. All truths, even these, are empirically acquired. The basis of Locke's ethics and politics is egoistic hedonism, according to which individual pleasure and pain act as the first arbiters of moral and socio-political judgment. That which is likely to produce pleasure is termed good, that which is likely to effect pain is termed evil. Though an empirical fact in first discovery, this principle can also be rationally demonstrated, and is given as well by divine revelation--it is inherent in experience, reason, and the law of God. The politics grows, of course, out of the ethics. Unlike Hobbes, Locke argues that, though bound to natural law, every man is otherwise free and equal in a state of nature--every man naturally seeks to preserve himself and others in peace and in goodwill. What compels man to enter a socio-political order is not, therefore, the impulse to preserve himself against the natural inclinations of others to the contrary, as Hobbes had supposed, but variously out of convenience, inclination, and security against those aberrant others not attuned to natural law. The end of government, by this view, is to secure the common good, or to extend the natural state of individualism, by preserving the personal safety and property of the governed, and so the socio-political order itself. The sovereign is installed by the people to protect their natural liberty. In the event of his acting contrary to this trust, a provision for his deposition by the people must be enacted. The otherwise excessive powers of the sovereign must also be limited by investing the legislative and executive energies of government in separate agencies. Locke thought monarchy inconsistent with civil liberty.

Locke's educational philosophy flows consistently and naturally out of his more fundamental allegiances. For him, the purpose of education is to progress inductively to happiness through pleasurable experience. This experience entails improving the sense-perceptual faculties (as the bodily source of all knowledge) by physical education, and the faculties of the mind (as the ultimate form of knowledge) by intellectual education. The results of such experience are a person of vigorous action, exemplary moral and socio-political character, practical good sense, and high intellectual prowess. Cornelia Edmondson's "A Continuum of Thought on the Value of Health, Physical Education and Recreation from the Time of John Locke Through the Early Twentieth Century" focuses mainly on Locke's view of physical education, and is likely the most important study of Locke's philosophy in this respect. It concludes that Locke's powerful and enduring influence on the philosophy of physical education has largely to do with his empiricist leanings and the high place of the body and arduous activities of the body in such leanings.

Locke's influence on modern thought and life has been immense. His comprehensive and systematic theory of knowledge picked up on the earlier forms of empiricist sentiment in Bacon and Hobbes, it launched the school of modern British empricism soon to be taken over by Berkeley and Hume, it would in the end have a significant hand in inciting Kant, and it would inspire as well much of the empirical psychology of the eighteenth and nineteenth centuries. This latter movement, usually called sensationalism, held that sensation is not merely the source of knowledge, but that, it is the only mode of experience. The most notable champions of this view were Étienne Bonnot de Condillac (1715-1780), Claude Adrien Helvetius (1715-1771), James Mill, and Bentham. And Locke's ethical, socio-political, and educational thought had a profound impact on no less a figure than Rousseau. At bottom, Locke was among the more conspicuous heralds of the modern European Enlightenment.

From Locke, the empiricist gauntlet was taken up most instructively by George Berkeley (1685-1753). In his trenchant analysis of the origin and nature of human knowledge, Berkeley attempts to dispel the then-raging skepticism over knowledge and religion, and to put an end to non-empirical speculations about the nature and significance of reality. With Locke, Berkeley argues that it is meaningless and self-contradictory to hold that there is anything else than what the senses provide. There are, therefore, no innate ideas: all ideas are abstracted from experience. With the rationalists and against Locke, however, Berkeley is convinced that we can know all that there is to know of reality. It is simply that there are no non-empirical facts to know of it. This establishes the limits of human knowledge as that derived from sense experience--all "else" is unknown to us. Berkeley also breaks with Locke's view that we can know bodies as material things persisting apart from our experience of them. He regards this view as unduly speculative in itself, and as contrary to Locke's own fundamentally empiricist principles. Moreover, since our knowledge is limited to what our senses provide, it is limited to ideas. Ideas cannot in any case be like material objects, but only like other ideas. Reality is thereby constituted by ideas, and only by ideas. According to Berkeley, these ideas are by their nature active and indivisible, they are thereby also indissoluble and so immortal. This argument for the immortality of ideas is taken to establish the immortality of the soul as well, and to also show that, even in the event of a passive, material world, such a world could not have an effect on the world of ideas. The apparent passivity of an "extended world" could not consequently be the cause of our perceptions, as Locke had held. All so-termed material things are, therefore, nothing other than the ideas we perceive "of them". "Their" existence consists in "their" being perceived by the mind--esse est percipi. Things exist only as complexes of ideas--there are no unthinking substances. This argument thereby collapses Locke's primary-secondary quality distinction into secondary qualities alone. Moreover, Berkeley is persuaded that the belief in an independent world of matter throws one into challenging the universality of God, and so also into skepticism, materialism, and atheism.

Among those "things" of which we have a "direct" perceptual experience, according to Berkeley, are the conscious operations "of mind". From this experience is deduced the existence of mind itself as that in which ideas, or conscious operations, exist, and that by which such ideas are perceived. The mind is consequently thought distinct from its ideas. Berkeley makes this basically rationalistic conclusion even though our consciousness of mind as such is inferred from our consciousness of "its" operations, or ideas; and further, from the implicity invoked principle that ideas inhere in a substance. Our direct experience is only of ideas, and not of mind itself. Moreover, though our ideas are private--we directly perceive only our own ideas--the existence of other minds is implied by the existence of our

own. Berkeley's acceptance of this implication saves him in this case
from the fall to solipsism, or the view that the invividual self alone
exists. Berkeley also admits to the existence of selves, bodies, and
God on rationalistic-tending grounds, which are in apparent violation
of his empiricistic allegiances. The self is thought a further ground
of mind, or that which possesses mind. The body is construed as a
discrete mosaic of ideas which we know to exist from our perceptions
of it, and which must exist else we be pure idea (a distinction befitting
only God). Though our minds then make ourselves what we are, our
minds are nonetheless inseparably connected to a corporeal notion, or
body. This formulation of the mind-body relation is reminiscent of
Spinoza's double aspect theory, in that a correspondence between sets
of ideas, and not between ideas and something other than ideas is suggested. Such a formulation also saves Berkeley's idealistic monism
from the dualistic clutches which so gripped such as Locke. Concerning God's existence, Berkeley adopts a version of the causal theory of
perception. That is, since he rejected Locke's material version of
this theory, since he nevertheless was obligated to explain the appearance of perceptions in us, since he was convinced that the cause of
this appearance is not in, but independent of us, and since he found
repugnant the notion of "unperceived objects", or particular events
which "depend" for their existence on a perception of them, but which
are nevertheless unperceived by finite minds; Berkeley invokes the
existence of an eternal, omniscient, omnipotent, active, indivisible,
and immaterial God as the cause of perception and the perceiver of all
"things". God is, therefore, presupposed as the cause of empirically
known effects. But it is again not clear that a strict interpretation of
Berkeley's empiricistic first principles allows that our perceptions be
known as effects, and so neither that any cause can be said to underpin
them.

Eighteenth century British empiricism is run to a sophisticated
end by the pragmatic-tending thought of David Hume (1711-1776).
Hume accepts Berkeley's esse est percipi and attempts to work out the
implications of this principle with a care, rigor, and consistency that
had eluded Berkeley himself. In this working out, Hume hopes to demonstrate the untenability of rationalism, and to show philosophy's
great need for the experimental method. Hume was convinced that the
rationalists' reconstruction of knowledge was unduly speculative, remote, abstruse, contrary to the real nature of things, and unachiev-
able. He holds that the negative function of philosophy is to reveal the
metaphysical excursions of rationalism for the masquerades that they
are. And for its positive side, Hume reserves an exploration of the
nature of the mind and human knowledge. For Hume, philosophy is
exclusively devoted, in its positive aspect, to giving a descriptive account of our epistemic faculties. Though Hume was little impressed
with the practical or existential significance of such an account, thereby differing greatly in this respect from such as Spinoza, he did consider philosophic truth valuable for its own sake and preferable to

illusion even if more limited and less useful in the course of mundane experience. He was highly skeptical, in particular, about the successful operation of philosophic insight in the mundane world where the forces of passion seem most prominent, and about the capacity of reason to effectively talk about such as ultimates, substances, causality, souls, and the external world. The first principle of Hume's empiricism is that all that can be known are our own sense perceptual experiences, and so that man cannot have knowledge of "things" outside such experiences. While we can speak of, and have "beliefs" about such "things", even if there be such "things", we can simply not have knowledge of "them". This is so because we have no sense perceptual experience of "them". One cannot, therefore, either establish that something exists independently of our sense perceptual experience, or that nothing so exists, let alone determining the constitution of this something or nothing, presumably either as spiritual or material. Hume thereby rejects both materialism and immaterialism as untenable theses.

According to Hume, sense perceptual experience, or things of the mind, are of two kinds. They are either sense perceptions, or impressions, or they are reflective entities, or ideas. The distinction between impressions and ideas is more so one of degree than one of kind. Impressions are considered the most vivacious and directly, or immediately known of the two, and ideas, the less lively copies or combinations of impressions which are, then, mediately known. Fictitious experiences are thought less clear and lively than veridical ones, and detectable by reason as discontinuous. Hume, therefore, argues that there are no counterexamples to the proposition that all ideas are drawn from impressions, or direct sense perceptual experience. It follows from this, for Hume, that all knowledge takes the form either of matters of fact, which are discovered by a correspondence between impressions, have opposites, and are only probable truths, or of relations of ideas, which are discovered by a correspondence between ideas as in mathematical truths, have no opposites, and are absolute or necessary truths. In order to explain the continuity and relations among and within these various forms of knowledge, Hume also has need of a doctrine of the association of ideas, according to which bits of knowledge have a natural tendency to associate with one another. This doctrine is particularly active in explaining such notions as resemblance, contiguity, and causality—notions which in the end apparently depend for their explanation on rationalistic invocations. That is, it is not very much clear that the strict empiricist thesis can handle these notions, nor that it can yield the doctrine itself. The most important of these notions for Hume is causality, for without it matters of fact cannot be explained. Our knowledge of causality, he argues, comes from an impression of events succeeding or conjoining one another in a uniform and recurring fashion. Though we cannot claim that these events are necessarily connected, for we have only an impression of their succession and not of their connection,

Hume wishes to nonetheless hold that the natural propensity to associate ideas leads us by custom (if not by experience) to expect the appearance of a particular event "with" the appearance of another. The instinct of custom, then, and not experience, brings us to the belief in a certain world order in which the present and future formally and substantially conform to the past. It is this instinct, in fact, which enables us to get on well in everyday affairs, even though it falls somewhat short of knowledge in the strict sense. That is to say, every good and practical purpose is served by acting in accord with it, and no good or practical purpose is served by acting contrary to it.

As earlier suggested, among the notions Hume thinks meaningless are substance, souls, and material objects. He nonetheless distinguishes the realities of mental and physical events, but withholds ascribing substance to them. Mind is thereby construed as nothing other than the collection of our perceptions, and body nothing other than the collection of impressions commonly, though wrongly conceived as existing intimately with, but apart from ourselves. Though we do commonly think of our bodies as existing independently of our perceptions, and they may well, we can simply not know if this is or is not the case, because we can rightly claim to know only what we perceive. We cannot likewise claim to have knowledge of self, as that collection of perceptions which we are, or to have knowledge of the means or manner by which bodies, minds and bodies, and minds "interact".

Despite Hume's strict interpretation of empiricist doctrine, he nonetheless allows that there is no truth so certain as the existence of God. In what gives the appearance of a highly rationalistic appeal, Hume argues for the existence of God from the principle of sufficient reason. By this principle, he is firmly persuaded that God exists as the absolutely perfect first cause and continued sustainer of the universe, and as the foundation of all happiness, morality, and sociopoliticality. Though His existence is indubitable, however, His nature cannot be known, for the only way it could be known is to ascribe human perfections to Him, and this would constitute the calamity of anthropomorphism. Moreover, the "truths" of religion, like those of ethics and politics, are "truths" of passion, or practical, and so active and free "truths" of the will, as distinct from intellectual truths. In religion, one seeks a happiness that is left unfulfilled by nature; that is, a happiness which, though it obeys the natural law of causality, seeks an active and free fulfillment of one's instinct for a coherent world. Morality also rests on an instinct, and not on an intellectual necessity according to Hume. By his view, the basic sentiment which leads us to live a morally just life is an altruistic sympathy for the happiness of man, or what Hume calls enlightened self-interest. His utilitarian ethic claims that those things are good which please oneself and are in sympathy with the interests of humanity in general. A social and political order is required in order to save man from the chaotic and self-destructive tendencies of his unenlightened years. As one's self-interest is educated, or enlightened by knowledge, it gives rise quite naturally to governmental convention, or enforced rules of cooperation and distribution of resource. In effect, this convention places necessary restraints on self-interest and reconciles it with the common good. And Hume's aesthetics argues for a universal standard of taste, or beauty, according to which beauty refers to those impressions which most emphatically arouse to pleasure the passions of persons with refined aesthetic sensibilities.

Though empiricism has formed the dominant allegiances of British philosophy since Roger Bacon and William of Occam, rationalistic developments were never silenced altogether. The most notable of those opposed to the modern empirical teachings were the Cambridge rationalists, Ralph Cudworth (1617-1688) and Henry More (1614-1687), and the Scotch common sense appellant, Thomas Reid (1710-1796).

Rousseau. The spirit of independent and free inquiry that had characterized the Renaissance and the seventeenth century spills also over into eighteenth century thought and life. Despite Hume's influence, there was about this period a growing spirit of optimism, and a burgeoning confidence in human reason to resolve even the most staggering of human problems and to render human life intelligible. The sciences and philosophy were consequently and increasingly marshaled to a consideration of social, political, and educational matters. These characteristically Enlightenment tendencies were nowhere more apparent, nor more fully developed than in the thought of the French reformers, Voltaire (1694-1778), Montesquieu (1685-1755), Denis Diderot (1713-1784), and Jean Jacques Rousseau (1712-1778). The lot of these thinkers argued tirelessly against ecclesiastic domination and social, political, religious, and philosophic oppression. They adopted an evolutionistic form of naturalism, or materialism, by which man is considered a participant in the natural order, and thereby "subject" to natural law and possessing the natural rights of equality, temperance, simplicity, fraternity, and liberty. The intellectual and moral-aesthetic-political aspects of man's life are thereby considered "products" of nature, and not as separate from nature.

The major philosophic figure in this trend was Rousseau, whose basic thesis revolved variously around the notion that socio-political institutions tend toward autocracy, or to impose alien requirements on persons, and so to enslave them; and that nature conversely tends toward democracy, or the free expression of will, and so to liberate persons. Largely through the use of property, these institutions have made man unequal and have thereby corrupted his natural inclination to equality and liberty. Contrary to such as Hobbes, then, Rousseau thinks nature the ideal condition--the condition invested with all the good and proper things that the soico-political condition lacks. He is nonetheless convinced that a form of socio-political organization is

necessary because the innocence of nature is not restorable, and because in the state of nature there are some aberrant persons who demand power and freedom for themselves at the expense of others.
Since the state of nature cannot, therefore, be recaptured, and owing
as well to the aberrant aspects of it, Rousseau argues that socio-
politicality itself must be upbuilt and reformed in the image of nature.
In enlightened, or natural socio-politicality, then, conventions and
laws must be freely and unanimously agreed to by all, and they must
be fashioned to promote equality and social justice for all. By this
view, socio-politicality is an organic unity, general will, or social
contract, which has as its end the realization of the common good.
Rousseau's social and political philosophy effectively represents an
attempt to reconcile utility and justice by demonstrating that freedom
is obedience to self-imposed law, which naturally conforms, in turn,
to the public interest. Socio-politicality is thereby construed as a
manifestation of that which is naturally and universally felt, willed,
and good.

Rousseau's educational philosophy is similarly disposed. It advocates a natural development of the individual personality in which
one is freed from bogus social and political expectation, and freed for
discovering one's basically natural inclinations as these inclinations
variously occur in natural environments of a more widely general sort.
Education is thought to make life in general intelligible, to give all
persons an understanding of what democratic citizenship in an ideal
state entails, and to make for the harmonious development of one's
various aspects, most notably one's so-termed mind and body. Physical education was consequently highly recommended, principally as a
means of protecting and enhancing health, and developing rich sense
experiences, but also for moral, social, and recreative purposes.
Throughout one's education--through the animal, savage, pastoral,
social, and adult stages--physical education plays a very prominent
role. The natural course of learning goes on through these stages,
which individually pass abruptly over into succeeding stages, and
which collectively recapitulate the entire sweep of human development.
In this course, the teacher "manipulates" the environment so as to
maximize an individual, free, and so natural experience of it. This is
necessary in order to make for an efficient and sufficiently short
introduction to nature and its socio-political extensions. In the beginning of this introduction, education is largely negative, principally involving the removal of contaminated socio-political obstacles to natural development. As it moves toward its end, conversely, it tends
more fully to a positive instruction in the materials and forces of nature and, derivatively, of socio-politicality. Perhaps the most important study dealing with the implications of Rousseau's thought for
physical education and sport is Mary M. Frederick's "Naturalism:
The Philosophy of Jean Jacques Rousseau and Its Implications for
American Physical Education". Discussed in this piece are Rousseau's
views of education and physical education, as well as the revolutionary

- 144 -

influence of these views on European and American physical education since the eighteenth century. The most significant of these views include Rousseau's insistence on vigorous, natural, and spontaneous movements for proper growth and development, his emphasis on the natural, as distinct from the socially maligned individual, his advocacy of the unity of mind and body, and his accentuation of the moral values of physical activity.

Kant. The modern era ends with the unexcelled genius of Immanuel Kant (1724-1804) and his resolution of the rationalist-empiricist dispute which had so marked the period. In his system, which exhibits both idealistic and realistic tendencies, Kant hoped to demonstrate the roles necessarily played by both reason and experience in our knowledge. This demonstration eventually succeeds, and with its success also come Kant's dispersion of the then somewhat fashionable skepticism with respect to the capabilities of either and both reason and experience, and such skepticism with respect to the free exercise of the will in moral and religious matters as well. Kant was at first most influenced by Leibniz and Wolff, later by Locke and Hume, and in the end broke independently away to a line of insight which summed one age, inaugurated another, and yet ranks with the highest triumphs of human civilization. As had been the case for most of the major figures of the modern period, the problem of knowledge remained the central problem of philosophy for Kant. With both the rationalists and empiricists, Kant held that experience provides the basic material, primitive data, or content of knowledge. He is further convinced, however, that the mind fashions that material in necessary accord with its own nature, or form, and so, that the structures of empirical reality correspond to the nature of mind--Kant's second Copernican revolution. Experience and knowledge are themselves possible for Kant only on such a view. With this, the long sought after mediation of rationalism and empiricism had been achieved.

In Kant's view, the traditional objects of philosophic inquiry, like nature, man, God, knowledge, and value, at least as these have been conceived as objective, universal, and necessary truths, are unknowable. All that can be known are what Kant calls possible objects of experience, or appearances. The character of the reality which lies beneath these appearances as their cause cannot be known for we have no experience of this reality as such. The concrete fact of appearance nonetheless presupposes the existence of such a reality for Kant. This reality is made up of what Kant calls material things-in-themselves, or transcendental objects--objects which themselves transcend our experience, but which our experience nonetheless presupposes. These objects provide our perceptions, or appearances, with a cause, and establish the limits of human knowledge. We know that they are, but we cannot know what they are. According to Kant, then, philosophy cannot aspire to a genuine knowledge of the ultimate nature of things, the noumenon, or discrete world corresponding to the form of our minds, as the rationalists had supposed; but only to a knowledge of what experience provides, the phenomenon, or world of appearances, which is nevertheless more than the empiricists typically allowed. Our knowledge cannot penetrate beyond the limits of experience--the world is nothing other than the sum of all possible object of experience. Kant's transcendental method of argument, which is itself somewhat unique among modern methods of philosophic argument in that it is not formed on a mathematical or natural scientific model, therefore, moves from the indubitable character of all possible objects of experience to what must be universally and necessarily presupposed by them in order to make experience possible at all. It moves from the empirical facts to the necessary conditions of their possibility.

The metaphysico-epistemic thrust of Kant's philosophy is to show that all ideas cannot be mere copies of impressions, but are in some sense reflections of the mind as well. This is done by pure reason, or by reason with all of the data of experience removed. And it is done in order to demonstrate the terms in which the mind, or understanding, structures our experience. Knowledge itself presupposes the existence of mind, the competence of reason to examine itself, and the cooperation of sensation, or the transcendental aesthetic, and thought, or the transcendental analytic, according to Kant. And all knowledge appears in the form of judgments in which something is either affirmed or denied. These judgments are either analytic, in which case the predicate merely elucidates what is inherent in the subject, or synthetic, in which case the predicate actually informs with respect to the subject. In order to strictly qualify as knowledge, however, judgments must do more than merely repeat themselves, they must extend our knowledge, and they must be necessarily and universally true. They must, therefore, be synthetic a priori judgments, and as such they are statements of a necessary and universal unity of possible objects of experience, or statements of a connection of appearances occurring in accord with certain formal ordering principles, called principles of the analogies of experience.

Kant also demonstrated that possible objects of experience are themselves made up of three constitutents: Hume's passive impressions (or, the manifold, multiple, material ingredients of our experience, its primitive data, in turn made up of external sense qualia, such as colors, sounds, and tastes, and internal sense qualia, such as emotional and volitional elements), the active forms of the sensibility, or intuitions, and the active forms of the understanding, or pure concepts or categories. It is these latter two constituents, together called the transcendental ego by Kant, which comprise the formal ingredients of experience, and so provide human knowledge with its two necessary stems. In his treatment of the forms of the sensibility, Kant eliminates the influence of both the impressions and the understanding in order to apprehend them as they are in themselves.

These forms, like those of the understanding, order all possible objects of experience, and are necessarily presupposed by such objects. Also like the forms of the understanding, they are neither derived inductively from our experience, nor are they inherent either in material things-in-themselves or in impressions; they are instead a priori forms of the mind for Kant. And they are exhausted by the forms of time (or causality, the form of inner sense, or psychic states) and space (or substance, the form of outer sense, or that which effects sensation). The forms of the understanding, moreover, raise the fragmented bits of spatio-temporal perception to conceptual knowledge, to synthetic a priori judgment. These forms are comprised of four general categories, each of which itself contains three particular categories: quantity (unity, plurality, totality), quality (reality, negation, limitation), relation (inherence and subsistence, causality and dependence, community), and modality (possibility and impossibility, existence and non-existence, necessity and contingency). It is further the case that the three constituents of possible objects of experience, impressions, intuitions, and concepts, are thought discrete. Kant, therefore, has need of a principle which links or mediates these constituents--a principle which accounts for the relationships among them. Though knowledge itself presupposes a union of these constituents, for Kant, he is nonetheless obliged to draw out the terms of this union, and he does this in what he calls the transcendental schema, which is at once pure, or of reason, and sensuous, or of sensation.

Kant terms the principles which apply to possible objects of experience, immanent principles, and those which extend to matters beyond the limits of experience, transcendent principles, or Ideas. The most important of these latter principles concern the existence of God, human freedom, the immortality of the soul, and the world as a purposeful order. Kant argues that, though the Ideas are not of possible objects of experience and, therefore, neither do they constitute synthetic a priori knowledge, they are nonetheless natural to reason in the sense in which they guide and organize it, assure its unity, and are methodologically useful to it. They are not, therefore, products of pure reason, nor presupposed by knowledge, but are known instead by what Kant calls practical reason, and are of great practical-ethical value. Among the most important laws of practical reason, and the law which forms the basis of Kant's ethics, entails our duty to act so as to deserve happiness. Inherent in the voluntary acts which form this duty is the freedom of the good will, and the constraint to choose what is highest and best in us by its exercise. Kant's conciliation of determinism and free will is also bound up in the foundations of his ethical thought. In this, he intuits man as a unified consciousness at once a participant in the world of sense by which he is determined, and in the world of reason by which he is free. Man is, therefore, considered free insofar as he acts in accord with the self-legislated laws of reason, and he is moral insofar as he submits to the universal and necessary moral law of reason which Kant calls the categorical

imperative. This law unconditionally, or categorically, commands
man to act always so that the determining principle of action becomes
universal law, and to intend this action out of a respect for one's duty
to the self-legislated law, and so to happiness alone. Such a law commands a treatment of every person always as an end and never as a
means. A socio-political order of persons commanded by the imperative results in a kingdom of ends, or a community of rational spirits
which is implicitly perfect, for it effects the perfect coalescence of
individual and common goods. Robert G. Osterhoudt's "The Kantian
Ethic as a Principle of Moral Conduct in Sport" attempts to show the
relevance of the imperative as the principle of moral conduct in sport;
that is, to reveal the imperative as forming an ethical posture proper
to persons as sportspersons. From a discussion of Kant's general
philosophic and ethical views, as well as the basic character of sport
itself, comes the conclusion that the free choice of entering sport
carries with it the moral obligation, not merely to abide by the laws
governing such activity, but to do so for the sake of duty to the self-
legislated law itself, which is in turn tantamount to treating one's
competitors with a respect one would prefer for oneself--that is, to
treating them as ends-in-and-for-themselves, and not as mere means
to the gratification of one's own egoistic desires and inclinations. The
invocation of such a principle, Osterhoudt argues, would encourage an
order of ideal conduct regrettably and increasingly absent from the
playing of modern amateur and professional sport.

The moral dimension just discussed introduces man to a world
transcending the phenomenal, and implies human freedom, as well as
the immortality of the soul, the existence of God, and the purposeful
nature of the world. Kant argues for the soul's immortality on the
somewhat dubious grounds that the necessary connection between
happiness and morality is left unrevealed in the world of practical reason, and that this incompleteness leads one to postulate the existence
of a future world where such a connection is fully realized. And Kant
insists that the existence of God is sought naturally by reason as the
omniscient, absolutely perfect, and unconditional guide of knowledge.
He holds that alternative arguments end in equally plausible, but
contradictory and experientially inaccessible conclusions, or antino-
mies. Concerning his view of the world as a purposeful order, Kant
argues similarly that reason is inherently disposed to such a notion,
and that a purposeful world order follows from the moral law. Kant's
aesthetics itself flows out of the Idea of purpose. He is of the view
that, though beauty is a function of one's response to objects, and not
a function of objects themselves as such, it is nonetheless of a universal, or of a common form for all who cultivate an informed sensibility
with respect to it. This response is distinctly aesthetic in virtue of its
entailing pleasure of an utterly disinterested, non-consumptive, non-
utilirarian, and free sort--a sort different than that characteristic of
theoretical and practical concerns. Though neither theoretical nor

practical, then, Kant argues that aesthetic pleasure mediates the tension between them. That is to say, it mediates the apparent antagonism between the rational and the natural, it effects an harmonious, free, and play-like interaction between the forms of the understanding and the forms of the sensibility, and it thereby raises one above the natural to a contemplative state in which the commitment to contending self-interests gives way in preparation for a genuinely moral condition. In any case, this is as may be supposed of disinterested purpose. Like his ethics in particular, Kant's philosophy of education was too greatly influenced by Rousseau. For Kant, education's principal obligation is to cultivate and advance man's unique and natural inclinations to acquire theoretical knowledge, to act morally, to apprehend God, and to form an aesthetic awareness. More synoptically, education was to develop an organism of sturdy body, alert mind, and moral, socio-political, and aesthetic sensitivity. Physical education was thought an important medium in which the lot of these objectives were to be worked toward.

The high place widely accorded Kant in the history of philosophy is as secure as the place of any other single figure. Much of the philosophy done since him has taken the form either of a response to, or an extension of his thought. A great deal of nineteenth century philosophy most especially was heavily occupied with the "completion" of the Kantian enterprise from its critical foundations. Kant's second Copernican revolution and his discussions of material things-in-themselves, freedom, immortality, God, and purpose gained most attention. Perhaps the most basic matter on which Kant is persistently challenged is his acceptance of "things" which we have no direct experience of, and which fail to conform to the forms of the sensibility or the forms of the understanding. It was widely thought that this acceptance without the realm of possible objects of experience was variously incompatible with, or contrary to the basic principles of his program. Among the most important, early replies to Kant came from the German Enlightenment poets, Johann Gottfried Herder (1744-1803) and Friedrich Schiller (1759-1805), and from the German intuitionist, Friedrich Heinrich Jacobi (1743-1819). Herder and Schiller both rejected Kant's dualism, discounted his unsympathetic treatment of nature, and argued for the balanced, or aesthetic education of man. Jacobi was convinced that the critical foundations of Kant's philosophy, and the sharp order of skepticism these foundations contain, could not yield a genuine knowledge of material things-in-themselves, freedom, or God. Jacobi argued instead that only a faith in the direct knowledge of the supersensible can give such a knowledge. The foremost educational disciple of Kant was the reformist Swiss thinker and educator, Jean Heinrich Pestalozzi (1746-1827). Pestalozzi worked out the theoretical and practical implications of Kantianism for education in general, and physical education in particular. His immensely influential work laid many of modern pedagogy's most important foundations. This work was most basically committed to a process of learning by direct, active involvement in subjects, in the beginning reduced to their most primitive simples, and progressively raised to more complex levels of learning. This process was to have been worked out through a rich variety of sense experience and intellectual challenge, and devoted ultimately to an harmonious development of the thinking, feeling, and willing aspects of man. Physical education figures prominently in all features of this working out, according to Pestalozzi. Perhaps the most important of those influenced by Pestalozzi was Friedrich Froebel (1782-1852), who advocated a playful, cooperative, natural, and self-expressive education having social and practical significance.

With Kant we have come to the terminal figure of the so-termed modern philosophic era. This period gives way to the distinctive and rich genius of nineteenth century thought.

Nineteenth century philosophy

The relatively brief one hundred years of the nineteenth century represents one of the most fertile, creative, and genuinely remarkable periods in the entire history of philosophic discourse. The passion for ultimate truth ran nowhere deeper, and the travail and frailty of the human condition was at no time more acutely felt and thought about than at this time. The variegated developments of nineteenth century philosophy are discussed in the following divisions: Fichte, Schelling, and Schleiermacher, Hegel, Marx, Herbart, Schopenhauer, Kierkegaard, Nietzsche, Neo-Kantianism, Positivism, Utilitarianism, and Evolutionism.

Fichte, Schelling, and Schleiermacher. Few movements have been so consumed with the spirit of speculative thought as post-Kantian German philosophy. It was a movement of great exuberance and encyclopedic scope beginning with the thought of Fichte and ending with that of Hegel. It developed in idealistic directions, aimed at achieving a sweepingly comprehensive system, and thought itself working out the completion of Kant's critical philosophy. Fichte, Schelling, Schleiermacher, and Hegel took as the beginning of their philosophy the free world of mind, or spirit, to which Kant's moral law points. For them, reality is intelligible only as self-determining spiritual, or rational activity--as an organic and historical evolution of spirit, or reason, toward itself, toward its knowing itself as such. In their systems, emphasis, therefore, rests on what was called the science of knowledge, or Wissenschaftslehre.

The earliest titan of this movement was Johann Gottlieb Fichte (1762-1814). Fichte sought the reform not only of science and philosophy, but of life itself. Perhaps it would be more strictly accurate to say that Fichte had hoped to show the terms of life's reform by, or in philosophy. According to Fichte's view, genuine knowledge is possible only by faith in an act of freedom, in a self-determining activity of will, ego, intelligence, or reason. In fact, knowledge necessarily presupposes such activity. Against Kant, then, Fichte argues that this activity cannot be caused by something external (Kant's material thing-in-itself), for we have no experience of such a something for one, and because, by the principle of sufficient reason, only that which is freely created by intelligence can be known by it. Otherwise the notion of freedom, and so of knowledge itself is upended. Fichte, therefore, attributed not only the form of knowledge to intelligence, or Absolute Ego, as had Kant, but the content of knowledge as well, as Kant had not. Our experience is accordingly nothing more than the concrete manifestation of Absolute Ego (Kant's transcendental ego). Fichte's views thereby end in absolute idealism, according to which there is Absolute Ego and nothing but Absolute Ego. It is the sole cause of its own content and the formal ordering principles of that content in one--the infinite ground of being and knowledge. The science of knowledge completes itself by becoming freely conscious of itself; that is to say, it completes itself in philosophy. This freedom of rational self-determination, not only makes knowledge possible, but also relieves humanity of being no more than an amoral link in a causal succession of natural event. It is this freedom which gives humanity a moral dimension. For Fichte, this dimension further implies that human experience is morally constrained for eternity, and that it is constrained to a universal purpose, or end. That is, for him, morality itself implies immortality of the soul and the existence of God, or universal purpose. Humanity is morally and socio-politically obliged to serve this at once individual and public purpose, this spiritual end, which guides concrete historical evolution. Education is likewise expected to contribute to the realization of this end, principally in the form of its giving directions for intellectual, moral, and socio-political (or nationalistic) development.

Also strongly attracted to the new idealism was Friedrich Wilhelm Joseph Schelling (1775-1854). Schelling holds that it is no more legitimate to argue that the transcendental ego, or Absolute Ego, and concrete human experience, or the phenomenal world, are causally related (as had Kant, and in less strict terms Fichte as well), than to conceive of the phenomenal world as causally related to some material thing-in-itself (as had Kant). He, therefore, conceived of the phenomenal world as the concrete realization of a principle (for him, the Absolute, or the fundamental principle of reality) which is by itself mere potentiality. The Absolute cannot consequently be said to exist prior to and independently of the phenomenal order (as Kant and Fichte had supposed), but as a potentiality actualized in that order--it has no "real" existence apart from its phenomenal "manifestations". Also against Kant, Schelling tends toward a view of nature as something other than barren determinations by which we are morally constrained. He thinks of it as itself possessed of purpose, life, and reason. For Schelling, then, nature is neither opposed to, nor is it utterly discrete from reason, but is instead an epoch in the organic evolution of the Absolute. This process of evolutionary development occurs dialectically in the form of opposing events (theses and antitheses) reconciling themselves in progressively higher syntheses. The end of this objective idealism and this development is reason coming to know itself in-and-for-itself, reason coming to self-consciousness, and so, to freedom. According to Schelling, the highest stage in this end, and the stage which intuitively completes it, is artistic expression.

Fichte's perfervid moralism and Schelling's ardent aestheticism are matched in early nineteenth century German philosophy by the zealous Protestant religiosity of Friedrich Daniel Ernst Schleiermacher (1768-1834). Schleiermacher's sweepingly comprehensive and systematic program sided with Schelling, and against Kant and Fichte, in its sympathetic regard for nature. It imputes reason and will, and so moral substance as well, to nature. With Kant, and against Fichte and Schelling, however, Schleiermacher holds to the existence of material things-in-themselves, though his position in this regard is not strictly Kantian. He holds that reality is not authentically known merely as phenomena (Kant's position), but in terms of a yet more fundamental nature. In this regard, Schleiermacher postulates the existence of two aspects of reality, thought and being, and proposes as well the existence of a transcendent ground, or principle, which brings these aspects into resolution and unity. This absolute principle, God, cannot be known by reason, but only immediately by religious feeling, or divining intuition, and is construed by Schleiermacher as the identity of thought and being--a spaceless and timeless unity of spatio-temporal plurality. According to this view, man is morally constrained to move in the direction of this infinite unity, to live the moments of his life as though extended into eternity. Though he thought the notion of personal immortality implausible, Schleiermacher envisioned the working out of general world purpose and individual moral obligation coming together in one's free movement toward God, or coming together in a vertical eternity.

Hegel. Post-Kantian German idealism comes to its highest development in the thought of Georg Wilhelm Friedrich Hegel (1770-1831). The foundations of Hegel's work owe most to Aristotle, Kant, Fichte, and Schelling. From these foundations, Hegel constructs one of the most imposing and encyclopedic systems in the whole history of philosophic reflection. Much in the spirit of harmonization that characterized Aristotle's thought, which he greatly admired, Hegel protests the fragmentation of man so evident in modern thought, most importantly for him in the thought of Kant. Though Hegel found much in Kant to his liking--most notably, the second Copernican revolution, the transcendental method, and the insistence on human freedom--he sides with Fichte and Schelling in rejecting Kant's material thing-in-itself as unduly speculative, in violation of Kant's own premises, and throwing man into a regrettable dualism. The monism which results also improves on Kant in its showing the creative flow and record, the development, of human knowledge and experience throughout history. Hegel's high regard for Kant's Copernician revolution, makes his epistemic inclinations very similar to Kant's, however. These inclinations persuade that, though all knowledge commences with, or has its source in experience, experience itself merely provides an occasion for thought, and so is not itself true knowledge. Hegel's view of knowledge is circular in the sense in which it depends on a mutual refinement of the rational and empirical parts which make it up. This leads Hegel to the conclusion that an understanding of all empirical parts of the rational whole is necessary to an understanding of the whole itself, and that an understanding of the rational whole itself is necessary to an understanding of its empirical parts. Thus, with Kant, Fichte, and Schelling most notably, Hegel overcomes both the strict rationalist thesis, according to which reality is construed as conforming to a formalistic mathematical or natural scientific model, and the strict empiricist thesis, according to which the mind is construed as conforming to the impressions of a mindless world.

Hegel's objective idealism seeks the harmony of such classically troublesome "polarities" as universality and particularity, reason and nature, thought and being. It holds to the unity of reason, and so to the view that a single Spirit permeates all individuated forms. By this account, what exists is consciousness and nothing but consciousness in its various forms. All existence reveals itself, and is constituted as conscious event--reality discloses itself as a mosaic of rational laws which explain such event. This system of rational, or spiritual laws, or laws of consciousness, is called Idea, and is differentiated as determinate substance and active self-actualizing principle. As manifest in the phenomenal world, or in our experience, this system is termed Spirit. With Schelling, however, Hegel holds that it is no more justifiable to regard the transcendental ego, or Absolute Ego, or Idea and the phenomenal world as causally related (as Kant and Fichte had), than to regard the phenomenal world as causally related to some material thing-in-itself (as Kant had). The relationship of Idea and the phenomenal world was instead conceived in terms of potentiality and actuality; that is to say, in terms of Idea, as potentiality, concretely actualizing itself as phenomena. The phenomenal world is, therefore, considered the product of neither Kant's transcendental ego, nor Fichte's Absolute Ego, nor Kant's material thing-in-itself, else it violate the principles of the critical philosophy, and be gratuitous as well. Nor, on the first grounds, can Schelling's Absolute or Hegel's own Idea exist in any sense prior to the phenomenal world, as had been the case for the Kantian and Fichtean principles. Thus, the phenomenal world is regarded as the first stage in the developmental actualization of Idea. And, unlike its precedents in Kant and Fichte, to finish the point, Idea does not exist prior to this actualization. In fact, for

Hegel, the system of reason does not actually exist at all except as it is embodied in phenomena--there are no noumenal entities. The system of reason is shown to exist only as revealed in human experience. According to Hegel, then, the concrete manifestations of Idea work their way toward an idealization, perfection, or progressively more adequate embodiment in time and as Spirit. In this development, various stages are passed through and to. These stages represent a hierarchy (in the form of a circular progression) from primitive forms of consciousness in which all things appear differentiated to absolute forms of consciousness in which all things are apprehended as a unity. Each of these stages necessarily depends on the previous one(s), and each develops toward pure rationality, or a rational consciousness of their universal participation, and in the end rational self-consciousness. All stages are both a product (a discrete result of prior development) and, except for the final one, a prophecy (only an intermediate development leading to higher ones). The Idea acquiring bare inanimate existence is the physical world, which, in turn, acquires animate existence becoming life. As life acquires subjective, individual, or personal consciousness it becomes Subjective Spirit. As Subjective Spirit acquires interpersonal existence it becomes Objective Spirit. And as Objective Spirit, in turn, acquires self-knowledge, or becomes conscious of itself as such, and so, exists in-and-for-itself, it becomes Absolute Spirit, or God.

Reality in the form of Absolute Spirit is the denouement of consciousness' development, a full embodiment of the system of reason-- it is consciousness knowing itself as consciousness. God is, therefore, the perfection of a world which exists prior to its becoming perfect, or fully rational, but which is moving inexorably in the direction of its own perfection. Moreover, Absolute Spirit itself assumes a number of forms, according to Hegel. These are art, religion, and philosophy, each of which invites a progressively higher expression of self-consciousness. The arts concern the self-consciousness of beauty in which the spiritual truth is revealed in sensuous forms, and sensuous forms themselves are imbued with spiritual significance. The three basic types of art, symbolic, classical, and romantic, represent the three orders of unity between the spiritual and the sensuous that have shown themselves in the historical evolution of the arts. Robert G. Osterhoudt's "An Hegelian Interpretation of Art, Sport, and Athletics" develops a discussion of Hegel's general philosophic commitments, emphasizing those of an aesthetic sort, and draws from these commitments implications for regarding sport and athletics as art forms. It tries to show the meaning of sport and athletics as art forms given the philosophic foundations of Hegelianism. Stressed are the fundamentally spiritual inclinations of sport and athletics, the sense of unity between the spiritual and the sensuous in sport and athletics, the enduring, rational, intrinsic, and disinterested character of sport and athletics, the terms in which sport and athletics embody

themselves in an expressive medium, as well as the likenesses between sport and athletics and the arts in these various respects. Also
considered in regard to the artistic character of sport and athletics
are the distinction between true and spurious forms of sport and athletics, the competitive, or agonistic motif in sport and athletics, training and records in sport and athletics, and the distinction between
amateur and professional forms of sport and athletics.

Religion is taken up with a tacit and symbolic expression of self-
consciousness. And philosophy obtains an explicit and complete apprehension of self-consciousness. Only in philosophy is the Idea, the
fundamental principle of reality, fully revealed as such. Philosophy
shows the reason in all things, and in this the development and the
unity of reason itself. Philosophy is at once the self-apprehension
and the self-actualization of Spirit and Idea. The network of rational
laws, the Logic, which is the actual and the actual, it, constitutes
Thought thinking itself as such, and so philosophy. Philosophy is
thereby considered the highest expression of Spirit, the highest manifestation of Idea, and the noblest form of human activity.

Hegel's brilliant philosophy of history was perhaps the most
genuinely serious and genuinely philosophic effort of the sort to that
time, or at least since Augustine. He envisioned world history as the
development of the world toward Absolute Spirit. World history, then,
is the consciousness of the self-actualization of knowledge, and so
freedom as well--man's freedom and the significance of his existence
ultimately reside in his being a manifestation of absolute knowledge.
The philosophy of history apprehends the patterns of this consciousness' development, and ultimately the unity of its subjective, objective, and absolute parts and stages--it notices the logical self-unfold-
ing of thought. According to Hegel, this development and unity occur
by a dialectic process in which events, or theses, give rise to separated opposites, and ultimately to a conciliation and a resolution of
opposition; whereupon further, albeit higher oppositions suggest themselves. For Hegel, the final stages in this process develop only in
terms of an ethical life, which is itself possible only within the state.
The fundamental obligation of the state is to establish and maintain
institutions which optimize man's progress toward self-knowledge and
freedom. The advance from Subjective Spirit to Objective Spirit depends on this, and, of course, the advance from Objective Spirit to
Absolute Spirit depends on the prior one. The state is, therefore,
conceived as a rational, self-actualized system of laws and institutions
concerning property, contract, and punishment which allow for such
progress--progress which informs our conduct with impartial reason
and establishes, preserves, and extends the common good by critical
refinement of purely subjective, egoistic interests.

The Hegelian system was an enormous influence on the early
nineteenth century, and it provided many of the most noteworthy

insights to which later thinkers of the period were so heavily indebted. The major responses to Hegel, most notably those of Marx, Herbart, Schopenhauer, Kierkegaard, and Nietzsche, constitute much of what remains of nineteenth century philosophy.

Marx. Few philosophic talents have so profoundly effected the course of human history as the German social and political theorist, Karl Marx (1818-1883). Marx' thought contains much of what would now be called philosophical anthropologic tendency, but it was for Marx himself a naturalistic mediation of what he took to be the equally untenable excesses of idealism and materialism. He rejected the idealistic view of reality as essentially spiritual owing to its undue abstractness, and dismissed the materialistic conception of reality as exclusively concrete in virute of its apparent mindlessness. Marx holds instead that man can be understood only in terms of what he has actively made of himself through his own practical activity, or labor. According to this account, consciousness is a faculty of natural man, and is, therefore, derivative of nature, and so not as Hegel had insisted, itself the constitutive principle of reality in general, and humanity and nature in particular. For Marx, then, unlike for Hegel, Schelling, and Fichte, there are natural entities which persist independently of consciousness. Marx does not make abundantly clear, however, how this can be known. Moreover, Marx is convinced that in a state of nature man is free and inclined to use his also natural milieu to actively further his own self-determination. Humanity is nonetheless inherently moved to social participation, principally because his self-determination cannot be autonomously realized. In any event, this social interaction is itself considered an expression of man's naturalistic constitution. Also bound up in this constitution, for Marx, is the distinctly human obligation to treat other persons in other than an exploitative fashion, as well as the distinctly human inclination to refine the productive activity which alone fulfills man beyond the animal impulse to merely provide for biological sustenance. Concerning this latter, Marx holds that such activity must be undertaken as an intrinsically creative act, or an act which sets one in the direction of self-determination. For Marx, however, prevailing economic circumstance was inadequate to the task of liberation. In fact, this circumstance, acting as it did out of feudal and civil, instead of natural allegiances, actively prevented the development of genuine humanity. For, the means available for such development were controlled by the few at the expense of the many, the many were consequently alienated from the means of their self-realization, and a perfervid egoism was everywhere apparent--an egoism which set men against one another, and allowed them to regard one another as little more than means to the satisfaction of one's own self-interest. This egoism and the alienation it produces cannot be overcome by a natural progression of thought beyond it, as Hegel had argued, but only by a revolutionary revision of the capitalist institutions which are at its foundation, according to Marx. Only a revision of this sort can emancipate the masses from the hold of capitalist exploitation, and propel social and political life out of its feudal and civil bondage and into the liberating possibilities of socialism and communism. The role of philosophy in this revision is not merely to make interpretive descriptions of past, present, and foreseeable future event, but to actively show the way of revision itself, and to give this way passionate and persuasive defense. Despite Marx' ostensible disagreements with Hegel, the dialectic of his program and the germ of many of his best insights are owed directly to Hegel. In fact, Marx apparently avoids Hegelianism "only" by denying the basic assumptions of modern philosophy which Hegel had embraced. Not unlike other of the major responses to Hegel, Marx' program begins wtih different principles than those worked out in the critical triumph of Kant.

Herbart. Johann Friedrich Herbart (1776-1841) was among the most vigorous opponents of post-Kantian German idealism. He regarded this movement as an aberration of the Kantian principles which it variously proposed to follow, refine, and complete. In its place, Herbart puts an empiricistic, pluralistic, and deterministic realism. With Kant, he argues that thought has its basis in experience, that experience reveals only phenomena, and that the fact of phenomena presupposes the independent existence of things-in-themselves which cause them and make them so many secondary qualities. Against Kant and the idealistic interpreters of Kant, however, Herbart denies the mind itself any formative power. He is, therefore, left with a strict empirical epistemology, according to which the mind unconsciously and passively receives sensations or ideas which, by the activity inherent in them and not in the mind itself, raise themselves to consciousness. Accordingly, systematic interconnections of ideas also occur unconsciously and involuntarily. This highly mechanistic conception of knowledge, together with his ethics (which argues for the formal union of will and reason in order to effect an harmonious sociopolitical order), form the basis for his highly influential views on pedagogy, applied psychology, or education. Herbart insists that the process of education must begin by disturbing the unconscious mass of ideas, by exhorting them to consciousness so to speak, and it must go on from this to an active involvement in an ongoing mosaic of new and unique experiences, an increasing assimilation of what these particular experiences reveal to general ideas, and an application of these ideas to practical concerns. This original disturbance of unconscious ideas is a function of interest, according to Herbart--the degree to which ideas associate with other ideas is a function of interest. The obligation to spark such interest and to thereby stir up the unconscious mass of ideas is consequently numbered among the more solemn pedagogical responsibilities; and this responsibility is best discharged through an established curriculum of integral disciplines explicitly designed to make for such interest and disturbance, and in the end for the cultivation of virtuous conduct. Much of the Herbartian pedagogy is heavily indebted to the educational philosophy of Kant and Pestalozzi.

Schopenhauer. Like Marx and Herbart, Arthur Schopenhauer (1788-1860) too considered himself an ardent opponent of the fashionable idealism of post-Kantian German philosophy. With many of the major figures who followed in the shadow of Kant, Schopenhauer accepted the master's second Copernican revolution, but rejected his paradoxical allegiance to the material thing-in-itself. In his system, which is run through itself with idealistic tendencies, reality is construed as Idea and Will. It is Idea insofar as all knowledge of it comes in the form of perceptions, which are themselves nothing else than ideas in the mind that show the world as a mosaic of ideas perceived by subjects. It is Will insofar as man is more than a mere knowing subject; he is also an active, doing, striving, craving, and yearning being, and a being who has a consciousness of this other dimension of himself which cannot be explained fully in rational terms. Schopenhauer is particularly obsessed with opposing Hegel's virtually complete appeal to reason, and holds, against Hegel, that the fundamental principle of reality is Will, and not Idea--the fundamental principle of reality is this blind, irrational force. In respect to the relative merits it gives reason and will, Schopenhauer's philosophy is a form of voluntarism. By this view, then, Will is primary, and all else, like body, mind, and nature, is derivative of it, in the form of being outward manifestations of it. Schopenhauer infers by analogy the existence of other wills, minds, and bodies from the existence of his own. Since, however, the Will is itself perceived as idea by the mind, and the mind as such is not apprehended in a fully explicit sense by Will; it is not altogether clear in what terms Will should be considered more primary than Idea.

By Schopenhauer's view, the most fundamental expression of Will is that of preserving one's existence--the will to live, or be. In the higher animals and in man, this primitive, blind, irrational willing may be touched and in some measure influenced by intelligence, for it sometimes objectifies itself in the world of ideas. In lower forms of existence, life proceeds by willing alone, and is as such utterly devoid of intelligence. It is the universal presence of willing in all forms of life, as distinct from the selective presence of intelligence, which persuades Schopenhauer that Will is more fundamental than Idea. There is presupposed in this view, however, a certain discontinuity between willing and thinking that is never fully resolved. In any case, the source and substance of Schopenhauer's infamous pessimism is rooted in the notion of Will's primacy over Idea, and the contention that the ceaseless will to live (as the most fundamental expression of Will itself) is the cause of all selfishness, sorrow, struggle, and evil in the world. Human life as such is, therefore, seen as predominantly evil, base, selfish, painful, miserable, meaningless, fruitless, and so unworthy of preservation. With neither a god nor immortality to support life, according to Schopenhauer, one is consequently left with nothing much other than the bottomless void, or despair of human experience itself. In this more so Eastern resignation than Greek affirmation of life, the perpetuation of life is equivalent to the perpetuation of pointless suffering, and is less preferred than eternal oblivion. Man can hope to free himself from the wicked will only by actively suppressing his inherent selfishness and acting out of a pure sympathy for others. This liberation may occur in a number of ways for Schopenhauer. Philosophy enlightens with respect to the character and limits of human understanding and action, and through this enlightenment shows the way to minimizing sensual engagements and other desires of willing, and so minimizing suffering itself. The arts suppress the will to live by viewing the world as it is in itself, as it is independently of the influence of willing, independently of a desire for its use or manipulation. In a phrase, the arts obtain a will-less circumstance by viewing the world as pure idea. The palliative effects of philosophy and the arts are nonetheless inferior to a more direct, a stoic denial of pleasure and acceptance of pain. In this denial and acceptance, life is abhorred and the impulse to be is annihilated. Even such an ascetic resignation gives only temporary relief from the incessant craving, however, and so it too fails in the end to make life palatable. For life is at bottom suffering, and happiness of an enduring sort it thereby made unrealizable. Accordingly, Schopenhauer's escape from advocating self-destruction is narrow at best. He holds that an act of such rational appeal as suicide is at odds with the fundamentally irrational nature of reality, and so an untenable denial of reality. Perhaps the most notable of the sympathetic responses to Schopenhauer was the attempt of Eduard von Hartmann (1842-1906) to reconcile Hegel's intellectualism with Schopenhauer's voluntarism. The result most closely resembled a blend of Schelling's idealistic metaphysics and Schopenhauer's pessimistic axiology.

Kierkegaard. Few of the replies to Hegelianism were so openly contemptuous of Hegel's philosophy as the thought of the magnificently talented Danish thinker, Sören Kierkegaard (1813-1855). Though most of what Kierkegaard knew of Hegel came from misleading secondary sources, or Schelling's equally misleading interpretations of him, Kierkegaard thought himself exploding the Hegelian demon no less in culture and religion than in philosophy. He sought a reform of human. life altogether by recalling the individual to himself, by working out a renaissance of human freedom, self-determination, and personal dignity, by making a basic transformation in individual human existence. He hoped to raise men from their public and complacent condition to an active, personal, and genuine reflection on life and happiness, and ultimately to Christianity, which he considered the highest mode of existence. Philosophy is not itself the capstone of this development, as for Hegel, but only that which shows the way to its end. The central issue of Kierkegaard's philosophy is the distinctive character of human existence. For him, man is the only authentic existential being, the one being endowed with freedom and a consciousness of its ominous responsibilities. For this emphasis and this view, Kierkegaard is widely remembered as the nineteenth century harbinger of what has become one of the most prominent and influential movements in twentieth century philosophy, existentialism. In emphatic opposition to Hegel, Kierkegaard's program proclaims that the essential nature of man resides, not in his impersonal and general features by which each person is like every other, but in his uniquely personal and particular features according to which each person is distinct from every other. Unique human subjectivity, or individuality, thereby forms the center of Kierkegaard's thought.

According to Kierkegaard, then, truth and happiness are individual or subjective matters, and are best obtained by self-governed, experiential confrontations. The highest of these confrontations, and the confrontation which signifies the culmination of unique human subjectivity, or personal identity, is the confrontation with the transcendent God of Christianity--not the God of reason realizing itself as such in man, as for Hegel. To be truly human, in Kierkegaard's view, is to orient one's life toward God, to freely choose the God relation, to freely choose a personal faith in, and obedience to Him. The achievement of unique individuality, truth, and happiness is, therefore, a function of one's free and personal relation to God. Effectively, this achievement is a constitutive expression of the logical impossibility of the Trinity, infinite God becoming finite man, which Kierkegaard calls the greatest of paradoxes, or the absolute paradox. The supreme test of faith is, therefore, that which requires belief in the most absurd conclusion possible, for it is this test which raises the greatest and the most individualizing passion. For Kierkegaard, then, Christian faith is the supreme existential allegiance, because in its "reconciliation" of the immanence of man's finite condition and his aspiration to the transcendence and infinitude of God is found the most revealing and uniquely personal of experiences, without which life falls over into a Schopenhauerian meaninglessness. It is not altogether clear, however, in what terms this can be considered a genuine, meaning a mindful reconciliation, or for that matter in what terms the entire position escapes calling true whatever absurdities raise the most individualizing passions, or falls into the paradox of gaining individuality only by giving it up.

For Kierkegaard the dialectic of human existence takes place in three basic modes: the aesthetic, ethical, and religious. Man enters the lowest of these three, the aesthetic, from an altogether public mode in which his conformity to convention, domination by others, and lack of individual autonomy and responsibility are central. In the aesthetic mode, he leaps from the utterly public to a conformity with his own sensuality, to a life dominated by the pleasures of sensual desire which ends in merely ephemeral accomplishment, doubt, emptiness, and despair. The barrenness of the aesthetic leads one to the ethical mode of existence in which life is seen through the relative categories of right and wrong. This mode exceeds the capricious pleasure of the aesthetic in virtue of the personal, passionate, and intrinsic choices it requires, and it, therefore, also engenders a more enduring happiness, peace, and tranquility than the aesthetic. It is yet finite, however, and so unworthy of ultimate devotion, and, like the aesthetic, ends in a form of devastation and despair. Its major significance resides in its presaging the faith relation of the highest mode of existence, the religious. In this mode, one rejects all thisworldly, self-interested inclinations in pursuit of a unity with God. For Kierkegaard, only this paradoxical leap of faith, unsppported as it is by anything thisworldly, only this quest for unity with an infinite and eternal, albeit personal being, delivers the complete individuality and happiness which are the end of life authentically lived. In some sense, Kierkegaard has inverted the metaphysical hierarchy of Hegel, in that the subjective of a sort reigns over the absolute of a sort. With Hegel, however, he holds that the three modes of human existence are not lived as mutually exclusive, nor are they suspended or abolished by assent to a higher mode, but do instead support the advance to a higher mode in the form of making such an advance possible.

Nietzsche. The most memorable stem of nineteenth century German philosophy ends with the consummate genius of Friedrich Nietzsche (1844-1900). Nietzsche took the basic insights of Schopenhauer and developed them in positive and optimistic directions. Like Schopenhauer, Nietzsche too wanted to come to grips with the implications of a Godless world for human existence. His penetrating account of modern thought and life concludes neither in Schopenhauer's pessimistic resignation, nor in Kierkegaard's Christian happiness. It ends instead in a rejection of Christianity, and all otherworldly positions, as well as with a joyful affirmation and enhancement of this life. The Darwinian denial of any qualitative difference between man and animal undermined many of the mid-nineteenth century's and Western civilization's most basic assumptions. These assumptions were principally of Christian origin, but even at this, and with nothing to replace them, Nietzsche foresaw a cultural crisis in which the fall to nihilism, or foundationlessness, was next to inevitable. Since, therefore, there is no Kierkegaardian God to redeem the world and to make man eternally happy, according to both Schopenhauer and Nietzsche, only a positive, non-theistic, or human standard of value saves man from utter despair. Both Kierkegaard and Schopenhauer had been convinced that human life can be meaningfully sustained only in relation to a transcendent God. Kierkegaard axiomatically embraced belief in such a God and thereby found the meaning he had sought. Schopenhauer rejected such a belief and thereby fell into the pessimistic torment for which he is so well remembered. Nietzsche effectively mediated these two views by adopting Schopenhauer's atheism and Kierkegaard's analysis of the devastating effect of Christianity's demise on human culture, as well as his optimistic affirmation of life. He denounced the notion popular with both, however, that only a belief in a transcendent diety saves man from groundlessness. Nietzsche argues instead that one

- 161 -

denies the will to live when admitting to the view that life is meaningful only as it related to God. The great crime of Christianity lies in
its demand for such a denial, and in its consequent deprivation of this
life. Nietzsche is convinced that human life is endowed with genuine
meaning and significance only to the extent that it is considered meaningful and significant on its own terms. He, therefore, holds that life
must be affirmed despite its suffering and its godlessness. Nietzsche
followed Schopenhauer in the view that the world is constituted as will
and idea. Perhaps the most elegant expression of this view is found
in his brilliant account of ancient Greek tragedy, which he viewed as
a fusion of the Dionysian (the reflection of the sensuous will most importantly in the form of music) and the Apollinian (the reflection of
idea most importantly in the form of sculpture) impulses in man.
Against Schopenhauer's Buddhist-like negation of the will, however,
Nietzsche argues in characteristically Greek terms for a celebration
of the joy and power inherent in human life. Also against Schopenhauer, Nietzsche holds that human life is more fundamentally rooted
in the will to power than in the will to be, for the latter is frequently
risked for want of the former, and the former, which expresses itself
in creative activity, produces the greatest happiness. For Nietzsche,
the creative expression of the will to power affirms life and gives the
courage and strength to oppose weakness, suffering, and evil, and to
promote goodness. Evil is, in fact, what diminishes the will to power,
goodness what enhances it. Even truth and beauty are worthily pur-
sued only insofar as they augment the will to power--only activities
which actively contribute to the quantitative and qualitative development of creativity, or the will to power, are ultimately worthy.
Nietzsche conceives of art as a world of idealized illusions which
heighten creativity, and so offers a palliative for life in the form of
importing a renewed enthusiasm for it. Wherein the will to power is
sublimated in the fullest measure and sense, and, therefore, developed away from the common tendency to express it as a basal brutality,
men of great creative and intellectual prowess (overmen, or super-
men) are the result. These are not ordinary men, for Nietzsche, not
men of the herd, not men who are human-all-too-human, men who are
more so animal than distinctly human, but those who embody the realization of man's highest possibilities, his ultimate enhancement.
Higher men are distinguished from lower both in terms of their quan-
tum, or strength of power, and in terms of their qualitative, or moral
superiority. According to this view, the only standard of value is the
overman, or the realization of human life's highest form--the highest
cultivation of the will to power. All other than overman is significant
only insofar as it contributes to man's highest possibilities. The herd,
or underman, is, therefore, something to be overcome, a bridge between animality and overman. For Nietzsche, however, even the
higher man--as approximated by the likes of Homer, Socrates, Plato,
Alexander the Great, Caesar, Dante, Leonardo, Spinoza, Frederick
the Great, Kant, Napoleon, and Goethe--are themselves largely insignificant as individuals. They are primarily significant as contributors

to the fulfillment of what is highest in the species man. Nietzsche's fundamental concern is, therefore, somewhat unlike Kierkegaard's, for he is more so interested in humanity as species, or lebensphilo-sophie, than in unique human subjectivity, or existenzphilosophie. As such, Nietzsche's thought represents the nineteenth century herald of what would become a prominent twentieth century movement, philo-sophical anthropology.

Though the meaning and significance of life is confined to this-worldly events for Nietzsche, it is not located in the social circum-stance of everyday life, in what is called a comfortable security. This meaning and significance is instead realized in a fellowship of uncommon men; not a commiserative fellowship, but a competitive gathering in which men assist one another in achieving a creative life, and in which only a mutual respect among participants is extended. Such uncommon individuals and gatherings have been deliberately sup-pressed by an impersonal public and institutional circumstance, how-ever. In its democratic inclinations, this circumstance has preferred the standardized, common, tranquil, complacent, and mediocre person who is unable to stand the whole truth of life, to the genuinely extra-ordinary person who is able to affirm and endure that truth. Much of Nietzsche's attack on Christianity, no less than his attack on demo-cracy, has to do with the distressing fullness with which they promote the ordinary and weak as over and against the extraordinary and strong. This promotion, Nietzsche argues, is fundamentally evil, for it diminishes the will to power and dignifies what he calls a slave mo-rality. For him, Christianity is the highest corruption, because it encourages man to believe in a myth which, once exploded, undermines life totally, leaving only despair. Christianity is, therefore, thought to renounce life, to renounce the will to power and its expression in the body and other thisworldly conditions, in the only terms which make it meaningful. Similarly, everyday socio-politicality, most particularly that of democratic inclination, too promotes a destructive and decadent weakness. Such socio-politicality is, by Nietzsche's view, the means by which the herd consolidates its mediocrity and preserves the con-ventional standards and myths which make life palatable for it. Effec-tively, it suppresses the unusual on the grounds that customary, albeit illusory, modes of existence are threatened by the extraordinary. Higher men conform to such standards only in the sense and to the de-gree necessary in order to enhance the will to power. Higher men fashion their lives around carefully self-chosen values which support and advance their creativity, and not around the inherited values of the herd. Though all higher men cultivate the common virtues of a noble human soul, such as courage, wisdom, sympathy, and solitude; they do, within the context of this cultivation, as a working out of this culti-vation, transfigure values in relation to their own will to power. And for higher men this is a transfiguration which coincides with--that is to say, constitutes--the working out of humanity's highest possibilities. If they allow the herd its illusions, however, they come to be pitied instead of destroyed, and though hardly understood or respected they are at least preserved, and the free pursuit of their creativity, which is the formal end of their life, is enhanced. The numerical superiority of the herd consequently requires a "submission" of this sort to the slave morality. Though it is, of course, a higher morality which is sought by this "submission".

As the end of striving in general is human creativity so too is this the end of education in particular for Nietzsche. He conceives of the educational process as inherently arduous (for life proceeds only at the expense of other life) and largely solitary (for the herd contaminates), as requiring an order of discipline and devotion far exceeding the capricious, and as successively entailing an unbiased understanding of one's cultural heritage, a critical assessment of that heritage, and ultimately a release of one's own creative faculties. In this process, one cultivates one's talents to the level of other higher men before thinking oneself prepared to surpass that level. Moreover, Nietzsche's extraordinarily sympathetic regard for the body, as much more than an instrument of the mind, as inseparable from the mind, and as one mode of the reality of a person, led him to advocate an active, intense, and courageous participation in daring and vigorous forms of physical activity. He was convinced that such a participation constitutes a prominent medium through which the will to power is fulfilled. In "The Philosophy of Friedrich Nietzsche as a Foundation for Physical Education", Gary C. Banks draws out the implications of Nietzsche's metaphysical, epistemic, ethical, and educational views for physical education. Banks concludes that Nietzsche's general philosophic program implies a highly favorable view of physical education, as a creative avenue through which one's knowledge of the body is enhanced, one's health and bodily beauty and strength improved and sustained, and one's Greek strife for a balanced and harmonious excellence in part fulfilled. Similarly, Esar Shvartz' "Nietzsche--Philosopher of Fitness" proposes the implications of Nietzsche's philosophy, most particularly his views about the nature of man, for physical education. Central to this discussion are what can be made of Nietzsche's talk about the body, his doctrine of the will to power, and his notion of the overman. Concerning the body, Shvartz emphasizes Nietzsche's view of the unity of man, the high significance of the body as one aspect of this unity, the need for an active cultivation of bodily event, and Nietzsche's attack on the despisers of the body. Stressed in Shvartz' examination of the will to power are the primacy of human initiative and self-determination as over and against mere adaptation, and the need to courageously throw oneself into life so as to carve it out for oneself, so as to self-determine it. And emphasized with respect to the overman are Nietzsche's views that higher men do not flee from life's tragedies but take them on straightforwardly, and that the natural instincts of such men are dominated by an allegiance to individual and species self-affirmation and fulfillment, and not by a loyalty to the political and religious institutions of the herd. Shvartz takes these ideas to imply that the likes of physical education and sporting activities allow man to fulfill himself in his body, to recognize, affirm, and enhance his will to power through the conquering of fear and danger in adventurous experiences, to fight against his alienation from the bio-physical reality of which he is a part, and to become a person of extraordinary accomplishment.

Neo-Kantianism. Aroused by a growing stream of materialistic response to the post-Kantian German idealists, greatly influenced by the achievements of modern science, and driven by an interest in reconciling scientific and philosophic insight, a talented group of late nineteenth century German thinkers again turned the gaze of philosophy on the problem of knowledge and on Kant's critical resolution of it. The most notable contributions to this movement include the idealistic pantheism of Hermann Lotze (1817-1881), the psychological idealism of Gustav Theodor Fechner (1801-1887), the variously idealistic- and realistic -tending view of Wilhelm Wundt (1832-1920), and the ethical idealisms of Rudolf Eucken (1846-1926) and Wilhelm Windelband (1848-1915).

Positivism: Comte. Nineteenth century French philosophy developed in an altogether different direction than had the German thought of the period. In significant measure, it represented a continuance of the eighteenth century concern for socio-political matters, as distinct from a reflection on the more basic issues of metaphysics and epistemology which had occupied the center of German philosophy. It nonetheless differed even from eighteenth century French tendencies in virtue of its preference for achieving social reform by evolutionary, as opposed to revolutionary process. That is to say, it thought a progressive modification of socio-political institutions by an institutional process itself superior to a radical destruction and reconstruction of such institutions by civil disobedience. The socio-political reform so ardently sought by this movement was based on a yet more fundamental reform of the sciences, most especially the social sciences, and was to have been achieved principally through education. Effectively, the philosophic program of this movement is founded on experience and the laws of science--the program's basic outline is that of a positive philosophy--and it is in the end devoted to defending the equal distribution of property, power, and happinees. Its earliest notable developments come from the work of Claude Henri de Saint-Simon (1760-1825). Saint-Simon's thought is more so an apologetic for reform than a systematic and well argued formulation of its terms, however. A comprehensive, systematic, and rigorously argued account of the position was left instead to Auguste Comte (1798-1857).

The pragmatic-tending thought of Comte sought an empirical knowledge of the natural laws of society, which Comte thought presupposed by all of the other sciences and by a philosophical orientation as well. He was convinced that human knowledge has evolved historically from a theological, to a metaphysical, to the ideal, or positive stage. According to Comte, theology and metaphysics both attempt to achieve the unobtainable; that is, both are engaged in the futile task of explaining the world in absolutistic and essentialistic terms. Conversely, the positive stage is dominated by an attempt to explain the uniform relations among phenomena. In this stage, the true nature of things is revealed, and it is revealed by direct experience and in relativistic and progressivistic terms. Comte's observations concerning the historical evolution of knowledge led him to a systematic classification of the sciences in the order in which they have appeared in the positive stage. The hierarchy progresses from the simplest and most specific science, mathematics, to the most complex and general form of knowledge, sociology, which is taken to include ethics. Though each level in the hierarchy presupposes each lower level, Comte escapes the charges of reductionism and materialism, which he disdained, by arguing that none is reducible to any other. Moreover, he holds to a view of the socio-political order in which the egoism of individual interests is cultivated in accord with the nobility of reason, and in the form of man's social impulse, or feeling of love. For Comte, the central ethical command, and the central principle of his religion of humanity is to live for others. He opposed popular representation in government, how however, for it makes the informed dependent on, and victim of the uninformed.

Utilitarianism: Bentham, J. S. Mill. Though deeply indebted to the classical British empiricists, Locke, Berkeley, and Hume, Jeremy Bentham (1748-1832) was the first to give a trenchant philosophic account of the modern ethical doctrine of <u>utilitarianism</u>. His pragmatic-tending thought importantly continued the empiricistic traditions of seventeenth and eighteenth century British philosophy. It was primarily devoted to establishing a principle of moral conduct for the individual, and a scientific basis for the legislative improvement of the socio-political order. His self-evident <u>principle of utility</u> approves of all actions which produce happiness in the form of pleasure, and disapproves of all actions which produce unhappiness in the form of pain. According to Bentham, the system of jurisprudence, legislation, or law which governs the socio-political fabric has as its primary obligation the direction of man's actions so as to produce the greatest possible quantity of happiness. His philosophy and concrete practice of education, his Chrestomathia, was likewise based on the principle of utility, and on a hedonistic calculus which, at once, determines the quantities of pleasure and happiness, and so the relative merits of alternative courses of action. Like the thought of the earlier British empiricists, Bentham's too provoked rationalistic-tending responses, most notably from the Scotch philosophers, William Whewell (1795-1866) and William Hamilton (1788-1856), who were most significantly affected by Kant. Bentham is, perhaps, best remembered, however, for his influence on the pragmatic-tending programs of James Mill (1773-1836) and his celebrated son, John Stuart Mill (1806-1873).

The genius of the younger Mill again entrenched British philosophy in its empirical roots, and in even greater measure than had Bentham's thought. Under the profound influence of Bentham, Comte, and the classical British empiricists, Mill's work formed the most significant contribution to nineteenth century British philosophy. Though he was primarily interested in socio-political reform, Mill nonetheless recognized well that a fully satisfactory treatment of such reform depends itself and greatly on a sound, probable knowledge of it, and that this, in turn, depends on the use of sound methods of inquiry. He, therefore, first concerns himself with fundamental logical and psychological matters. For him, this comes to establishing a valid and reliable system of inductive logic. Assuming the uniformity and universality of nature and the doctrine of the association of ideas, Mill attempted to demonstrate that all knowledge, all inference and proof, save self-evident truths, consists in inductions. That is, it consists in inferences from known to unknown particulars. By his view, deduction ends at its beginning, for it only repeats what is already known by induction--it reveals no a priori truths because there are none. He nonetheless holds with Kant that only phenomena, and not noumenal things-in-themselves, are known, but that material things-in-themselves must be thought to exist in order to explain the cause of our sensations. Mill's empiricistic allegiances keep him a notable distance from Kant on other matters, however. He conceives of mind as nothing other than a series of feelings, and of the self as a permanent possibility of feelings which has its character formed through the liberal exercise of its own free will--that is, through the science of education. And he is persuaded that even the most basic laws of logic and mathematics are explained exclusively by reference to experience. Mill's sought after reform of the socio-political sciences and institutions then rests on these more fundamental insights. The terms of this reform are guided by a curious correspondence between social and political event, and by a Benthamesque ethics which insists that the measure of goodness, or happiness, is pleasure, and that the sine qua non of morality is bound up in the principle, the greatest good of the greatest number. Mill's hedonism differs from Bentham's, however, in that, pleasures are taken to differ not only in quantitative, but also in qualitative respects. This allows Mill to hold that intellectual pleasures reign over sensuous ones and are readily recognized as superior by all those well informed with respect to the nature of both. The utilitarianism of Mill is further distinguished from that of Bentham by virtue of its interpretation of happiness as being more than a pure self-interest; namely, as being a disinterested social sentiment, or a desire for the unity and welfare of all men.

Evolutionism: Spencer. The naturalistic-tending philosophy of Herbert Spencer (1820-1903) brings this discussion of nineteenth century philosophy to an appropriate close. Spencer primarily devoted himself to overcoming the fragmentation and inconsistency of common sense orders of thought. In this, he sought a fully unified knowledge of reality, a universal knowledge, a synthetic philosophy. His program was given to discovering the highest truths, the truths from which the principles of the particular sciences could be deduced. For Spencer, these principles are deducible from such self-evident truths, but they are also empirically accessible and so having the faculty of introducing themselves into the unified system. His alleged resolution of the rationalist-empiricist dispute, therefore, suggests that while knowledge is based on a priori forms of the mind (relation, difference, and likeness) which have evolved as products of the species experience, it is nonetheless also owing to empirical source. In fact, it is this empirical source which has progressively and variously upbuilt itself to the form of the a priori categories, and has made them visible. Accordingly, all knowledge is only of finite and limited things, and is thereby also relative. Despite this claim, however, Spencer embraces the existence of an Absolute Being as the objective correlate of man's subjective feeling of activity, power, and force, and as underlying and explaining the activity of nature and all experience. By Spencer's view, the indestructible persistence of this subjective feeling is independently expressed in mind, or subjectivity, and in matter, or objectivity. The basic terms of Spencer's evolutionism, the fundamental basis of the species' development, is thereby grounded in a continuous adaptation of internal, or psychological, to external, or physical events. The crown of Spencer's synthetic philosophy is his ethics, however. Like Bentham and Mill, Spencer held that happiness in the form of pleasure is the first principle of morality. More so like Mill than Bentham, however, he was convinced that the end of the evolutionary process, the ideal of the process, is a permanently peaceful socio-political order in which every constituent achieves his self-interest and assists in achieving the self-interest of others. In this process, the notion of justice dictates that all men are free to do as they will, except interfere with the freedom of others to do likewise. This essentially individualistic thesis, which aims at reconciling the extremes of egoism and altruism, regards the welfare of socio-politicality as a means of promoting the welfare of its units. It, therefore, tends to prefer the least feasible interference of the state with respect to the exercise of individual freedom. Somewhat surprisingly, and unlike either Bentham or Mill, however, Spencer's ethics is taken as having a rational, as distinct from an empirical origin. That is, it is deduced from the basic principles of the various sciences. Moreover, his naturalistic inclinations are nowhere more conspicuous than in his philosophy of education. Owing much to Pestalozzi, Spencer opposes the classical tradition in education and advocates a fiercely individualistic curriculum, which is science-dominated and ultimately obliged to give a preparation for complete, intellectual, moral, and physical living.

With Spencer this discussion of nineteenth century philosophy ends. Though less can be conclusively said about twentieth, than about nineteenth century thought, a brief treatment of the current century's philosophic development nonetheless follows. Our historical perspective on this period is simply too limited for this treatment to be other than cursory and inconclusive, however.

Twentieth century philosophy

Our propinquity to the events of this century, together with the astounding diversity of these events, make a characterization of the philosophy of the period doubly difficult. Perhaps this diversity and the consequent difficulties it raises is itself the most salient characteristic of twentieth century thought. The following discussions of this thought are worked out in the following divisions: English and American idealism, French and Italian idealism, Intuitionism, Existentialism, Phenomenology, Philosophical anthropology, English and American realism, Pragmatism, and Analytic philosophy.

English and American idealism: T. H. Green, F. H. Bradley, Royce.
Late nineteenth and early twentieth century British philosophy turned dramatically away from its empirical traditions. It even regarded nineteenth century British empiricism as a regressive interlude in the development of European thought. It much preferred Kant and Hegel to Locke, Hume, Bentham, and Mill. The movement effectively comes to an independent reformulation of early nineteenth century German idealism.

Easily the most prominent figure in this development was Thomas Hill Green (1836-1882). Green held that an all-uniting, universal self-consciousness, a noumenal or spiritual world, is presupposed by, and makes possible, the existence of the phenomenal world and our knowledge of it. The mechanistic order of nature is, therefore, a product of this consciousness, and not itself the source of consciousness as the empiricists had argued. Green conceives of man, or self, as a free and eternal unifying consciousness, not unlike the universal mind, which organizes impressions or sensations in such a way that they are made intelligible and qualify as knowledge. According to this view, man is a moral agent in virtue of his capacity to conceive of an idealized state of himself, and to willfully aspire to that state. Man is so endowed, for Green, because he is a replica, albeit an imperfect one owing to his participation in nature, of the eternal self-consciousness--a participant in the consciousness of God, as well as in the order of nature. Moreover, according to Green, the good is the best thing, a perfection to be attained or fulfilled, something absolutely desirable, intrinsic, independent, and supreme. Ultimate moral and socio-political duty has to do with an active moving in the direction of the good--a movement which implies a form of universal equality and respect among all men; that is, implies the categorical imperative. In this, all men must be treated as ends-in-themselves; such that, no self-interest can be realized apart from, let alone at odds with the common good. The perfection of others is thereby included in the conception of oneself as perfect, and morality is thought a function of a rational community with others. There can consequently be no notion of political obligation without a notion of this organic ideal in which all rights are mutually recognized and honored in a world brotherhood. The glimpse that man gets of this ideal is incomplete and, therefore, limited, however. He moves toward it in bits and pieces, obtaining with each bit and each piece a progressively better, though never a full view of it. Green thus accounts for man's less than divine status in the world, while nonetheless showing the terms of his constraint to a regulative moral standard. The philosophy of Green most resembles the thought of Fichte among those to whom he is most indebted.

Like Green, Francis Herbert Bradley (1846-1924) too argued that man has an inherent, but incomplete insight into the Absolute, and that this insight is contrary to his apprehension of the world as fragmented appearances. Also like Green, Bradley is convinced that this spiritual Absolute, or unifying principle of all things, is necessarily presupposed by our knowledge and disparate sentient experience. This is tantamount to claiming that a knowledge of particular things entails a knowledge of them as harmonious participants in one reality --a knowledge of them in the unity of all experience. Bradley's predictably organic ethics and politics also resemble Green's. By this view, man is a moral agent in virtue of his possessing an intent to realize himself as an infinite whole; that is to say, as a self-conscious part of the Absolute. The ultimate ends of morality, socio-politicality, and reality thereby converge for Bradley. The philosophy of Bradley is most like Schelling's among those to whom he is most beholding. Perhaps the strongest Hegelian tendencies in this movement are found in the work of Bernard Bosanquet (1848-1923), who argued that human fulfillment resides in man completing the system of knowledge, morality, and beauty--resides in man coming to one with Absolute unity. Also contributing significantly to this movement was the pluralistic and personalistic idealism of John Ellis McTaggart (1866-1925) and the subjectivistic aesthetics of Robin George Collingwood (1889-1943).

Neo-Hegelianism also had a significant impact on late nineteenth and early twentieth century American philosophy. The leading figure in this movement was Josiah Royce (1855-1916), who construed the whole of reality as consisting in ideas. For Royce, the fundamental interpretive principle of reality is an orderly, rational, omniscient, and knowable Logos which includes all finite selves and all finite consciousness (and is as such, personalistic), but which is also more than any or all of the finite selves and consciousness comprising it, insofar as it completes, unifies, and makes self-conscious these selves and consciousness. The moral dimension of human existence is then bound up in one's faith in, and loyalty toward this universal omniscience, or highest good.

French and Italian idealism: Renouvier, Boutroux, Croce, Gentile.
The development of idealistic tendencies in late nineteenth and early
twentieth century French philosophy was more so the product of a
negative response to Comte than a reconsideration of the post-Kantian
German insights. The major contributions to this movement included
the pluralistic and personalistic system of Charles Renouvier (1815-
1903), which denied the existence of a noumenal world and confined
knowledge to the relativity of phenomenal relations; the voluntaristic
and evolutionistic reconciliation of idealism and materialism of Alfred
Fouillée (1838-1912), which interprets reality as a singular, active,
psychic force, or idées-forces; and the program of Émile Boutroux
(1845-1922), which envisions reality as an hierarchy of existential
levels from highly determinate, to progressively more indeterminate
and free, to ultimate freedom, or God.

The idealistic movement in twentieth century Italian philosophy
is principally a response against what is considered the unduly static
world views of the British Hegelians. Unsurprisingly, it, therefore,
emphasized the historical, as distinct from the logical or metaphysical aspects of Hegel's thought. As such, it concentrated on an interpretation of reality as the evolution of active and creative thought, as
the progressive evolution of human achievement. The most prominent
exponent of this view was Benedetto Croce (1866-1952). Embracing
the central principle of idealism that reality is spiritually constituted
and manifest in thought and experience, Croce interpreted the manifestations of spirit in concrete, human, and present, as distinct from
transcendent, absolute, past or future terms. He took as central the
nature and significance of the concrete human experiences of thinking
(humanity's theoretical aspect) and willing, or acting (humanity's
practical aspect). Croce further bisects the theoretical aspect into its
intuitive, or aesthetic, and its conceptual stems. The intuitive process is that by which the material of human experience is obtained.
It entails both perception and the expression of perception in imaginative media—the basal impressions from which all experience and
thought springs, and the patterning of those impressions in artistic
images. The conceptual process organizes the material which intuition places in evidence. And the willing process impels us to action;
that is, impels us to act out of the theoretical insights on which the
will itself depends. According to Croce, education is nothing other
than a cultivation of the theoretical and practical aspects of experience.
Though sharply influenced by Croce, the thought of Giovanni Gentile
(1875-1944) more closely resembles the absolutistic temperament of
German high idealism, than had that of Croce. Gentile was convinced
that Croce's unity of experience and his discussion of this unity's
multiple expressions in various spheres are incompatible. He, therefore, opts for a view which, in his judgment, better accounts for the
ideal unity of subject and object in self-conscious experience. His philosophy, as the fulfillment of self-consciousness, thereby represents

the synthesis of all disparate manifestations, most notably, of art, education, religion, and history.

Much of what remains of twentieth century philosophy goes as a mosaic of responses to, variations on, or extensions of nineteenth century developments. The multi-faceted reaction against idealism is likely the most prominent of these. The most pervasive consequence of these efforts has been to bring philosophy "nearer" to concrete experience, and so, by the view of the time, to make it more instructive of this experience.

Intuitionism: Bergson. Among the most influential of these attempts was the philosophical anthropologic-tending work of the French philosopher, Henri Bergson (1859-1941), who proposed a strict cleavage between proper objects of scientific, logical, and mathematical inquiry, and those befitting philosophic reflection. According to Bergson, science apprehends only matter, or the inert, static, predictable, and determined, which is without memory and creativity, and so incapable of penetrating to the essential character of reality. Philosophy, conversely, is capable of such a penetration, revealing the world as free, conscious, living, evolving, moving, remembering, creating, and individualizing force, or élan vital. Philosophy obtains a direct vision, or intuition, as distinct from a rational understanding, of the vital force which uses matter for its purposes and is at the center of all things. The moral and religious command of this view is to cultivate the pure vitality which is the fundamental interpretive principle of reality. Predictably, Bergson's notions of intuition, change, and creativity also form the basis of his philosophy of education.

Existentialism: Heidegger, Jaspers, Sartre, Marcel. Another of the highly influential movements in twnetieth century philosophy is the Kierkegaard-inspired existentialism, or existential philosophy. Among the earliest and most articulate proponents of this view was the German philosopher, Martin Heidegger (1889-1976). Like others of this persuasion, Heidegger was principally concerned to explain the meaning of distinctly human existence--to show what constitutes this existence and what the significance of being human is. He thinks most important the existential, as distinct from the objective traits of human existence. In his existential analytic, Heidegger erects the doctrine of ontological difference, according to which Being is the determining ground of beings, the determinate basis of all thought and experience. The human mode of existence is then taken as at once swept up in Being, and as the guardian of Being. That is to say, the human circumstance is determined by its "residence in" Being, and Being is itself realized only in the form of human circumstance. For, only in the human circumstance, or being, is there the sort of Being which can understand itself and the world as such. In this sort of Being, or Dasein, which is the highest form of human action for Heidegger, reality, or Being, becomes aware of itself per se. This highest form of human action is variously dominated by what Heidegger calls essential thinking, or the form of thought proper to philosophy, and poetic thinking, or the form of metaphorical expression proper to the arts. A subordination of essential and/or poetic thinking to social and practical imperative is consequently considered an inversion of life authentically lived, and so a perversion of thought and experience itself. Such a subordination is formally equivalent to frustrating the experience of Being. Moreover, according to Heidegger, Being is not a theologic transcendent, as "it" had been for Kierkegaard, but a consciousness embodied in the world as finite and temporal. It is, in fact, man's awareness of his finitude and temporality that makes his existence unique.

Heidegger's program emphasizes the anguish and dread of man caught between the dead world of religious faith and the unborn world of authentic existence. By his view, only an abiding attention to the fundamental terms of one's existence can "relieve" such an anguish and deliver one to an authentic state of being, to a distinctly personal state, or existenz. Authenticity is basically conceived as a freely chosen living in accord with one's fundamental, existential nature. Effectively, it is a living in recognition of one's highest possibility, as well as one's death. The call to authenticity is a call to recognize how things basically are, to thereby avoid self-deception, and to freely make oneself over into what one is most fundamentally. The prospect of falling into inauthentic modes of existence, or das man, is nonetheless great. In such modes, dominated as they are by everydayness and impersonality, one fails to recognize the full nature and significance of the distinctly human mode of existence, one acts primarily out of a conformity to one's environment thereby alienating oneself from one's own potential for authenticity. In a state of inauthenticity, one is lost in publicness, other-directed, and so living in accord with one's natural, being-in-the-world, and social, being-with-others, expectations as though interchangeable with and thereby like other persons. One is living out one's ontic possibilities as a functional and impersonal part of other than distinctly human modes, in this circumstance. Only anxiety, guilt, and death arouse from the inauthenticity of the everyday, and allow one to live out one's ontological possibilities as a free, self-directed, individual personality. Heidegger characterizes anxiety as a peculiarly human discomfort arising from the realization that, relative to the human condition, the world is meaningless --man is simply thrown into it as a concrete fact. Guilt is taken as a peculiarly human discomfort which results from man's choosing to fulfill certain of his alternatives, and consequently and regrettably being unable to fulfill others. One's personal confrontation with death is the most radically individualizing and humanizing possibility of Dasein for Heidegger, however. According to him, it is only through the urgency established by death that man is capable of authenticity at all. What is required of an authentic response to these features of distinctly human life is a resolute confrontation to them, a seeing them for what they are. What is seen in such a confrontation is that they are not publicly manageable, impersonal events, not events the responsibility for which can be displaced or shared; but, events faced in the solitude of oneself which bring one to self-knowledge. In John H. Walsh's "A Fundamental Ontology of Play and Leisure" the implications of Heidegger's existentio-phenomenologic ontology for play and leisure activities are examined. Walsh concludes that authentically, as distinct from spuriously, engaged play and leisure activities, such as sport, serve to repair, maintain, and perfect Dasein's being genuinely anxious, free, responsible, finite, and temporal.

The philosophy of the German thinker Karl Jaspers (1883-1969) begins in much the same place as Heidegger's. According to Jaspers, the tragic conflicts of our age are due largely to an excessive dedication to the ends of merely empirical being, and the tendency of this excess to disregard the ultimate problems of human existence as such. It is an age with neither spiritual purpose nor personal autonomy--an age "between", an age of basic purposelessness, as for Heidegger. For Jaspers, one is led out of the despair created by such a state by philosophy. This is most apparent in his highly sympathetic, charitable, and appealing account of the history of philosophy, or philosophizing, as the development of a community united in the common search for the personal meaning of reality in general, and human existence in particular. Jaspers, in fact, makes unusually much of man's realizing himself only in such a community, and only in relation to the other-than-oneself in general, and so only by the sort of communication which characterizes such communities and such relationships. Moreover, Jaspers thinks human existence intelligible only as free subjectivity: it is not a knowable object. Though they mutually develop one another, and though reason arouses distinctly and authentically human subjectivity, or Existenz, from its slumber; reason and Existenz are nonetheless the poles of Being. Existenz is infinite in the sense of its being unto itself, unconditioned by finite things, and so not as such determinable objectively, or rationally. The limits of Existenz, called boundary situations, are, therefore, inherent. The most important of these situations, death and guilt, are accepted freely and lovingly as the fulfillment of Being. Existenz is, therefore, a general consciousness of the uniqueness of the individual self--an impulse to self-determination, to independence, or Transcendence. Jaspers is further convinced that sport, though typically a trapping of purposelessness, can contribute to the vitality of this consciousness. It can participate in the revolt against the self-destructive tyranny of the objective and the everyday; it can function as a form of uniquely human expression; and it can affirm and enhance, as distinct from merely sustain it.

The leading French figure in the existentialist movement was Jean-Paul Sartre (1905-   ). Sartre's early thought claimed a radical distinction between the mode of existence which is unaware of itself (the non-human mode, in-itself, or en-soi) and that which is aware of itself (the distinctly human mode, for-itself, or pour-soi). The en-soi mode is determined by the causal order of things, and is, there-fore, incapable of free choice and exhausted by its empirical qualities. The pour-soi, conversely, is determined by free choice, by what man makes of himself, by man's transcendence of the causal order. As such, the pour-soi lacks the permanence of the en-soi which the pour-soi nonetheless seeks but can never attain. In fact, the human cir-cumstance is itself characterized as a passionate but futile quest for the synthesis of en-soi and pour-soi, for the unattainable absolute. The inescapable tension which results explains man's condemnation to freedom, negation, isolation, and frustration. According to this view, man and the world are ontologic opposites: Being is identified with the positive character of the world, and Nothingness with the negative character of human existence. Only Nothingness is free to choose as it might, only human actions, which themselves entail freedom, are, therefore, significant. For, only by the free choice of self-determin-ation does one escape being a merely causal event, an inauthentic pro-ject. Man's awareness of this freedom, and the personal and grave responsibility that come with it, leads him to the dread, anguish, and solitude which reveal the basic nature of pour-soi. That is to say, in his choosing for himself, as though choosing for all mankind, he enters such states and thereby puts himself in for such revelation. The lot of this is, of course, not to argue that man is altogether and in every sense free. Sartre holds that man is conditioned and limited by the terms which he finds himself in, by the terms in which he has been thrown into, the world; in a word, by his facticity--for one, man is not free not to be. What the lot of this does demonstrate, however, is that man does exist within limited alternatives which themselves hold no intrinsic value. While the circumstance in which human life persists is in many ways determined, then, its value is not among those ways. This gives rise to Sartre's famous notion that existence precedes essence--value is a function of human choice, not an inher-ent feature of the determined order.

By Sartre's view, it is man's excessive absorption in the inau-thentic demands of the everyday which keeps him away from the rigors of dread, anguish, and solitude, and so obscures his vision of freedom and the responsibility for genuine truth. This flight to the everyday, to a being with the determinations of the natural and social orders in-stead of a being with oneself, is tantamount to being what one is not and not being what one is. Sartre calls this flight into which man all too commonly falls, a state of bad faith, or self-deception. It is ulti-mately man's authentic response to death--the most radically individ-uating event in his life--which brings him to a forthright confrontation with human life and himself. It is facing the solitude and absurdity of death which in the end unveils himself to himself, makes him fully and authentically human, and preserves his dignity through a circumstance which seems actively opposed to such a preservation.

Sartre's notion of the body, play, and sport have been of particular interest to the philosophy of physical education and sport. By
this view, the body is considered the pour-soi engaged in the world.
This engagement takes three forms: what the body is immediately for
a given subject (as a center of self-reference with respect to the
world), what the body is as an object for others (as an object which
figures in the experience of others), and what the body is as an awareness of one's body being observed by others (as a regarding onself as
others would, as en-soi, which goes as a form of self-alienation).
Sartre considers play a basic expression of one's subjectivity, and so
a turning resolutely away from an objective characterization of oneself. And sport, as a form of play, is thought an act of appropriation
toward the absolute permanence of the en-soi. James W. Keating's
"Sartre on Sport and Play" regards Sartre's treatment of the ontological foundation of play and sport as the most ambitious and exciting
account yet given on the subject. According to Keating's interpretation of Sartre, the fundamental motive force of things--the pour-soi
vainly but relentlessly desiring the non-temporal permanence of the
en-soi, or being--is vividly acted out in such activities as play and
sport, no less than in art and science. Though variously working
their way through the other categories of desire (to do or make, and
to have), play and sport authentically undertaken are basically devoted
to the appropriation of being itself. This appropriation is not a making
oneself objective, however, but an earnest attempt to secure the elusive permanence of one's personal and free subjectivity.

Somehwat unlike the secular brands of existential philosophy put
forward by Heidegger, Jaspers, and Sartre, the thought of the French
thinker, Gabriel Marcel (1889-1973), develops in a religious direction.
Like Heidegger, Jaspers, and Sartre, however, Marcel too strenu-
ously objects to the intolerable modern preference for the impersonal,
functional, and technical, as over and against the personal, aesthetic,
and affective. For Marcel, body-mind, subject-object, thought-being
polarities, though having some basis in experience, are basically inaccessible, most especially to the objective inquiries of science. The
relation of mind and body, for one, must simply be taken as given and
accepted as mystery if it is to be talked about at all, according to
Marcel. Insofar as satisfactory discussions of such mysteries are
possible, they are possible only through philosophic reflection. This
is so because the self is more than the sum of its empirical qualities,
and can thereby be only reflectively, and not scientifically known.
One's unique human subjectivity cannot be scientifically verified, but
only born witness to--it is mysterious, repulsed by objective analysis,
the self-evident foundation and source of experience, as distinct from
the consequence of experience. One's relations with what one has,
consequently differ from one's relations with what one is and others
are. In the case of one's body, however, there is an ultimate blending
between having and being, for the body is evidently both a part of the
world of objective things, and a constituent of one's basically subjective

self as well. The concrete and immediate participation of one's body in the objective world provides an access to this world, through which the mind grasps being in its existential fullness. Moreover, Marcel also holds that, though man's response to being, and so man himself, is fundamentally free, this response and man himself are nonetheless conditioned in significant ways and measures by one's character, one's past, and God. In fact, the supreme ontological mystery, according to Marcel, is the union of the self with the transcendent Being, or God. This union is the result of renouncing one's self-sufficiency and affirming God's transcendence. It is only through this renunciation and this affirmation that man makes himself what he is. That is, Marcel conceives of man's direct and authentic participation in being as depending on such a renunciation and affirmation, as well as on a sympathetic regard for nature and community.

Other major influences on twentieth century existential philosophy have included the Sartre-like atheism of Albert Camus (1913-1960), and the theistic views of Nicolas Berdyaev (1874-1948), Martin Buber (1878-1965), Jose Ortega y Gasset (1883-1955), Rudolph Bultmann (1884-   ), Karl Barth (1886-1968), Paul Tillich (1886-1965), and Reinhold Niebuhr (1892-1971). Though few of these figures, or the others, have had much to say of education, physical education and sport, the modern humanization of these phenomena owes much to the general influence of the movement they represent. Two pieces in particular have instructively examined the implications of Buber's and Ortega's thought for sport, however. R. Scott Kretchmar's "Meeting the Opposition: Buber's 'Will' and 'Grace' in Sport" argues that a viable test and a minimal second person's confrontation of that test designate the objective framework of sport. This insight fails, however, to touch on the qualitative aspects of sporting encounter, according to Kretchmar. For this, use is made of Buber's notions of "will" and "grace", as these notions operate in the context of personal (I-Thou, as distinct from I-It) relationships in sport. "Will" is understood as a psychological readiness to enter an I-Thou relation, and "grace" is construed as an inclination to meet one's "opponent" as a dynamic and unique subject, and so not as a mere object among other objects to be used in the gratification of one's own egoistic ends. For Kretchmar, the successful coming together of "will" and "grace" in sport promises human affirmation in it. And, in Nelson R. Orringer's "Sport and Festival: A Study of Ludic Theory in Ortega y Gasset", sport is unveiled as Ortega's central philosophic datum. By this interpretation, sport is that mood which positively describes authentic doing and living, and which negatively demonstrates the achievement of freedom from the responsibility of everyday experience. It is the mood of self-determination, self-renewal, spontaneity, and exuberance which delivers the activities of life, and life itself, to a blissful, an instrinsic satisfaction. Accordingly, existential fatality is translated into an active liberty, freedom, and joy. For Ortega, then, it is the spirit of sport which genuinely subordinates reason to the existential reality of the individual life.

Phenomenology: Brentano, Meinong, Husserl, Merleau-Ponty. The foundations of modern phenomenology are variously found in the realistic-tending aspects of Plato's metaphysics and epistemology, in Descartes' subjectivistic analysis of self, in Kant's view of the phenomenal world, and in the medieval discussions about universals. The movement has typically embraced the realistic notion that objects of knowledge persist independently of the knowing mind. Franz Brentano (1838-1917) established a true empirical psychology which examines the nature of mental acts by which the mind apprehends objects. By his view, such a psychology is founded on the only basis which will support a science of the mind. Brentano distinguishes this sort of reflection from the psychologism of ninettenth century British empiricism which focuses on the unknowable, psychological genesis of thought. His analysis concentrates on an examination of the mind's essential characteristic, of the characteristic which defines it, and of the products of this characteristic. For Brentano, this characteristic is the mind's referential capability, or its ability to refer to something beyond itself, to an intentional object. The form of this inquiry was carried further by Brentano's talented student, Alexius Meinong (1853-1921). Meinong constructs a theory of intentional objects as such from a conception of such objects as anything that can be thought or intended In his system, the various kinds of intentional objects, together with the characteristic properties of each, are distinguished. Principal among these kinds are particular (e.g., tables), ideal (e.g., numbers), and imaginative (e.g., golden mountains, square circles) objects.

This form of phenomenologic reflection reaches its highest development in the thought of the German philosopher, Edmund Husserl (1859-1938). Husserl concerns himself with both the method and the content of phenomenologic anslysis. For him, pure phenomenology is the description of subjective processes, or phenomena--the description of what is found in, or presented to experience. Phenomenology thereby differs from psychology in virtue of its limiting itself to describing what is displayed in experience, as distinct from giving an explanation of such displays in causal or genetic terms. Phenomenology takes no more, and pressuposes no more than what it finds in experience, according to Husserl--psychological inquiries that pretend to do more than this fall over into an excessive speculation. The objects of phenomenologic reflection are consequently intentional objects, and Husserl's interest in them is in their pure, or ideal essences-- in what they are when the particular facts encumbering them are eliminated, or bracketed away. For Husserl, only a knowledge of such essences qualifies as genuine knowledge. The phenomenology of the brilliant French philosopher, Maurice Merleau-Ponty (1908-1961), takes a different turn than in the German thinkers, Brentano,

Meinong, and Husserl. Merleau-Ponty's system is more so a synthesis of existential and phenomenologic themes, as distinct from a pure phenomenology as such. In his celebrated reflections on perception, Merleau-Ponty emphasizes the active and free nature of distinctly human experience, and sharply opposes objective, scientific, and mechanistic characterizations of it. He holds that such objective, causal characterizations cannot explain bodily experience. This experience cannot be explained by a view of the body as a participant in the causal order, as an object among other objects. It must be explained instead as the embodiment of mind or consciousness, as a subject actively and meaningfully existing in the world, as a lived experience. His phenomenologic-tending discussions are devoted to recognizing and demonstrating the terms of this experience.

Philosophical anthropology: Scheler. Principally from Marx, Nietzsche, and Bergson comes the twentieth century movement of philosophical anthropology. This movement takes the species man, the personal, social and cultural character of man, as its starting point and its formal end. The most notable twentieth century advocate of the position is Max Scheler (1874-1928), whose ethico-religious interpretation of Husserl's phenomenology led him to a view of man as a concrete unity of acts. For Scheler, this unity, as man's being, is disclosed to him by love. William J. Morgan makes particular use of this notion in his "A Philosophic Analysis of the Audience-Athlete Relationship Utilizing Scheler's Phenomenological Paradigm of Sympathy and Love". The intent of this essay is to establish the ontological basis, limits, and possibilities of the audience-athlete relationship. Through Scheler's paradigm of sympathy and love, Morgan defines the nature and function of the audience as it relates directly to, and has significance for the athletic realm of Being. The analysis distinguishes authentic from inauthentic audience-athlete relationships, and concludes that the fundamental basis of the audience-athlete relationship is constituted in sympathetic response, on a rudimentary level, and is ultimately founded in loving response. Other major contributors to the program of philosophical anthropology include Ernst Cassirer (1874-1945), Helmut Plessner (1892-   ), and Susanne K. Langer (1895-   ).

English and American realism: G. E. Moore, Russell, Alexander, Whitehead, Santayana. Among the most significant developments of the twentieth century has been the resurgence of a mature form of realism, most notably in English and American thought. This movement was not so much an independent triumph as a virogous response to what it considered the excesses of earlier forms of idealism. It has been most heavily influenced by these excesses (in negative ways), and by Hume's epistemology and twentieth century advances in logic and mathematics (in positive ways).

The earliest and among the most profound thinkers of this persuasion was George Edward Moore (1873-1958). Acting out of a notion best developed by Meinong, and opposing Berkeley in particular, Moore expanded the distinction between the act of knowing and that, object, which is known. According to this early view of Moore's, the object of knowledge exists independently from any act of consciousness by which it is known--it exists irrespective of its perception. In his later philosophy, Moore modifies the severity of independence objects enjoy in relation to sense perceptions of them. This is done in order to show that there is a relationship of any sort between man's impressions of physical objects, or sense data, and physical objects themselves. He comes in the end to adopt the view that while sense data may persist unsensed, physical objects do so in only a naive and hypothetical fashion. That is, in order to explain man's knowledge of physical objects, such objects must be construed as permanent possibilities of perception--a significant recantation on his earlier views of strict realist tendency.

Much influenced by Meinong and Moore in particular, Bertrand Russell (1872-1970) held to the strict realistic position that physical objects persist in-themselves irrespective of any perception or awareness of them. Though he conceived of these objects in various ways in different periods of his thought, and though aware that the independent existence of such objects cannot be proved, Russell nonetheless clung throughout to the strict realistic view as the simplest and most tenable explanation for sense perception. With Moore, Russell argues that sense data are distinct from man's conscious sensation, but, against Moore, that they do not exist unsensed, and that they are private, or immediately known only by individual subjects. Man's a priori knowledge is explained by the independent existence--that is, the extramental and extraphysical existence--of qualitative and relational universals, which enjoy a direct relation with mind, but are nonetheless distinct from mind. The precise relations among these universals, sense data, objects, and minds is not made altogether clear, however.

Likely the most systematic thinkers of this persuasion were Samuel Alexander (1859-1938) and Alfred North Whitehead (1861-1947). Both developed what could fairly be called a realistic epistemology within a naturalistic metaphysics. For Alexander, the fundamental interpretive principle of reality is Space-Time, which he conceives as a natural, infinite, continuous, and irreducible union of space and time. The primordial properties of this union are identity, diversity, existence, relation, substance, causality, quantity, intensity, and motion. But for Alexander, these are not contributions of the mind to experience, as Kant had taught; they are instead empirically obtainable understandings. They do not prescribe laws to nature, but are themselves features of nature. In fact, mind is itself construed as a naturally evolved event. By these basically naturalistic tendencies and his doctrine of emergent evolution, Alexander argues that the universal space-time matrix is the fundamental medium within which all qualitative levels of reality emerge or develop--most notably, the highest of such levels, life, mind, value, and Deity. It is within this metaphysical framework that Alexander develops his realistic epistemology. In this latter, two forms of knowledge, both provoked by sense perception, are distinguished: enjoyment, as the mind's direct awareness of itself, and contemplation, as the mind's awareness of objects other than itself.

The process philosophy of Whitehead takes on much of the naturalistic tendency of Alexander's thought. According to this view, nature, as the whole of things, is conceived as an organism, or organic system of spatio-temporal events, occasions, actual entities or particular objects, and eternal objects or universals which appear in particular objects. Whitehead construes God as the ground of reason, or the principle which selects eternal objects for appearance in actual entities. Thus, experience flows from objectivity to subjectivity, and not, as for Kant, from subjectivity to objectivity. Like Alexander, then, Whitehead thinks himself to have inverted Kant's second Copernican revolution. Moreover, his realistic and empirical epistemology considers prehension the fundamental form of knowledge, or the characteristic pattern of knowledge recurring at all levels of abstraction. Prehension is conceived as unconscious, pre-cognitive perception, or as the rudiments of taking account of the essential character of particular events, occasions, and objects. Perception is then viewed as a cognition of prehension, an attending to the terms of prehensive experience; and cognition is regarded as that which relates perceptual events to one another and thereby unifies them. Whitehead rejects the sense datum theories of perception and knowledge, most prominently advocated by Moore and Russell, as excessively abstract; that is, as being guilty of treating abstractions of concrete experience as though they were themselves concrete. This is Whitehead's celebrated fallacy of misplaced concreteness. For Whitehead, the theory of prehensions avoids such an error by bringing the fundamental origin and nature of knowledge into present experience. His philosophy of education flows easily and consistently out of these more general views, and is considered among the landmarks of progressivistic thought in modern education. It is effectively a protest against dead, inert, useless, or insignificant ideas and knowledge. Whitehead conceives of education as the use of knowledge; that is, as the concrete, intelligent doing which defines self-development. The process of actively doing is more so emphasized than the product of such doing, and the relations of ideas are stressed more fully than their isolation.

While the thought of the English philosophers, Moore, Russell, Alexander, and Whitehead, forms the center of twentieth century realism, a new American form of realist sentiment also works its way into a prominent place in twentieth century philosophy. This movement

was most devoted to giving a sharp analysis of the origin and nature of
human knowledge, and, as such, it cultivated a close association with
the revolutions in twentieth century science. It first took the form of
an epistemological monism, according to which objects of knowledge
are directly apprehended by conscious agents, but developed later
along more critical lines which held to a form of epistemological dualism, in which material objects are thought to exist independently both
of mind and of the sense data by which they are known. The foremost
exponent of critical realism in American philosophy was George
Santayana (1863-1952). Like both Alexander and Whitehead,
Santayana's thought is variously naturalistic and realistic. By his
view, all things have their source in the mechanism of nature, even
rational interpretations of man's scientific, social, religious, artistic,
and philosophic activities. Science, society, religion, art, and philosophy are, therefore, seen as expressions of nature, and it is man's
creative engagement in such activities which serves to distinguish and
dignify him. In his epistemology, Santayana takes as self-evident the
independent existence of physical objects and consciousness. Knowledge is explained as a system of universals, or essences, which persist independently of physical objects (but are nonetheless representations of these objects) and which are themselves known indubitably by
direct apprehension. Santayana, therefore, argues that matter is the
primary of the three principal realms of being (matter, essence, and
spirit), that the three realms exist independently of one another, and
that the three are nevertheless complementary. Santayana's aesthetics ranks among the best American discussions on the subject of
beauty. For Santayana, the sense of beauty is the highest human capacity, for it is capable of evoking greatest pleasures. According to
this view, beauty is not a quality of objects, nor an intellectual, moral,
or practical matter, but a function of one's unmediated, emotional response to things—it is a function of vital, free, spontaneous, and intrinsically valued response. Although referring only to an ephemeral
moment, and pertaining only to conditions peculiar to that moment,
aesthetic judgments establish an absolute ideal. That is to say, though
everyone responds in his own way, though everyone thereby establishes
his own aesthetic standard, and though there cannot, therefore, be a
common standard of taste with respect to aesthetic content for all persons; the form of aesthetic response is the same for all persons, and
all persons make such responses as though judging for all persons.
The common form of such response, according to Santayana, and so
the form which makes the response aesthetic, is constituted by a
unique sort of subjective pleasure. The objective features of an art
product may arouse such pleasure, but they do not constitute this pleasure, for these features do not raise peculiarly aesthetic responses in
all persons. The differentia of aesthetic pleasure, for Santayana, is
the illusion of objectifying pleasure. Though its disinterestedness and
universality are prominent among its features, it is this illusion which
makes it what it is. By this view, then, beauty is disinterested, universal pleasure which is thought to be inherent in the qualities of

objective things, but which is, in fact, a subjective response that we make to such qualities. Among those activities Santayana numbers as particularly capable of a great aesthetic development is sport. He considers sport, together with such as science, religion, and art, as an end-in-and-for-itself, as a basic form of human expression, as a vital feature of a liberal education, and as a conspicuous opponent of instrumentalism. Other noteworthy contributions to the general development of twentieth century realism include the neo-Thomist theology of Jacques Maritain (1882-1972) and the panentheistic theology of Charles Hartshorne (1897-   ).

<u>Pragmatism: Peirce, James, Dewey</u>. Pragmatism fashions one of most pervasive influences on twentieth century philosophy. This movement is perhaps the most important contribution of American philosphy to the history of philosophy in general. Though its major figures are American, however, it has some of its most basic roots deep in ancient, modern, and nineteenth century philosophy. It owes particularly much to nineteenth and twentieth century advances in the empirical sciences and in analytic and positivistic philosophy. Its founder and one of its most profound interpreters was the brilliant American philosopher, Charles Sanders Peirce (1839-1914). Peirce emphasized the analytic function of philosophy in clarifying the meaning of concepts and propositions; and he developed the notion that such meaning is obtained only from an analysis of the practical consequences of concepts and propositions. His metaphysics is phenomenologic-tending; it describes phenomenal experience as it is given immediately to consciousness. His epistemology inherits similar inclinations; it is principally taken up with a theory of signs, or <u>semiotic;</u> that is, a theory about that which refers to an object independent of itself. In this, Peirce defends a correspondence theory of truth according to which a concept or proposition, as a sign, is true in virtue of its corresponding to its referent object. The fairly high order of skepticism apparent in Peirce's thought shows through most graphically in his <u>doctrine of fallibilism</u>, which persuades that no synthetic proposition--no proposition about the so-termed world--can ever be verified absolutely, by correspondence or otherwise. Peirce ranks among those titans in the history of philosophy who have spawned intellectual revolutions, or at least put the mark of philosophy on such revolutions. He gave twentieth century pragmatism its germinal principles--principles which were later and more systematically and elaborately worked out by James and Dewey most importantly.

For William James (1842-1910), as for Peirce, philosophy is principally an analytic matter of clarifying ideas so that they are made useful in leading from parts of one's experience to other parts. The test of knowledge, by this view, is the expediency of its practical consequences in life, its problem-solving capacity. According to James, reality is best conceived as pure experience, as passionate, instinctive vision from which consciousness emerges. Consciousness merely explains such experience in a posterior fashion. This experience demonstrates the world as multiple, diverse, and comprised of novel and opposed events. James' system is, therefore, pluralistic-- a view which best explains the most important sorts of experience, practical moral and religious ones, according to James. Moreover, James' pluralism is theistic, for theism is the only conception of God which satisfies man's emotional disposition; and it is melioristic, for the world is inherently neither good nor evil, but inclined in the direction of its constituents actively striving either for its success or its failure. His epistemology, or rational psychology, is among the most notable of his contributions to philosophic thought. He construed the mind as the unity in, and of the stream of conscious process, and he employed the method of investigating conscious activity which turns the mind, and so consciousness itself, to an examination of such activity (the method of psychological introspection). James also developed a unique interpretation of the doctrine of free will which conceives of the will as the ability of the mind to focus on a freely chosen, single idea, exclusive of other ideas. For James, this focus itself entails action. The deeply psychological tone of James' thought also drew him to a trenchant examination of the educational process. Acting out of his characteristically progressivistic inclinations, James opposed what he took to be an exaggerated intellectualism in modern education. He advocated an experience-centered, and an individual-centered education in which learning occurs fundamentally through instinct, and in which the goods of society and individuals are mutually enhanced.

Much like James, John Dewey (1859-1952) too describes the world as constituted by change, indeterminacy, and evolution, as being a mosaic of particular, relative events unknowable in the absolute terms of "traditional philosophy". For Dewey, these events are, and are knowable only in virtue of their being consequential, or useful, in the consciously experienced lives of men. He thereby takes human experience as the starting point of his philosophy, and considers philosophy itself the basic method of analysis used to obtain a fundamental understanding of concrete experience. His pragmatic program may be described as instrumentalistic and experimentalistic. It is instrumentalistic owing to its perfervid concern for verifying useful, anticipated or hypothesized consequences of experience. It is experimentalistic in that it hopes to erect a theory of concepts or operations which can empirically determine future consequences. Dewey was convinced that this interpretation had achieved the reconciliation of rationalism and empiricism so daringly, but unsuccessfully undertaken by Kant in particular. Further to this point, experience is not alien to nature, but the means of discovering nature: it is the confrontation of the unified self--the knowing and willing moral, social, aesthetic, and religious self--with its environment. The culmination of human experience and happiness is found in an aesthetic refinement and intensification of ordinary experience, according to Dewey. Such a refinement and intensification entail a bringing order and harmony to disordered experience--the aesthetic resolves the disparate aspects of experience and thereby enhances the general experience of living.

Dewey's influence on contemporary thought has been enormous. This influence has been nowhere more widespread than in the philosophy of education. Dewey's meliorism, like James', holds that only by active social and educational involvement can the ideal of man as living in harmonious community with others be realized. Also like James' educational philosophy, Dewey's is progressivistic, and it is experience-centered and individual-centered. It advocates the development of an integrated personality--a unified moral, social, aesthetic, and religious individual--through a psychologically ordered curriculum and a natural method of inquiry. By Dewey's view, education is the experimental study of man and his world. Education must, therefore, not only be brought into contact with everyday learning situations, it must be itself an experience in democratic living. It must itself acculturate by giving instruction in the skills and knowledges of intelligent doing and effective social living. Dewey consequently reserved a high place in the curriculum for physical education and sport, considering them an excellent medium for learning such skills and knowledges, as well as themselves a possible source of aesthetic experience. The major studies dealing with the implications of Deweyan thought for physical education and sport are Carolyn Ann Cramer's "John Dewey's Views of Experience: Implications for Physical Education," Francis W. Keenan's "A Delineation of Deweyan Progressivism for Physical Education," and Richard A. Larkin's "The Influence of John Dewey on Physical Education." Cramer's work emphasizes Dewey's theory of experience and its meaning for education in general, and physical education in particular. The notion of experience talked about construes it as a process of doing, reflecting, and undergoing the consequences of an event. In its educational aspect, it, therefore, entails a continuity and interaction between the learner and that which is learned. Education revitalizes and humanizes the learner by progressively reconstructing or reorganizing experience in order to make subsequent events more purposeful and meaningful. The principal contribution of physical education to this process has to do with its unique way of integrating the mental, physical, social, and emotional aspects of one's life, and the acting, thinking, and feeling operations by which these aspects function. Keenan's study reveals the implications of Dewey's views on knowledge, value, mind, and education for physical education. Most prominently considered are: the educational process, as an intelligent reorganization of movement knowledge in reference to the self and the world; learning, as a going beyond one's utterly private sense of physical activity to a higher awareness of such activity in relation to oneself, the world, and the social order; interest and effort, as the inherent appeal of physical activity to the learner's intelligence; curriculum, as the intimacy of theory and practice in physical education; the teacher, as the expert of, and model for physical movement phenomena; the individual, as a unified being in physical education; and the intimate relationship of school and society. Keenan concludes that physical education can contribute much to the basic aim of education, to fashion intelligent and democratic individual and social growth through experience, by making provision for understanding and appreciating human movement phenomena. And Larkin's commentary emphasizes the implications of Dewey's philosophy of education for physical education. It concludes that the Deweyan notions of man as an organic unity and as the primary agent of experience, are well served, or cultivated, by physical education; and that, physical education thereby contributes significantly to the good life.

Perhaps the most notable of Dewey's many followers in the philosophy of education was William Heard Kilpatrick (1871-1965). And his most prominent disciple in a general philosophic sense was Clarence Irving Lewis (1883-1964), who is best remembered for his conceptual pragmatism. According to this view, experience is best explained as human needs embodied in a priori conceptual categories.

Analytic philosophy: Wittgenstein. Like the other prominent forms of twentieth century philosophy, analytic philosophy too has been greatly influenced by the genius of contemporary science. Somewhat surprisingly, however, this movement has tended toward anti-realistic inclinations. It has held that, while scientific concepts and theories are indispensably useful conventions which allow man to understand his practical life and to live out its terms, there is no sufficiently good reason to suppose these concepts and theories literally accurate representations of the objective world. The fullness of this skepticism leads the analysis to reject "traditional metaphysics" as unduly speculative and meaningless. The earliest developments in this movement are the conventionalist doctrines of Ernst Mach (1838-1916), Richard Avenarius (1843-1896), and Henri Poincare (1854-1912). This conventionalism holds that the knowable world consists solely in pure experiences, sensations, or perceptions, and that our knowledge is, therefore, nothing other than a description of such experiences. Scientific concepts and theories are consequently regarded as convenient definitions, or conventions, which are apparently consistent with the unknowable facts, but which cannot, of course, be verified by such facts. Also noteworthy, in the early development of contemporary analytic philosophy, is the fictionalism of Hans Vaihinger (1852-1933). According to this somewhat extreme position, scientific concepts and theories are considered useful practical insights, but they are thought contradictory of reality. For Vaihinger, they are useful fictions--the doctrine of the 'as if'.

The later analysts emphasized discussions about the criteria of verifying knowledge, and owed particularly much to Hume and the earlier conventionalist thinkers. This logical positivism has been most widely devoted to an examination of the direct, or in practice, as

- 186 -

well as the indirect, or in principle, verifiability of experiential knowledge. It attempts a clarification of the meaning of all cognitively significant statements, and in this is principally concerned with investigating the structure and function of language. Moritz Schlick (1882-1936) and his Vienna Circle were the first such thinkers. The movement was introduced to American philosophy by Rudolf Carnap (1891-1970), and to English philosophy by its most notable exponent, Ludwig Wittgenstein (1889-1951). Wittgenstein was convinced that most philosophical statements, most particularly those of a "traditional" metaphysical sort, are not so much false as nonsensical, meaningless, and so unanswerable. In his early analysis of a logically structured language and his later treatment of ordinary language, Wittgenstein outlines the proper function of philosophy as simply making our propositions clear. Other noteworthy contributions to this movement include the rigorous mathematical logic of Gottlob Frege (1848-1925), the philosophy of mind of Gilbert Ryle (1900-   ), the aesthetics of Nelson Goodman (1906-   ), and the ethics of Alfred Jules Ayer (1910-   ).

Our treatment of twentieth century philosophy, together with our general discussions of the major philosophic periods and figures and their implications for physical education and sport, ends here. What has been demonstrated is the ebb and flow of philosophic discourse as it has been carried on by its most accomplished proponents, its progressive development and refinement through its major periods and the genius of its greatest figures, the terms in which philosophic thought concerning physical education and sport is necessarily instructed by the broad dimensions of philosophy in general, and the terms in which physical education and sport themselves cannot be understood and appreciated in a fully adequate way apart from the larger context of human knowledge and experience of which philosophy is the formal end.

CHAPTER VI

SOME REFLECTIONS ON CONSENSUS

The great emphasis that has been put here on differences among various disciplines, concepts, issues, systems, periods, and figures could easily obscure the genuine agreements which also prevail among them. Some profit may come from now accentuating the terms of these agreements, and calling more explicit attention to them. What sparks this discussion is a concern for the individual and cultural affairs which are in significant measure governed by such disciplines, concepts, etc. That is to say, if the notion, that philosophic insights provide a major guide to our individual and cultural actions (in general terms, as well as in terms particular to physical education and sport), can be taken seriously, and if little other than distinctions, however important in themselves, can be found in these insights; then one may have occasion to inquire, how a sufficient consensus among, and continuity of individual and cultural actions can occur in order to secure palatable and constructive forms of individual and cultural existence. Insofar as ourselves, our culture, education, physical education and sport, are reflectively guided, they can neither escape the capstone influence of philosophy, nor can they be independent of a concern for consensus as a determinant of the quality of institutional life. This is not to adopt the view that absolute agreement on all matters is either necessary, desirable, or even possible. For it is quite the case, it seems, that the vitality of our personal and institutional lives depends as heavily on some measure of disagreement, as it does on some measure of agreement. To expect full consensus on such inherently intricate and individual humanistic concerns is simply not to understand very well the character of such concerns in any case. Owing to all of this, and since the disagreements have already received sufficient attention, the task here will be to show the terms in which consensus is proper, desirable, and necessary. It is not to spuriously make diverse views agree where they do not, but to recognize an order of consensus which is required as a genuine ground for cultural unity, while nonetheless making provision for the integrity of divergent, individual views. This is effectively to rise above divisions that are not sufficiently substantial and decisive to the integrity of individuals and cultures to set them apart utterly. Neither is this an entreaty to eclecticism; it is instead a demonstration of the provisions that must be made in order both to preserve the integrity of all individual participants in a necessarily institutional process, and to preserve as well the institutions themselves.

Among the various philosophic views are found great differences at the level of fundamental allegiance. These differences in some significant measure arise from the differences in skeptical inclination apparent in such views. Some philosophic programs may, therefore, be fulfilled within the context of other, less widely skeptical programs. Such programs, then, are compatible with these more widely visionary perspectives, but limit their inquiry so as to exclude the wider vision. There are also views which disagree in fundamental commitment, but which are nevertheless mutually instructive with respect to their treatments of various "non-fundamental" issues, and may even be mutually helpful in providing greater insight into the character of their respective primacies. Observations such as these may furnish at least a partial basis for conciliation among philosophic views-- views which typically emphasize their dissimilarities. Moreover, the enriched understanding of the world which a serious study of philosophy promotes, and the tolerance for views other than our own, as well as the humility with respect to our own views, which grow out of this understanding, further inspires the notion that a variety of philosophic visions may make compatible contributions to our understanding of, and appreciation for reality generally, physical education and sport more particularly. This all too frequently unrecognized or underestimated possibility allows for the view that all responsible and rigorously argued positions, however disparate, have a rightful place in the pantheon of philosophic discourse, and that all such positions contribute in some measure to the enrichment of our thought and life. Under the actualized terms of this possibility, the mutual intolerance and antipathy so common among philosophers, not to mention persons generally, give way to a view of philosophers and persons as sympathetically united in a common search for truth. By this notion, philosophic truths are not mutually destructive, not in their most significant dimensions at any rate, but are accumulated and integrated-- they contribute to the cohesive sense of community necessary to serious thinkers, and to serious persons of every stripe.

None of this is to veil the lingering recognition that wide differences, even utterly unreconcilable ones, among many philosophic views nonetheless remain. Most notable of these is the fundamental order of cleavage apparent between views of progressivistic-relativistic emphasis and those of essentialistic-absolutistic tendency. The differences between views of these two general forms are severe, and usually make even utterly practical expressions of them incompatible. These forms together, however, contain all particular order of view, and the views contained in each do allow for a certain order of practical agreement and tolerance. Each holds within it views of the same general form expressed in different ways. That is to say, while the modes of practical action typically suggested by positions of a progressivistic-relativistic tendency are characteristically different than those typically proposed by notions of an essentialistic-absolutistic inclination, the modes of practical action fashioned within each of these tendencies are sufficiently alike to make them at least mutually tolerable. While institutions (or forms of cultural life) built on the principles of one tendency cannot, therefore, long tolerate institutions built on the principles of the other, institutions which share at least the basic principles of one of these tendencies can find themselves participants in a single vision--a vision which at least, manages to avoid falling into self-contradiction, and so self-alienation and self-destruction. These, then, are the terms in which consensus is proper, desirable, and necessary. These are the recognitions which both allow for the necessary integrity of differing individual views, and secure as well the necessary integrity of institutional forms. The welfare of individual and cultural life depends heavily on both kinds of integrity, and so on such a consensus.

APPENDIX A

SOME THOUGHTS ON A PROPER NAME

At bottom, the subject of this text is sport. Few expressions raise such a sense of ambiguity as this one, however. It is fashionably conceived either as in some sense exlcuding, in some sense including, or in some sense serving as the basis for distinguishing such as dance, exercise, movement, physical education, play, and recreation. But it is not very much clear as to in precisely what sense this is so in any of these cases. This essay will attempt to lay away some of this ambiguity by concisely saying what sport is. First, it will be necessary to give an account of what is expected of terms, or linguistic expressions in general. Then it will be possible to demonstrate in what the term 'sport' consists, and in this to show as well the basic nature of dance, exercise, movement, physical education, play, and recreation. The distinctions between sport and these others, and in significant measure the basic character of sport itself will thereby be made explicit.

A term, or linguistic expression which names a spatio-temporal particular (a person, place, or thing) signifies that particular. That is to say, it utters a conventionally (or esoterically) accepted phrase which represents that particular. Such expressions thereby symbolize a mutually and continuously held, as well as an informed understanding with respect to the particulars to which they refer. In this way, these expressions fulfill their general communicative function, and recognize as well their aesthetic obligations. The search here is for a linguistic expression which adequately signifies the phenomena fashionably known as physical education and sport. This expression must be sufficiently general to refer to all of the sorts of activity properly included by these terms, yet sufficiently specific so as to avoid mention of all of the sorts of activity properly excluded by them. It must include explicit or tacit mention--it must recognize--all of the major forms of activity designated by the term(s) 'physical education and sport', and only these forms. The attempt here is to determine the expression(s) which is most aptly descriptive/prescriptive of these phenomena; not for the purpose of arbitrarily reforming or revising them, but for the purpose of promoting a more fully and carefully developed understanding of, and appreciation for them as such. Moreover, this discussion will confine itself to talk about the logico-linguistic bases of these determinations; thereby avoiding comment on the status of even prominent historical traditions, and the socio-politico-economic exigency, or administrative implication of such determinations.

The difficulty in successfully completing such a treatment is substantial. The precise meaning of the phenomena and terms considered is elusive. For the stipulations which distinguish each of these, themselves wait significantly on yet more basic presuppositions about reality in general—elaborate presuppositions which it is neither the purpose nor the capability of this essay to uncover, and presuppositions to which not even every rational, informed, and insightful person will agree. The "provocations" which follow thereby represent what, within the limits of a few pages and moments, can be plausibly said about the most preferred alternatives from among all of the many others.

Perhaps the most basic phenomenon prominently talked about in discussions concerning the basic character of sport is movement. The notion of movement implies a sense of mobility, as distinct from a sense of immobility; a sense of the dynamic, as distinct from the static; a sense of activity, as distinct from inactivity. Further implied by this is the view that movement entails an interpenetration or interaction, whereby "something" comes to displace or succeed "something else". In spatial terms, then, movement is tantamount to displacement; in temporal ones, it is equivalent to succession. The yet more basic presupposition of these notions is <u>change</u> itself. All of this comes to saying that, spatially, change, as the ground of movement, expresses itself as a "something" coming-to-occupy-the-place-of a "something else"; temporally, it takes the form of a "something" preceeding or following a "something else".[1] Apparently, the spatial characterization is closely related to the temporal in that displacement and succession entail one another. That is to say, displacement carries with it the notion of preceeding or following, and succession carries with it the idea of coming-to-occupy-the-place-of. Since "everything" is in this sense changing,[2,3,4] movement needs to be considered the universal principle of change, or history—as the motive force inherent in the entire fabric of things. According to this account, then, the notions of displacement and succession together make up change, and change, in turn, reveals itself as the constitutive basis of movement.

When prominently expressed in the form of "bodily" displacement-succession of a particular objective and intentional sort, movement evidently provides such as dance, exercise, physical education, and sport with a primary medium. But movement, as the general principle of change in the world, refers in some sense to all phenomena, and not merely or distinctively to an animating presence in dance, exericse, physical education, and sport. Movement as such, therefore, excludes little and is, consequently, insufficiently discriminating to conclusively secure the sorts of distinctions here sought.

Among the other basic phenomena considered in discussions of this type, play is perhaps the most prominent. Play is not itself a concrete activity in the sense in which such as baseball, boxing, and gymnastics are concrete activities, for play does variously "attach" itself[5] to these and other activities, and provides these activities with an axiologic, or value guide. Play, then, is of a different order than concrete activities as such. It is of a more general order than these activities. It is a quality of concrete activity by which the activity(ies) to which it is "attached" (or in which it inheres) is intrinsically valued, or valued in-and-for-itself, and so voluntarily engaged, of an extraordinary or supra-mundane and disinterested character, and aesthetically ordered. Play is, therefore, a function of our regard for activities, as distinct from a function of the objective mosaic of characteristic which distinguishes activities themselves. And its conceptual opposite, work, or the instrumental mode of valuing, is the result of saying what not-play is, and is as such secondary to play. The notion of intrinsicality is needed prior to, and as a basis for the notion of instrumentality; for the latter is effectively a flying away from the former. Play is positive, independent, and primary; work is negative, dependent, and derivative.

Insofar, then, as dance, physical education, and sport assume a genuinely human posture, they are primarily played. But this is what can and must be said of all types of human activity authentically disposed; that is, disposed to a fulfillment of human beings, as distinguished from being disposed to an instrumental regard for, and use of them. The notion of play, like that of movement, is nonetheless helpful here in its carrying out some fundamental distinctions; but it is not decisive in the end of this carrying out, because it as such fails to discriminate between the phenomena that it is our charge to discriminate between, and that it is in the character of our experience to distinguish.

The notion of recreation is closely associated with the notion of play. It is commonly conceived as that collection of activities, voluntarily undertaken in the time unobligated to work--in leisure time-- and primarily for the "enjoyment" it evokes. This is tantamount to characterizing recreation as the category of concrete activities conducted at play, or intrinsically valued. Though this characterization implies an inversion of the play-work relation earlier discussed, it does not, on further inspection, actually carry out such an inversion. The negative reference to recreation as occurring in the time unobligated to work simply reinforces the previously adduced insight that play and work are mutually exclusive. This reference does not, therefore, penetrate to the basic constitutions of play and work themselves except to observe that the two are qualitatively distinct. This needs to be so because the contrary results in a confusion (in the form of an inversion) with respect to what is meant by positivity and negativity. In any case, recreation conceived in this way is virtually as inconclusive in making the distinctions tacit in our experience which it is the objective of this essay to make evident, as play itself. For it is nothing other than the concrete substance in which the play spirit resides. And insofar as recreation is thought a category of concrete activities which is not distinguished by the terms of its concretion, but by a mode of valuing this concretion, recreation may be understood as including any sort of particular concrete activity--dance, physical education, and sport being perhaps among the more prominent of these --which has the intrinsic mode of valuing at its axiologic center. And this is in prospect the case for any and all concrete activities.

Unlike recreation, exercise is by its nature instrumental; referring to the category of concrete activities conducted at work, or extrinsically valued. Insofar as it has to do with physical education and sport, it entails an organization of "bodily" movements preformed primarily for the purpose of enhancing the structuro-functional disposition of the self. As such, the principle interest in these movements is in their external effects, as distinct from in the movements themselves and their possibilities for human fulfillment. Though it is of concern to such as dance, physical education, and sport, then, in the form of its producing effects which are useful in these, it is of such concern largely as a preliminary or preparatory tool, and not as a part, let alone the whole of these as such.

With the lot of prior discussion now in hand, adequate foundation has been laid for a productive conversation about sport itself. All sporting activity is governed by an elaborate mosaic of rules which stipulate the material goals aimed at, and the means permitted in attempting to achieve these goals. These rules individually define particular sporting activities, and collectively contribute much to saying what sport in general is. For one, the goals they posit serve no utilitarian purpose. These goals, and the means to them, merely make possible an experience of a certain, compelling sort; namely, an experience of standing in viable relation to the performance of another (or others), and/or a stipulated standard of performance. As such, they are accepted merely because they make this experience possible, and in this they serve the spirit of play. And for another, these rules embody an emphasis on the "physical" which makes the way in which movements are made highly significant. The final outcome of these movements does not exhaust their significance, as is so in the movement of chess pieces and in other board and card games as well, in which the terms of movement themselves are incidental, in any interesting sense, to the position (or state) moved from and to. In sport, the movements themselves are idealized and become an engaging part of the activity. This is so on two principal counts. Firstly, these movements require great skill to perform well--one's success in sport thereby depends primarily on the skillful execution of these movements, as distinct from any chance occurrence of them (which counts most in such as dice). And secondly, these movements (together with their connections to final outcomes) constitute the concrete substance of sport's aesthetic appeal.

Even at this, however, we come upon activities which apparently satisfy these conditions, but which it is nonetheless our inclination to exclude from any strict and full notion of sport. Such activities as horseshoes, hurling, orienteering, and hula hooping, among similar others, have an insufficiently wide basis in our historico-cultural experience to be included. They have not affected the human circumstance in sufficient measure to have gained anything more than a geographically or historically isolated practice. And activities involving self-propelled mechanical contrivances (e.g., automobile and hydroplane racing) and animate non-humans (e.g., bull fighting, rodeo, horse racing, hunting, and fishing) do not meet the voluntary and self-conscious requirements of playful and peculiarly human endeavor. So-termed "conquest" or "nature" sports (e.g., mountain climbing, sky diving, and surfing) apparently persist on the edge of these distinctions and must be considered sport insofar as they obtain sufficient historico-cultural, or institutional grounding.

The activities which most unequivocally satisfy these conditions are the individual, dual, and team sports[6] which follow:

-individual sports:

-classical forms of individual sport:

-gymnastics: classical forms of aerial movement.
-swimming and diving: classical forms of aquatic movement.
-track and field athletics: classical forms of grounded movement.

-individual winter sports: alpine skiing, biathlon, bobsledding, cross country skiing, figure skating, luge, ski jumping, and speed skating.
-other individual sports: archery, billiards, bowlling, canoeing, croquet, curling, cycling, golf, modern pentathlon,[7] rowing, shooting, weightlifting, and yachting.

-dual sports:

-dual combative sports: boxing, fencing, and wrestling.
-dual court sports: badminton, court tennis, handball, squash, and table tennis.

-team sports: baseball, basketball, cricket, field hockey, football, ice hockey, lacrosse, rugby, soccer, volleyball, and water polo.

The problems with this conception are not yet at an end, however. For dance, too, apparently meets all of the conditions here laid out for sport, and yet it is not consonant with our experience of either sport or dance to consider dance a sport.[8] The two grounds on which dance and sport are most commonly distinguished have to do with the alleged competitive emphases of sport (and the absence of such emphases in dance), and the typically more numerous, elaborate, and inflexible rules of sport (than those which "govern" dance). Insofar as sport has competition in the strict sense as a necessary characteristic, it must be considered qualitatively distinct from dance, which is strictly competitive in only an accidental way. What is usually made of this is that the intention of dance is basically expressive, and the intention of sport basically competitive. But this characteristic (the competitive characteristic) was reduced in our prior discussion of it to a being constrained by standards of variously expressed (by the performances of other participants, or by other "independently" stipulated standards of performance) excellence, and in this basic constraint dance shares, though perhaps in different degree than sport. This reduction is also and further supported by the earlier argued conclusion which has sport a peculiarly human undertaking—an undertaking which is by its nature basically expressive; that is, variously searching after and finding the human "in" it. The second basis on which sport and dance are thought fundamentally, or qualitatively different is similarly reduced to a difference in degree. It does quite seem to be the case that the rules of sport are typically more numerous, elaborate, and inflexible than those of dance. This latter observation has lead to the fashionable notion that dance is basically more creative than sport.[9] Even if this claim goes through, however, it yet fails to drive a qualitative wedge between sport and dance. The most that can, therefore, be made of the differences between sport and dance apparently has them distinct as to degree, but nonetheless of the same kind. As such, the two evidently constitute the movement arts, as being those art forms, and only those art forms,[10] which make movement (in the sense earlier ascribed to sport) their medium of expression.

This leaves physical education, which in modern history has undergone the transformation from physical training, in which it was thought an agent of bio-psychological health and fitness; to physical culture, in which it was conceived as an acculturative agent; to physical education itself. Through the former two elements, systems of calisthenic and gymnastic exercise, and the motif of exercise itself, were predominant. Physical education was on the way to becoming itself in these elements so to speak. With its development to physical education as such, these systems and the basic motif underlying them were left behind, and the possibilities of a genuinely playful treatment of sport and dance moved into the foreground as the dominant, even the constitutive element. Under the terms of this conception, physical education may be plausibly characterized as sport and dance in pedagogical garb, or sport and dance in the trappings of a formal development toward human fulfillment. This conception seems superior to the former two in virtue of its drawing the former two into a higher unity, and in virtue of its accounting for our highest experience of physical education in a way that the former two conceptions do not. This conception has not abandoned these other two, so much as included them as preliminary notions and showed the way to their distinctly human development. The former two notions are, therefore, simply too limited in themselves to satisfy the contemporary view of physical education as an expression of man's highest possibilities. If physical education can be plausibly considered a form of sport (and dance), then--i.e., its educational form--the term 'physical education and sport' is itself redundant, for it implies a more substantial difference between physical education and sport than can be delivered. Physical education is by this account included by the notion of sport (and dance), and so of a different, a less general order than sport (and dance).

In recent years, such terms as 'anthropokinetics' and 'kinesiology' have been advocated as more suitable to the phenomena taken up by physical education than the term 'physical education' itself. But these effectively refer to the study of man in movement, or to the study of a "moving" humanity, a reference previously dismissed as insufficiently discriminating. These terms do not distinguish endeavors such as sport and dance from others which employ movement only incidentally (e.g., music, drama), in a widely general fashion (e.g., human engineering), or in a mundane way (e.g., house painting, truck driving).

With this the circle comes closed, the basic character of sport, dance, exercise, movement, physical education, play, and recreation shown, and the key significance of sport demonstrated. Even at this, however, only tentative judgments, based significantly on unexamined foundations, have been obtained--embryonic provocations for another time.

Notes

1The "something else" here refers to "anything", however slightly different than the "something" it displaces or succeeds; even an "anything" which so closely resembles that "something" so as to be thought synonymous with it. The mere fact that "something" has passed through another moment-expanse is sufficient to call it "something else" in the sense here intended. For this "something else" now has "something" in its experience in a way in which "something" itself does not.

²This is so even of so-termed "absolute" conditions like temperature-less (absolute zero) and pressureless (absolute vacuum) environments, which are themselves swept up in a universe now widely thought to be moving (on balance, expanding) in "every" moment and through "every" expanse.

³The more primary status of movement, as over and against its conceptual opposite, statis, is further demonstrated by the terms in which statis requires movement as a prior notion. The concept of statis is no more than the result of a vain attempt to say what movement is not--it is the negative of movement. And as such, it depends on movement in a way in which movement does not depend on it.

⁴This is not, however, to claim that there is nothing but change as such, but that change in the form of displacement and succession is the state in which "everything" finds itself. The formal characteristics of this "everything" nonetheless endure as the substance in which change occurs. Otherwise there would be "nothing" undergoing change. Change itself thereby presupposes that "something" changes.

⁵This is not to say that play is, or can be experienced apart from its concrete "attachments", but that insofar as it is experienced, it is experienced as a way of regarding concrete activities, and not as a concrete activity itself. For if this latter were the case, we would not think and talk as we do about playing "things".

⁶The criterion which distinguishes these categories is the number of persons required to claim participation in an activity, and so the number on whom the responsibility for performance directly depends. In individual sports only one is required, in dual sports one giving "opposition" to another is required, and in team sports several giving "opposition" to several others is required. These distinctions are not as empty, inconsequential, and purely quantitative as first appears. For they establish the qualitative possibilities of personal and interpersonal reference in these activities, and they provide the most general, exhaustive, and conclusive means of distinguishing them. Neither are they altogether unproblematic, however. Such as doubles tennis and massed wrestling seem most troublesome. But here one has a massed circumstance which has been upbuilt in the image of, and remains a variation of the dual form of activity. The same form of argument apparently holds in classifying other-than-singles bobsledding, canoeing, figure skating, luge, and rowing as individual sports. In the case of relay events in what are otherwise unequivocally individual

- 198 -

sports, one has individual segments of performance which are simply put together. The form of action and interaction remains fundamentally individual.

[7]Modern pentathlon is a difficult case owing to its equestrian component. It is nonetheless included because its four other components are rather indisputably sporting in character.

[8]Nor is it consonant with our experience of either sport or dance to consider sport a dance, drawing attention to the converse possibility.

[9]But if this is so on the grounds here adduced, it is so out of a negative concept of creativity as being heightened by a lack of, or a decline in constraint. And while this is likely so in some, even important respects, such a concept has nonetheless to demonstrate its positive side, and to show as well the relation between its negative and positive sides.

[10]Only these highly complex forms of movement expression have interested us sufficiently throughout our historical development to have moved us to making widespread, formal, institutional provision for them. This is a fact which is not incidental to understanding both them and us.

APPENDIX B

CURRICULUM CONCERNING THE PHILOSOPHY
OF PHYSICAL EDUCATION AND SPORT

Though the merits of a formal study of the philosophy of physical education and sport have been demonstrated, curricular provision for such a study has not been discussed. Restitution for this omission is made here in the form of a brief advocation concerning the general character of undergraduate and graduate preparation in the discipline, as well as a presentation of course outlines devoted to the concrete execution of this preparation.

At the undergraduate level is found a course experience and opportunity for independent study in the philosophy of physical education and sport, as well as provision for the study of philosophy in general. At the graduate level are four course experiences and opportunity for independent study in the philosophy of physical education and sport, in addition to extensive provision for the study of philosophy in general. While the general philosophic electives for those emphasizing the philosophy of physical education and sport in their undergraduate and Master's studies can be freely selected in accord with students' interests, this selection ought to be moving in the direction of establishing the expert competency aimed at in Doctor's preparation. Such a competency entails a formal understanding of the major philosophic sub-disciplines ("logic", metaphysics, epistemology, ethics, aesthetics, politics, and the major departmental philosophies, religion, science, history, and education), the major historico-philosophic periods (ancient, medieval, modern, nineteenth century, and twentieth century), the major philosophic systems (those examined in Chapter IV), the major philosophic figures (those examined in Chapter V), as well as an expert competency in one or several such issues, periods, systems, or figures of particular interest to the candidate.

The three course outlines which follow signify an instructional progression from introductory, to advanced, to "terminal" levels of understanding and appreciation. The introductory course is conducted in a lecture-discussion fashion in order to assure the efficient and explicit presentation of the ideas which provide the basis for the more refined accounts of the advanced and "terminal" levels. The advanced course is done in a lecture-seminar context, and the "terminal" course in a purely seminar way, so as to encourage a progressively more relaxed exchange of ideas as the capacity for informed, philosophic discourse improves, and so as such an exchange becomes substantivally profitable. A pedagogically viable progression in the complexity of notion and argument considered is also apparent across the three levels. That is, each course provides a basis on which succeeding courses heavily depend. This line of progression virtually, but naturally breaks the literature into short essay contributions (taken up in the introductory course), the great books (which provide the content for the advanced course), and the extended essay and dissertation pieces (the subjects of the "terminal" course). There is, moreover, an attempt to consider all of the crucially important literature concerning the philosophy of physical education and sport in the collection of these courses. The course requirements reflect a similar concern for instructional progression. The introductory experience requires a "personal" expression of philosophic views concerning reality, knowledge, and value generally, as well as the nature and significance of physical education and sport. The advanced course requires a critical examination of major texts, and the "terminal" experience, a genuine research essay. This approach has the effect of first introducing to the rigors of philosophic reflection concerning physical education and sport, then gently informing with respect to the expectations of creative scholarship concerning such, and finally refining the skills requisite to such scholarship. This general scheme allows for a systematic and comprehensive examination of the philosophy of physical education and sport as well as the general philosophic insight which underlies and surrounds it.

Introduction to the Philosophy of Physical Education and Sport
(introductory undergraduate course, preferably offered in three, one hour sessions per week)

Course description:
    An introduction to the form and content of the philosophy of physical education and sport. Attention is given to general notions of reality, knowledge, and value as such notions inform with respect to physical education and sport.

Course objectives:
    1. To advance an introductory understanding of the fundamental nature, significance, and method of the philosophy of physical education and sport.
    2. To fashion an introductory appreciation for the contributions of philosophic reflection to physical education and sport.

Textbooks:
    1. Osterhoudt, Robert G. An Introduction to the Philosophy of Physical Education and Sport.
    2. Gerber, Ellen W. (ed.). Sport and the Body: A Philosophical Symposium.

<u>Course requirements</u>:
1. A mid-term examination consisting principally in essay forms of question; the results of which determine 30% of the final mark.
2. A philosophic essay or expression of one's "personal" views concerning the nature and significance of physical education and sport (as well as dance, exercise, movement, play, and recreation) as such views reside in the fuller perspective of explicitly stipulated metaphysical, epistemic, and axiologic allegiances. It ought to approximate 10-20 double-spaced typewritten pages in length, and demonstrate a growth through the course. The results determine 30% of the final mark.
3. An art project in the form of sculpture, painting, literature, poetry, drama, cinema, dance, or music expressing the essential character of physical education and sport. The results determine 5% of the final mark. Since there is no formal provision for acquiring a glimpse into the artistic dimension of physical education and sport, and since philosophy approaches this dimension more fully than other disciplines studied with respect to physical education and sport, this opportunity is included here.
4. A final examination consisting principally in essay forms of question; the results of which determine 35% of the final mark.
5. Lecture-discussion attendance-participation: An exhortation to attend and participate in lecture-discussion sessions.

<u>Course plan and reading assignments</u>:
I.   Introduction: the nature, significance, and method of philosophy generally, the philosophy of physical education and sport more particularly:
     A. The general character of philosophy: Osterhoudt, Chapters 1 and 2.
     B. The nature, attractions, and method of philosophic reflection concerning physical education and sport: Osterhoudt, Chapter 3 and Appendix C:
         1. Zeigler, "A True Professional Needs a Consistent Philosophy".
         2. Kleinman, "Toward a Non-Theory of Sport".
II. The metaphysical status of physical education and sport: Osterhoudt, Chapter 3 and Appendix A; recommended (as a prominent example of metaphysical inquiry in general): Mourant and Freund, Aristotle, Chapter 4:
     A. Metheny, "Only By Moving Their Bodies".
     B. Hyland, "Athletic Angst: Reflections on the Philosophical Relevance of Play".
     C. Kaelin, "Being in the Body".
     D. Suits, "The Elements of Sport".

E. Santayana, "Philosophy on the Bleachers".
F. Harper, "Man Alone".
G. Coutts, "Freedom in Sport".
III. The epistemic status of physical education and sport: Osterhoudt, Chapter 3; recommended: Mourant and Freund, Plato, Chapter 3:
    A. Brackenbury, "Physical Education, An Intellectual Emphasis ?"
    B. Keenan, "The Concept of Doing".
    C. Henry, "Physical Education: An Academic Discipline".
IV. The axiologic status of physical education and sport: Osterhoudt, Chapter 3; recommended: Mourant and Freund, Kant, Chapter 2, and Hume, Chapter 7:
    A. The ethical status of physical education and sport:
        1. Keating, "Sportsmanship as a Moral Category".
        2. Pearson, "Deception, Sportsmanship, and Ethics".
    B. The aesthetic status of physical education and sport:
        1. Maheu, "Sport and Culture".
        2. Reid, "Sport, the Aesthetic and Art".
        3. Kaelin, "The Well-Played Game: Notes Toward an Aesthetics of Sport".
V. The implications of major philosophic systems and the thought of major philosophic figures for physical education and sport: Osterhoudt, Chapters 4 and 5; recommended: Mourant and Freund, Lucretius and Berkeley, Chapter 4, Russell, Chapter 3, Peirce, Chapter 8, and Heidegger, Chapter 4:
    A. Zeigler, "The Implications of Experimentalism for Physical, Health and Recreation Education".
    B. Shvartz, "Nietzsche--Philosopher of Fitness".
VI. Summary and conclusions: Osterhoudt, Chapter 6.

Advanced Philosophy of Physical Education and Sport
(introductory graduate course, preferably offered in two, one and one-half hour sessions per week)

Course description:
An advanced examination of the metaphysical, epistemic, and axiologic status of physical education and sport. Effectively, a critical study of the most systematic and comprehensive contributions to the literature concerning the philosophy of physical education and sport.

Course objectives:
1. To provide an advanced insight into the fundamental nature, significance, and method of the philosophy of physical education and sport.
2. To fashion an advanced appreciation for the contributions of philosophic reflection to physical education and sport.

Textbooks:
1. Herrigel, Eugen. Zen in the Art of Archery.
2. Huizinga, Johan. Homo Ludens: A Study of the Play-Element in Culture.
3. Metheny, Eleanor. Movement and Meaning.
4. Slusher, Howard S. Man, Sport and Existence: A Critical Analysis.
5. Weiss, Paul. Sport: A Philosophic Inquiry.

Course requirements:
1. A philosophic essay critically examining the views of one or several of the authors studied. Although appropriate passages from the chosen work(s) ought to be cited, the essay is primarily an insightful examination of that work by the student himself, and should be considered a research paper in no other sense. It ought to approximate 15-25 double-spaced typewritten pages in length, and conform to standard format specifications. The results determine 40% of the final mark.
2. A final examination consisting in essay forms of question, from which a choice of some sort will be possible. The examinations are distributed several days before they must be written, and any manner of preparation is acceptable, but they must be written during a designated period and without the use of notes or any other form of external assistance. The results determine 60% of the final mark.
3. Lecture-seminar attendance-participation: an exhortation to attend and participate in lecture-seminar sessions.

Course plan and reading assignments:
I. Introduction: the nature, significance, and method of philosophy generally, the philosophy of physical education and sport more particularly: Osterhoudt, Chapters 1 and 2 and Appendix D.
II. Huizinga, Chapters 1, 2, 3, 11, and 12.
III. Metheny, Chapters 1 to 8.
IV. Herrigel, text.
V. Slusher, Chapter 1.
VI. Weiss, Chapters 1, 9, 12, and 15.
VII. Summary and conclusions.

Seminar: Philosophy of Physical Education and Sport
(advanced graduate course, may be thrice repeated, preferably
offered in two, one and one-half hour sessions per week)

Course description:
A "terminal" examination of the metaphysical, epistemic, and
axiologic status of physical education and sport. Effectively, a
critical and scholarly study of student selected issues with respect to the most sophisticated philosophic bases of thought concerning physical education and sport.

Course objectives:
1. To provide a "terminal" insight into the fundamental nature,
significance, and method of the philosophy of physical education and sport.
2. To erect a "terminal" appreciation for the contributions of
philosophic reflection to physical education and sport.

Textbooks:
1. Osterhoudt, Robert G. (ed.). The Philosophy of Sport: A
Collection of Original Essays.
2. Journal of the Philosophy of Sport, Vol. 1.
3. Journal of the Philosophy of Sport, Vol. 2.

Course requirements:
1. A philosophic discourse of research proportions concerning
a major concept or issue, figure, period, or system of
thought in the philosophy of physical education and sport as
supported by rigorous argument and reference to the general philosophic literature. It ought to approximate 20-30
double-spaced typewritten pages in length, and conform to
standard format specifications. The results determine 50%
of the final mark.
2. Evidence of insightful examination and discussion of matters
under scrutiny in seminar sessions. The results determine
50% of the final mark.

Course plan:
I. Introduction.
II. The major philosophic concepts and issues, systems,
periods, and figures and their meaning for physical educa-
tion and sport.
III. Independent reflection on the metaphysical, epistemic, and
axiologic status of physical education and sport.
IV. Presentation, defense, and critical review of student re-
search essays.
V. Summary and conclusions.

APPENDIX C

ABSTRACTS OF THE MAJOR TRANSITIONAL WORKS

Abstracted here are the major transitional works in the literature concerning the philosophy of physical education and sport, as these works are characterized in Chapter III.

Best, David. <u>Expression in Movement and the Arts</u>.
This volume is devoted to exploding the orthodox, dualist notion of the mind-body relation (as well as the solipsistic, behaviouristic, mystic, empiricist, rationalist, and intuitionist excesses which are the consequences of this notion), and to showing the importance of this explosion for a satisfactory understanding of expression in movement, most particularly in the dance. This is accomplished principally by appeal to the monist views of Wittgenstein's later work which hold that, inner mental events, as standing qualitatively apart from outer physical events, cannot be inferred from outer physical ones, for one has no direct experience of such events. And that, the meaning of words or emotions is neither an object nor a private sentiment as such, but determined by their use or place in the ebb and flow of one's experience. Consequently, expression in the arts, in dance more particularly, is given only in the movement itself, and can be understood, 1) only in the context of concrete cultural and social convention, 2) only as a publicly observable event, and so not as the exclusive province of the dancer, 3) as learnable only by mastering certain techniques, and 4) as being unique to particular media. The meaning of these insights for the likes of sport is not much developed by Best, though he is ostensibly of the view that such meaning is fairly apparent from what else has been said.

Gerber, Ellen W. (ed.). <u>Sport and the Body: A Philosopical Symposium</u>.
The Gerber anthology brings together much of the most important short essay literature concerning the philosophy of sport and the body. This literature is organized into what Gerber takes to be the most significant dimensions of such a study: the nature of sport, sport and metaphysical speculations (the reality of sport as a phenomenon, and the effect of the sport encounter on individual existence), the

body and being (the mind-body problem), sport as a meaningful experience, sport and value-oriented concerns, and sport and aesthetics (beauty in sport, aesthetic pleasure and experience in sport, sport as art subject, and sport as art object).

Metheny, Eleanor. Connotations of Movement in Sport and Dance.
In this work, Metheny explores the nature of, and relationships between distinctly human forms of voluntary movement and the distinctly human thought with which such forms are connected. Revealed in the end are her interpretation of the philosophy of symbolic transformation as explaining the character of, and relations between movement and thought, as well as her view of human movement kinesthesia which issues from this philosophy. Variously articulated are:

> -the common characteristics of all forms of sporting competition, as embodied in the principle of overcoming inertia, the principle of finite limits, the principle of nonconsequential effect (on sporting facility and implements), and the principle of human control (the boundaries of sport are conventional, as distinct from natural)
> -the distinction between the competitive "good strife" (winning the contest) and "bad strife" (beating the opponent)
> -the qualities common to sport and dance; as a similar order of physical skill and movement pattern, and substantially the same disciplined control of complex neuromuscular functions
> -the principal attribute which differentiates sport and dance, as the purposes of the participants in each--the primary purpose of dance is the creation of beauty and the expressive interpretation of reality; whereas the primary purpose of sport concerns the efficiency and utility of performance
> -and, the meaning of human movement, as making life more articulate, as enhancing distinctly human inclinations, and as being inherently compelling.

Neal, Patsy. Sport and Identity.
Neal here exposes an existential-tending interpretation of sport which demonstrates the terms of human actualization in it. The book's most persistent emphasis concerns the organismic unity of man, the resultant totality of man's genuine involvement in sport, and the predominantly intrinsic, unique, extraordinary, and so play-like character of

this involvement. There is in such an involvement a
certain movement toward the self, a certain becoming
authentically one's self, a certain revelation of the utterly
personal, creative, and true self. Sport genuinely undertaken thereby exemplifies man's noble search through
anxiety and suffering for beauty, freedom, harmony, and
the extraordinary and boundless joy of authentic existence.
It is in this search that the creativity of being, the living
of life in the fullest sense, self-actualization is accomplished. Moreover, the moral actions presupposed by
such actualization require a rejection of the instrumental
and external values commonly advocated for sport, and so
entail a playing with, instead of a playing against other
competitors--a mutual pursuit of self-realization and a
mutual respect for the freedom of all persons.

Osterhoudt, Robert G. (ed.). The Philosophy of Sport: A
Collection of Original Essays.
This volume contains a collection of major unpublished,
essay contributions to the literature concerning the philosophy of physical education and sport. These essays
variously consider ontological, ethical, and aesthetic matters with respect to sport.

VanderZwaag, Harold J. Toward a Philosophy of Sport.
VanderZwaag variously explains man's fundamental attractions to sport in terms of its physical, cognitive, attitud-
inal, psychological, social, and cultural values. Sport is
itself characterized as a pursuit of excellence, a stimulating form of recreation, and an intrinsically engaging
form of activity or individualizing experience; and as
deriving its central values from play, competition, and
physical prowess. Also examined are such foundational
philosophic concerns as the nature of philosophy (metaphysics, epistemology, ethics, aesthetics, and logic) and
the relation of philosophy to science, art, religion, and
sport; as well as the relation of sport to movement, play,
games, physical education, and athletics, and the role of
the sportsperson in sport (most importantly as amateur
and as woman).

Webster, Randolph W. Philosophy of Physical Education.
In this volume, Webster attempts to unveil the underlying
truths of physical education by determining its origin, nature, meaning, aims, and objectives; and by distinguishing
it from physical culture, athletics, health education, recreation, safety education, camping, and outdoor education. Philosophy is used in order to promote a better
understanding of physical education, as well as to exhort

all professionals to a systematic formulation of their philosophic views. Importantly considered are the biological, economic, historical, political, psychological, religious, and sociological factors influencing one's philosophy of physical education, the procedure for constructing such a philosophy, the manner of applying philosophic notions, the establishment of a system of values as the culmination of philosophizing, and the implications of the four major educational philosophies (idealism, naturalism, pragmatism, and realism) for physical education and sport.

Whiting, H. T. A. and Masterson, Don W. (eds.). Readings in the Aesthetics of Sport.

This is an anthology of original essays which variously show the connections between art and sport, the associations of aesthete and athlete.

APPENDIX D

ABSTRACTS OF THE GREAT BOOKS

Abstracted here are the so-termed great books in the literature concerning the philosophy of physical education and sport, as these books are characterized in Chapter III.

Herrigel, Eugen. Zen in the Art of Archery.
        The Herrigel volume sketches out a "characteristic-ally" Eastern view of life, education, and sport. That is, it tends toward a spiritual emphasis, and is of a monistic and synthetic inclination. It accentuates the likenesses among, and the unity of the various aspects of reality, and so develops in the direction of a comparatively refined religiosity, and away from a relatively sophisticated technology. Conversely, the Western view, with which this is contrasted, "typically" tends toward material inclin-ations, and is of a pluralistic and analytic bent. It empha-sizes the differences among things, is, therefore, more so divisive than unifying in effect, and exhibits a compar-atively impoverished religiosity and well developed tech-nology.

        The basic tenets of Buddhist thought, of which Zen is a form, hold that existence consists most fundamentally in suffering, that the origin of suffering is egoistic desire, that suffering, therefore, ceases when desire ceases, and that the chain of desire, suffering, and being may be brok-en, and "oneself" annihilated, only by living in accord with prescribed maxims. Zen thereby seeks a single end, pur-pose, or goal--it is metaphysically absolute--and this end is the true, the spiritual, or Zen self. This self is ego-less or impersonal, natural or extraordinary, undifferen-tiated or without parts, and so techniqueless, mystical, and intuitively or immediately known. This end may be pursued in many ways, however--the doctrine of multiple means, or methodological relativism. In the process of these ways, wherein the goal is being sought but is not yet achieved, the self is not true, spiritual, and Zen, though it is moving in this direction; it is instead empirical or material. That is, it is egoistic or personal, willed or ordinary and mundane, differentiated or having parts, and so of technique, bodily, and rational. Though Zen is of the view that the goal is reached only through direct expe-rience and under the conscientious guidance of a skilled teacher and Master, the major intent of the Herrigel tract is to "describe" one prominent way that has been known to lead to the goal. Insofar as it is a mere description, then, it cannot actually perform such an act of concrete leadership. But it can at least instructively ask, according to Herrigel, whether or not it is the sort of experience that one might wish to pursue.

The primary purpose of archery, as well as the other "Far Eastern arts", is neither utilitarian nor aesthetic, but religious. That is, the purpose of archery is to bring the self into contact with ultimate reality. By archery, one understands a religious ritual, and not an innocuous pastime or a sporting form of prowess (at least not such a form of prowess as it is commonly conceived in the West). The contest in archery is, therefore, not between archers, nor is it between man and natural constraint; it is a contest of the archer with himself--it is a spiritual exercise in which one takes aim at oneself. The archer is consequently both aimer, or material subject, and that which is aimed at, or spiritual object. The ultimate reality sought by the practice of archery is the true, spiritual, or Zen self, also variously referred to as the Unconscious (for it is intuitive and egoless), the bottomless Ground of Being (for it is the most fundamental interpretive principle of reality), and as the unnameable Qualitylessness (owing again to its utterly fundamental character and so its undifferentiated nature). Becoming one with this ultimate reality, or becoming a Zen artist of life, entails a mastery and a subsequent transcendence of technical skills, in this case of such skills pertaining to archery. And these techniques must be sufficiently demanding to provide an experience of personal ordeal and suffering by which the terms of their transcendence, and so the terms in which they give way to a higher insight are revealed. In this sense, archery becomes an artless, or techniqueless art, and the archer a selfless, or egoless self. By this account, then, archery is one medium through which religious fulfillment is achieved.

Also instructively discussed is the necessary role of the teacher and Master in this experience. Practice of the art as such requires a teacher in that the end fashions the means used to obtain it, and the means must be passed through in order to realize the end; that is, a vision of the end cannot be obtained but through a difficult-to-master technique with which it has an intimate relation, and this technique must be fashioned so as to lead to the envisioned end. In this, the teacher must be teacher and Master in

one--he must have reached the end in order to understand
the realation in which means stand to it, and so the full
nature of means and ends themselves. In the beginning,
the student has no insight into the nature of the end, and
so is gradually led by the inspirational example and pedagogical skill of the teacher. The order of faith necessarily invoked by the student in this experience is virtually
complete, and without it the experience is not possible at
all. In such a circumstance, the relationship of student
and teacher grows gradually closer, and in the end the
distinction between them collapses as the student passes
over into the undifferentiated Zen. Most troublesome
about this entire view are its "dualistic" tendencies, its
unsympathetic view of "nature", and its unarticulated absolute.

Huizinga, Johan. <u>Homo Ludens: A Study of the Play-Element</u>
<u>in Culture</u>.
          Though play has been most commonly treated as a
pure biological or psychological event, Huizinga here
undertakes a philosophic anthropologic-tending explanation
of it as a primarily socio-cultural phenomenon. This
demonstration effectively integrates the concept of play
into that of culture, and shows the fundamental character
of play, shows play as it is in-and-for-itself. According
to Huizinga, the biological and psychological conceptions of
play have mistaken some of the prominent, but nonetheless
secondary consequences of play for play itself, and have
consequently missed the basic nature and significance of
play. They have also failed to exclude alternative conceptions, like one another and Huizinga's view, as well as
failed to show the unity of these alternatives--their reach
and their grasp have been altogether too prosaic. By this
account, the true nature and significance of play transcends
the mundane, utilitarian, and mediate qualities referred to
by biological and psychological conceptions--these qualities are themselves expressions or manifestations of a
more basic impulse. This impulse Huizinga variously
calls the play-impulse proper, pure play, fun-element,
sacred ritual, non-seriousness, and the play-element.

          Pure play is characterized as the absolutely primary
category of life familiar to everyone at a glance. As such,
it resists any strict analysis or logical interpretation, any
examination which pretends to reduce it to terms other
than its own (as most prominently and perniciously done in
the biological and psychological conceptions). Owing to the
the primacy of play, it has no parts, nor "anything" not
its own, it is nowhere totally absent, and it is known only

immediately and intuitively (though theories about it are in some sense rationally accessible, as the presence of his own work testifies). Play is then even more fundamental than culture itself and antedates it, as animals have not waited for man to teach them their playing, nor has human civilization added anything essential to play. Such civilization is in any case a manifestation of play according to Huizinga. Play itself is constituted as aesthetic intrinsicality; that is, as that quality of action by which the activity with which it becomes associated is intrinsically valued, and so without need or possibility of reference to that without it, and so also aesthetically appealing. This notion issues from what is presupposed of the main characteristics of play as such characteristics appear in play's social manifestations. These characteristics are, therefore, direct consequences of pure play, and expressions of its basic character. They are:

> -voluntariness, or undetermined and uncoerced
> entry into, and continued participation in ac-
> tivity
> -extraordinariness, or a being distinct from
> the utilitarian and "serious" demands of the
> everyday--it fulfills and not merely sustains
> life--it is consequently uncapricious, intent,
> absorbing, having a special or lived (as dis-
> tinct from a merely objective) spatio-tempo-
> rality, and creating and demanding a har-
> monious and aesthetic order
> -and, disinterestnedness, or standing apart
> from the satisfaction of simple, appetitive
> pleasures and desires, as being of a higher,
> more synoptic order--it has no material
> interest as such.

Huizinga attempts to further demonstrate the universal primacy of play by showing its essentially singular character in all major linguistic expressions of it, and by revealing that in these expressions play is always thought more fundamental than its opposite, work. He concludes that though linguistic conceptions of play superficially vary, the underlying character of play is essentially the same in the most diverse languages and cultures. And that, play's opposite, work, earnestness, or seriousness- as that quality of action by which the activity with which it becomes associated is extrinsically, or instrumentally valued, and so having its fundamental reference without itslef--is derivative of, and so secondary to play in terms of its being the consequence of expressing the concept, not-play. Since play and work, together with the capricious misuse of play (or folly), exhaust the general manners of valuing, since they are all pre-cultural impulses, and since play is positive and work negative; Huizinga has gone impressively far in a successful defense of his basic position that play is the primary basis of civilization. The full terrain of this position is further sketched in by historico-anthropologic accounts of play's participation in establishing and sustaining such archetypal modes of cultural activity as law, war, knowledge, poetry, philosophy, and art. In this, play functions as the most fundamental of civilizing agents; that is, as preceeding civilization, accompanying its emergence in the form of providing its primary basis, and in significant measure sustaining civilization once emerged. In this relationship of play and culture, play is not one among the activities of civilized life, nor has civilization evolved from play in the sense of its being a transformed playing; culture rather arises in the form of play itself and is in its most sublime moments played.

Civilization has not uniformly cultivated and preserved the play-impulse throughout its development, however. Since the early nineteenth century at least, Western civilization has increasingly assigned play a secondary function—cultural life has grown progressively more "serious" in this period. Though the cultural practice of such as sport and athletics (activities particularly receptive of playful tendencies) has accelerated throughout this time, giving the appearance of an increased allegiance to playful inclinations, the converse of such an increase has, in fact, occurred. Even sport itself, let alone cultural life in general, has become more and more intensely instrumental, and so sterile and profane. The old play-element has undergone almost complete atrophy. The highly competitive and utilitarian regard for culture, man, and sport have been left wanting for the play quality which forms the center of their authentic lives, and without which neither culture, nor man, nor sport can prosper. Culture must foster its basis more vigilantly, life must be lived more fully in accord with its playful ground, sport must be more completely played; for only in this way can civilization preserve and fulfill itself.

Metheny, Eleanor. Movement and Meaning.

This volume gives the most systematic and complete elaboration of Metheny's interpretation of Cassirer's and Langer's philosophical anthropologic-tending notion of symbolic transformation as it bears on human movement phenomena. Examined is the general meaning of all non-verbal forms of human activity, most particularly the meaning of the movement forms of dance, sport, exercise, and physical education. The basic outlines of Metheny's position are provided by its realistic-tending metaphysics which ostensibly admits to the independent existence of objects and minds, as well as to the capacity of the latter to accurately apprehend the former. The realm of objects is variously termed reality, forms of reality, or material forms. This realm further consists in natural forms, or material objects or events which take their course apart from human intervention, and presentational forms, or man-made or -influenced materializations of ideas. The realm of minds consists entirely in forms, or cognitive images of that which comprises the whole of material objects; namely, their structural (the materials and their organization) and functional or operational qualities, as well as the relationships which arise among these qualities. Moreover, these qualities appear to varying degrees of clarity in each of the three levels of abstraction through which forms develop in their migration to full understanding. In the first level of abstraction, comprised of perceptual elements, the most primitive, uninterpreted impressions are taken into the sense-perceptual faculties-- one is merely standing in a viable perceptual relation with material forms, the particular character of which is not yet recognized. These elements are presupposed by higher levels of abstraction and required by the empiricistic and abstractionistic epistemology Metheny adopts. The second level of abstraction is made up of perceptual forms, or coherent arrangements of perceptual elements, which recognize material forms as distinctive wholes. The third and highest level of abstraction is comprised of conceptual forms, or coherent arrangements of perceptual forms, which reveal the distinctive nature of material forms. This level signifies the culmination of recognizing and understanding a material form. It is here that ideas are translated into verbal forms or words, that consciously distinctive levels of clarity appear (conceptions, ideas, and concepts), that ideas are recognized as connotational (personal, unique, and unpredictable) or denotational (public, repeatable, and predictable), meaningful (having personal, affective interest) or meaningless (without such interest). In this scheme, movement provides the functional link between the domains of objects and minds, getting them together as it were. It is the medium through which ideas obtain content, and objects, life--the medium through which the subjective awareness is filled and becomes other

than an empty void, and the objective domain animated
thereby becoming more than a lifeless expanse. It is
through this medium that conceptual forms receive objective expression in the character of presentational forms,
prominent among which are such as dance, sport, exercise, and physical education.

As presentational forms developed and as an understanding of their scientific, technologic, artistic, and
philosophic dimensions improved, they were formulated
in a widening diversity of materials. Eventually included
in these materials was man himself. Movement patterns
as such were first thought significant in virtue of their efforts on concrete objects, then regarded as means of com-
municating ideas, and ultimately seen as genuine expressions of the human character, and so of value in themselves.
In this latter, the moving performer is one with the materials performed on or with--ideas are given material form
in the sense of the subjective giver of ideas coming together with their objective materialization. The remain-
der of the text deals with the denotational and connotational
aspects of the principal forms of human movement phenomena, dance, sport, exercise, and physical education,
and the terms in which these phenomena are and are not
meaningful. These phenomena differ, or can be said to
differ largely at the denotational level of meaning, leaving
the connotational aspects of each as undetermined abstractions of this level.

Dance is conceived as a complex composition of
movement patterns effectively distinguished by naming,
describing, notating, or demonstrating them. Despite
changing styles of dance, the primary purpose of dancing
remains unchanged, and that purpose is to evoke connotational meanings. The role of the choreographer in this
evocation is to define a movement pattern with connotation-evoking possibilities. This pattern provides a denotational outline within which the expressive faculties of the
dancer and audience work. Although the substantive character of these expressive or connotative faculties or experiences is private, unrepeatable, and so not capable of
being shared or communicated, their general form is
known and shared among a coterie of sufficiently well informed and sensitive percipients. This preserves both
the utterly individual character of the substance of connotations, as well as the interpersonal nature of intuitive
or poetic insight commonly experienced among the likes
of painters, poets, dancers, and musicians. Whatever

connotation-evoking possibilities are seen by the choreographer in the movement patterns he prescribes (and the best of these are the most universal and basic), he must nonetheless avoid the paradoxical trap of denoting these possibilities as such. To be able to do this is, for one, not possible wherein one has genuine connotations in the first instance, and, for another, it is to mistake the expressive, unique, and individualizing dimensions of human life for the technical, common, and anonymous ones. In this latter, according to Metheny, one falls into the peril of obscuring, or failing to recognize at all the most important aspect of our humanity--what is at the center of humanity itself. The dancer then brings the patterns of movement prescribed by the choreographer into a visual image which can, in turn, be made available to an audience. Like the choreographer, the dancer too, must avoid attempting to denote the substance of connotations, though he must intuitively share and express the form of connotation-evoking possibilities suggested by the choreographer.

Through the great number and diversity of sport forms, each with distinctive rules, movements, vocabulary, and performing groups, Metheny attempts to determine the meaningful characteristics common to all sport forms. Principal among these characteristics are the voluntary choice of participation in it, its rule governed character, its entailing an attempt to temporarily overcome the inertia of certain substantial masses in carefully stipulated ways, and its producing a conception of honorable behavior, a conception of the performance of the task, and a score which denotes the quality of that performance in quantitative terms. The only major feature of sport left undesignated by its rules is the proficiency with which participants are able to perform the prescribed task. In a sense, then, sporting performance serves as a test of a participant's ability to accomplish a useless task --a task likened to that of Sisyphus in that, like Sisyphus, one has no formally permanent, or utilitarian effect on the materials of sport. Metheny argues that this ostensibly "useless futility" partially, but importantly explains sport's difference from ordinary life, and our attractions to it. That is to say, characteristically unlike ordinary life, in sport one is free to focus one's full attentions on a well-defined task and to marshal the whole of one's energies to its effective performance. In this sense, one is free from the imperatives of the everyday--a negative freedom. In another sense, however, one is also free to be, to recreate oneself, to restore one's sense of wholeness and well-being--a positive and genuine freedom.

When sport is most authentically human, it values this
sense of integration even more highly than the score itself,
though it is only through the constraint of making the best
possible score that such a sense comes available in sport.

Moreover, Metheny characterizes exercise as an
organization of repetitive movements denoted by their own
performance and devised for the purpose of producing
certain positive, future effects on the functional (bio-
psychological) capacity of the performer. Wherein the
performer foregoes the conception of functional good he
may derive from the exercise in favor of the meanings he
finds in performance itself, however, exercise is transformed into dance or sport. And, education is conceived
as a potentially limitless process, that may well include
such as dance, sport, and exercise, and that serves to
activate meanings or meaningful learning. Insofar as this
process activates meanings of movement phenomena, and
concerns itself with how such meanings are learned, it is
called physical education.

Though the full sweep of Metheny's view posits the
high metaphysical status of movement in the form of
postulating its functional significance, the view leaves the
character of movement itself largely undetermined. Also
troublesome are its dualistic tendencies, and the discontinuity these tendencies promote between denotations and
connotations, technique and expression, public and private
events, and substance and form. Such tendencies have
also failed to allow for a fully satisfactory account of the
necessary contributions of the mind to experience.

Slusher, Howard S. Man, Sport and Existence: A Critical
Analysis.
By subjecting sport to existential interpretations,
Slusher shows the unification of man, sport, and existence,
which goes as demonstrating sport in a new dimension--a
dimension in which man learns of sport's potential in the
development of a meaningful humanity. Despite the
hostility of present institutions to such a potential, Slusher
ascribes to sport the possibility of providing authentically
personal and meaningful experience.

According to this view, man is an organic unity of
aspects whose manner of being-in-the-world defines his
existence. Man is his being in this sense, though the
world into which he is thrown resists his reason and humanity and makes itself hostile to him. In this being, the
body is one with the self, or is the personal location,

reference, or context of experience. And "it", and so the self itself, can be known only by its activity, only by its active involvement or movement in the world with other bodies. Unsurprisingly, then, the likes of sport, as entailing the vigorous forms of movement that it does, is a particularly rich medium for the fashioning of such knowledge. That is, in sport the prospect of developing an awareness of body, self, and world--of the conciliation of man's unique subjectivity with the objectivity of the world --is unusually high. When this opportunity is seized, and sport authentically undertaken, it provides the challenge of existence. Slusher conceives of genuine sport itself as a personal function, or expression of the individual's basically subjective constitution. By this view, sport is more than a mere link with life, it is a vital aspect of existence which opens the self to the mystery of being.

An authentic engagement in sport is taken as one in which man is totally and seriously immersed in it, and thereby free to fulfill his uniquely human self. In sport, the search for authentic being is facilitated by a confrontation with the fullness of responsibility for one's acts, and by the paradoxical experiences of pleasure, ecstacy, heroism, delight, joy and anxiety, anguish, despair, pain, death, and immortality with which sport is copiously sprinkled. Underlying this search is an intrinsic regard for sport, a regard which actively resists its use as a means to something without itself. What makes it worthy of human involvement resides within the character of sport as such; that is, within the ground of sport as a basic expression of human individuality. Its use as a biological, psychological, social, or educational instrument thereby goes as a misuse or exploitation of it, and as an indictment of those inclined to such treatment.

Also instructively discussed are:

> -the role of technique in sport: though the mastery of technique does not guarantee being, more refined skills carry with them a greater opportunity to attain being than less refined ones
> -the role of objective results in sport: in sport authentically undertaken, being takes precedence over results--it is prior to results
> -the role of competition in sport: the competitive character of sport is not so much thought a restriction of human action as providing an

opportunity, or a context for the concentrated marshaling of energies in sport--insofar as this character is allowed to obscure one's vision and realization of being, however, as it commonly has been, it is in violation of man, sport, and existence
-the audience-athlete relation in sport: the athlete is considered the primary agent in sport in that the experience of sport itself is reserved for him--the choices of sport and the responsibility to achieve self in it are his
-the relationship of sport and religion: both are archetypal forms of human activity which express or demonstrate a view of, and a relation to the common good
-and, the relationship of sport and art: sport is fundamentally different from art in that its product entails the maintenance of a form as distinct from its creation, and its medium is rational rather than emotional.

Slusher concludes that the only hope for sport, no less than for such as art, drama, and music, to overcome the dehumanizing tendencies under which it has fallen, is to cultivate the utterly personal possibilities of its experience. Most troublesome of the view adduced here is its occasionally ambiguous treatment of the relationship between individual subjectivity and the objective requirements of social life.

Weiss, Paul. Sport: A Philosophic Inquiry.
        In this volume, Weiss attempts an examination of sport in terms of principles which reveal its basic nature and significance as a participant in the whole of things, and which show its rightful place in the life of man. In such a treatment, sport is taken seriously as a legitimate object of philosophic inquiry. By Weiss' view, the authentic sportsperson shows us what we ideally are as bodies. He demonstrates what man can be and do through a disciplined mastery of his body. He displays mind in a body well made, and gratifies the uniquely human search for bodily excellence by placing himself in a viable relation to such excellence. Underlying this display and this gratification, as necessarily prior notions to them, is a conception of sport as an end-in-itself--an end which uniquely withholds the prospect of harmonizing and unifying one's bodily and intellectual aspects. As such, sport is detached from the everyday and the practical, and represents an

idealization of the universal human impulse to physicality. The freedom inherent in this detachment allows the athlete, not unlike the artist, religious person, and scholar, to apprehend ultimate finalities. Weiss characterizes sport as intensely serious, performed within a well established tradition preserved by rules, records, and histories, directed toward high achievement, possessing a sharp sense of spontaneity, demanding of dedication, appropriate skills, and considerable training, and an activity in which persons are tested with other persons. And games are thought a particular instance of sporting activity.

Also profitably discussed are:

-the role of the coach in sport: as being peculiarly between the concrete involvement of the player and the largely passive participation of the spectator--as having a keen influence on the strategy of play without actually playing

-the role of spectators in sport: as being largely passive respondents to the more significant involvement of athletes themselves

-the role of records in sport: as not only taking note of, but also providing a means for comparing achievements at different places and at different times

-the role of training in sport: as a progressive and rigorous preparation for, or process of becoming master of oneself

-the misuse of sport: as most notably embodied in such as military, propaganda, entertainment, and conquest motifs

-the amateur-professional controversy in sport: the amateur is likened to an artist who is occupied with the spontaneous making of something excellent, while the professional uses sport as a means for producing goods

-women in sport: holds that sport is equally an end-in-itself for both men and women, and that the union of mind and body is more fully recognized and felt by women than men, thereby explaining the apparently greater tendency of men to participate in such overt for forms of bodily expression as sport

-and, standardization of sport: advocates
such a standardization in order to make possible better comparisons of sporting results
achieved at different times, in different circumstances, and by different types of contestants.

Weiss concludes that the athlete most significantly unifies
a personal ideal with the meaning of mankind itself, and
is enriched by the excellence he seeks to embody relative
to this ideal and this meaning. Most vexing about Weiss'
view are its dualistic inclinations and its largely insufficient recognition of the intellectual dimensions and requirements of sporting activity.

BIBLIOGRAPHY

Abernathy, Ruth and Waltz, Maryann. "Toward a Discipline: First Steps First," Quest, No. 2 (April, 1964), 1-7.

Ahrabi-Fard, Iradge. "Implications of the Original Teachings of Islam for Physical Education and Sport." Unpublished Doctor's dissertation, University of Minnesota, 1974.

Aiken, Henry D. (ed.). The Age of Ideology: The Nineteenth Century Philosophers. Boston: Houghton-Mifflin, 1956.

Aldrich, Virgil C. Philosophy of Art. Englewood Cliffs, N. J.: Prentice-Hall, Inc., 1963.

Allard, Ronald J. "Sport: Tyranny of the Mind." Unpublished Master's thesis, University of Massachusetts, 1970.

Aquinas, Summa Theologiae. 2 vols. Thomas Bilby (ed.). Garden City, N. Y.: Image Books, 1969.

Archambault, Reginald D. (ed.). Philosophical Analysis and Education. London: Routledge and Kegan Paul Ltd., 1965.

Aristotle. Nicomachean Ethics. Martin Ostwald (trans.). Indianapolis: The Bobbs-Merrill Co., Inc., 1962.

Armstrong, Arthur H. An Introduction to Ancient Philosophy. Fourth edition. London: Metheun, 1965.

Aspin, David N. "Sport and the Concept of 'the Aesthetic'," Readings in the Aesthetics of Sport. H. T. A. Whiting and Don W. Masterson (eds.). London: Lepus Books, 1974.

Augustine. The City of God. Marcus Dods (trans.). New York: Random House, Inc., 1950.

Augustine. Concerning the Teacher and On the Immortality of the Soul. George G. Leckie (trans.). New York: D. Appleton-Century Co., 1938.

Austin, Patricia L. "A Conceptual Structure of Physical Education for the School Program." Unpublished Doctor's dissertation, Michigan State University, 1965.

Avedon, Elliott M. "A Philosophical Inquiry Into the Essence of Recreation." Unpublished Doctor's dissertation, Columbia University, 1961.

Bacon, Francis. Advancement of Learning and Novum Organum. Revised edition. James E. Creighton (ed.). New York: The Colonial Press, 1899.

Bair, Donn E. "An Identification of Some Philosophical Beliefs Held by Influential Professional Leaders in American Physical Education." Unpublished Doctor's dissertation, University of Southern California, 1956.

Baley, James A. and Field, David A. Physical Education and the Physical Educator: An Introduction. Boston: Allyn and Bacon, Inc., 1970.

Banks, Gary C. "The Philosophy of Friedrich Nietzsche as a Foundation for Physical Education." Unpublished Master's thesis, University of Wisconsin, 1966.

Bannister, Roger. "The Meaning of Athletic Performance," International Research in Sport and Physical Education. Ernst Jokl and E. Simon (eds.). Springfield, Ill.: Charles C. Thomas, Publishers, 1964.

Barbour, Ian G. Issues in Science and Religion. Englewood Cliffs, N. J.: Prentice-Hall, Inc., 1966.

Barrow, Harold M. Man and His Movement: Principles of His Physical Education. Philadelphia: Lea and Febiger, 1971.

Bayles, Ernest E. Pragmatism in Education. New York: Harper and Row, Publishers, Inc., 1966.

Baylis, Charles A. (ed.). Metaphysics. New York: The Macmillan Co., 1965.

Beardsley, Monroe C. (ed.). The European Philosophers from Descartes to Nietzsche. New York: Random House, Inc., 1960.

Beck, Robert N. (ed.). Perspectives in Philosophy: A Book of Readings. New York: Holt, Rinehart and Winston, Inc., 1961.

Bell, James W. "A Comparative Analysis of the Normative Philosophies of Plato, Rousseau, and Dewey as Applied to Physical Education." Unpublished Doctor's dissertation, Ohio State University, 1971.

Bentley, John E. Philosophy: An Outline History. Revised edition. Paterson, N. J.: Littlefield, Adams and Co., 1963.

Bergson, Henri. Matter and Memory. Nancy M. Paul and W. Scott Palmer (trans.). New York: The Macmillan Co., 1911.

Berkeley, George. The Principles of Human Knowledge, Three Dialogues Between Hylas and Philonous. G. J. Warnock (ed.). Cleveland: The World Publishing Co., 1963.

Berlin, Isaiah (ed.). The Age of Enlightenment: The Eighteenth Century Philosophers. Boston: Houghton-Mifflin, 1956.

Berry, Elmer. The Philosophy of Athletics: Coaching and Character With the Psychology of Athletic Coaching. New York: A. S. Barnes and Co., 1972.

Best, David. "The Aesthetic in Sport," The British Journal of Aesthetics, Vol. 14, No. 3 (Summer, 1974), 197-213.

Best, David. Expression in Movement and the Arts. London: Lepus Books, 1974.

Boas, George. Dominant Themes of Modern Philosophy. New York: Ronald Press Co., 1957.

Bookwalter, Karl W. and VanderZwaag, Harold J. Foundations and Principles of Physical Education. Philadelphia: W. B. Saunders Co., 1969.

Boyd, William (trans.). The Émile of Jean Jacques Rousseau. New York: Bureau of Publications, Teachers College, Columbia University, 1956.

Brackenbury, Robert L. "Physical Education, An Intellectual Emphasis?" Quest, No. 1 (December, 1963), 3-6.

Brameld, Theodore. Philosophies of Education in Cultural Perspective. New York: The Dryden Press, Inc., 1955.

Brandt, Richard B. The Philosophy of Schleiermacher: The Development of His Theory of Scientific and Religious Knowledge. New York: Harper and Brothers, 1941.

Bretall, Robert. A Kierkegaard Anthology. New York: Random House, Inc., 1936.

Brightbill, Charles K. Man and Leisure: A Philosophy of Recreation. Englewood Cliffs, N. J.: Prentice-Hall, Inc., 1961.

Broekhoff, Jan. "Physical Education and the Reification of the Human Body." Essay presented at the American Association for Health, Physical Education, and Recreation, Annual Meeting, Houston, Texas, March 24-28, 1972.

Broekhoff, Jan. "Sport and Ethics in the Context of Culture," The Philosophy of Sport: A Collection of Original Essays. Robert G. Osterhoudt (ed.). Springfield, Ill.: Charles C. Thomas, Publisher, 1973.

Brooke, J. D. and Whiting, H. T. A. Human Movement: A Field of Study. Lafayette, Ind.: Bart Publishers, 1973.

Brooks, Betty W. "Views of Physical Fitness from Four Educational Philosophies," The Physical Educator, Vol. 24, No. 1 (March, 1967), 31-32.

Broudy, Harry S. Building a Philosophy of Education. Second edition. Englewood Cliffs, N. J.: Prentice-Hall, Inc., 1961.

Brown, Camille. "The Structure of Knowledge of Physical Education," Quest, No. 9 (December, 1967), 53-67.

Brown, Camille and Cassidy, Rosalind. Theory in Physical Education: A Guide to Program Change. Philadelphia: Lea and Febiger, 1963.

Brownell, Clifford L. and Hagman, E. Patricia. Physical Education --Foundations and Principles. New York: McGraw-Hill Book Co., Inc., 1951.

Brubacher, John S. Modern Philosophies of Education. Fourth edition. New York: McGraw-Hill Book Co., 1969.

Buber, Martin. Between Man and Man. Ronald Gregor Smith (trans.). London: Kegan Paul, 1947.

Buber, Martin. I and Thou. Second edition. Ronald Gregor Smith (trans.). New York: Charles Scribner's Sons, 1958.

Bucher, Charles A. Dimensions of Physical Education. Second edition. St. Louis: The C. V. Mosby Co., 1974.

Bucher, Charles A. Foundations of Physical Education. Fourth edition. St. Louis: The C. V. Mosby Co., 1964.

Bucher, Charles A. Foundations of Physical Education. Fifth edition. St. Louis: The C. V. Mosby Co., 1968.

Burtt, Edwin A. The English Philosophers from Bacon to Mill. New York: Random House, Inc., 1939.

Butler, J. Donald. Four Philosophies and Their Practice in Education and Religion. Revised edition. New York: Harper and Brothers Publishers, 1957.

Butler, J. Donald. Four Philosophies and Their Practice in Education and Religion. Third edition. New York: Harper and Row, Publishers, Inc., 1968.

Butler, J. Donald. Idealism in Education. New York: Harper and Row Publishers, Inc., 1966.

Cahn, L. Joseph. "Contribution of Plato to Thought on Physical Education, Health, and Recreation." Unpublished Doctor's dissertation, New York University, 1941.

Caillois, Roger. "The Structure and Classification of Games," Sport, Culture, and Society: A Reader on the Sociology of Sport. John W. Loy and Gerald S. Kenyon (eds.). London: The Macmillan Co., 1969.

Caldwell, Stratton F. "Conceptions of Physical Education in Twentieth Century America: Rosalind Cassidy." Unpublished Doctor's dissertation, University of Southern California, 1966.

Carlisle, Robert. "Physical Education and Aesthetics," Readings in the Aesthetics of Sport. H. T. A. Whiting and Don W. Masterson (eds.). London: Lepus Books, 1974.

Carlson, Reynold E., Deppe, Theodore R. and MacLean, Janet R. Recreation in American Life. Belmont, Calif.: Wadsworth Publishing Co., Inc., 1963.

Carver, Julia. "A Study of the Influence of the Philosophy of the Church of Jesus Christ of Latter-Day Saints on Physical Education in Church Schools." Unpublished Doctor's dissertation, University of Oregon, 1964.

Cassidy, Rosalind. "The Cultural Definition of Physical Education," Quest, No. 4 (April, 1965), 11-15.

Cavanaugh, Patric L. "A Delineation of Moderate Realism and Physical Education." Unpublished Doctor's dissertation, University of Michigan, 1967.

Chamberlin, J. Gordon. Toward a Phenomenology of Education. Philadelphia: The Westminster Press, 1969.

Childs, John L. Education and the Philosophy of Experimentalism. New York: D. Appleton-Century Co., Inc., 1931.

Chisholm, Roderick M. Theory of Knowledge. Englewood Cliffs, N. J.: Prentice-Hall, Inc., 1966.

Chryssafis, Jean E. "Aristotle on Physical Education," Journal of Health and Physical Education, Vol. 1, No. 1 (January, 1930), 3-8, 50; Vol. 1, No. 2 (February, 1930), 14-17, 46-47; Vol. 1, No. 7 (September, 1930), 14-17, 54-56.

Clark, Margaret C. "A Philosophical Interpretation of a Program of Physical Education in a State Teachers College." Unpublished Doctor's dissertation, New York University, 1943.

Cobb, Louise S. "Philosophical Research Methods," Research Methods Applied to Health, Physical Education, and Recreation. Louise S. Cobb, Ralph B. Spence, Jesse F. Williams, and Kenneth D. Benne (eds.). Washington: AAHPER, 1949.

Cobb, Robert A. and Lepley, Paul M. Contemporary Philosophies of Physical Education and Athletics. Columbus, Ohio: Charles E. Merrill Publishing Co., 1973.

Cohen, Marshall (ed.). The Philosophy of John Stuart Mill. New York: Random House, Inc., 1961.

Collins, James. The Existentialists: A Critical Study. Chicago: Henry Regnery Co., 1952.

Copleston, Frederick. A History of Philosophy. 8 vols. Garden City, N. Y.: Image Books, 1962-1966.

Costner, Clay E. "Contributions to Thought on Physical Education by Selected Contemporary Educational Philosophers." Unpublished Doctor's dissertation, George Peabody College for Teachers, 1971.

Coutts, Curtis A. "Freedom in Sport," Quest, No. 10 (May, 1968), 68-71.

Cowell, Charles C. "Interpreting Physical Education Through Contrasting Philosophies," The Physical Educator, Vol. 20, No. 4 (December, 1963), 147.

Cowell, Charles C. and France, Wellman L. Philosophy and Principles of Physical Education. Englewood Cliffs, N. J.: Prentice-Hall, Inc., 1963.

Cramer, Carolyn Ann. "John Dewey's Views of Experience for Education: Implications for Physical Education." Unpublished Master's thesis, Drake University, 1970.

Croce, Benedetto. Aesthetics: As Science of Expression and General Linguistic. Revised edition. Douglas Ainslie (trans.). New York: The Noonday Press, 1922.

Curtis, S. J. and Boultwood, M. E. A. A Short History of Educational Ideas. Fourth edition. London: University Tutorial Press Ltd., 1965.

Daly, John A. "An Indentification of Some Philosophical Beliefs Held by Australian Physical Educators." Unpublished Master's thesis, University of Illinois, 1970.

Davis, Elwood Craig. The Philosophic Process in Physical Education. Philadelphia: Lea and Febiger, 1961.

Davis, Elwood Craig (ed.). Philosophies Fashion Physical Education. Dubuque, Iowa: William C. Brown Co., Publishers, 1963.

Davis, Elwood Craig. "The Power of Beliefs," Quest, No. 1 (December, 1963), 7-11.

Davis, Elwood Craig and Miller, Donna Mae. The Philosophic Process in Physical Education. Second edition. Philadelphia: Lea and Febiger, 1967.

Delattre, Edwin J. "Some Reflections on Success and Failure in Competitive Athletics," Journal of the Philosophy of Sport, Vol. 1 (September, 1975), 133-139.

Delfgaauw, Bernard. Twentieth-Century Philosophy. N. D. Smith (trans.). Albany, N. Y.: Magi Books, 1969.

DeSantillana, Giorgio (ed.). The Age of Adventure: The Renaissance Philosophers. Boston: Houghton-Mifflin, 1956.

Dewey, John. Art as Experience. New York: G. P. Putnam's Sons, 1934.

Dewey, John. Democracy and Education. New York. The Macmillan Co., 1916.

Dewey, John. Experience and Education. New York: The Macmillan Co., 1939.

Dewey, John. "The Need for a Philosophy of Education," John Dewey on Education. Reginald D. Archambault (ed.). New York: Random House, Inc., 1964,

Doherty, J. Kenneth. "Why Men Run," Quest, No. 2 (April, 1964), 60-66.

Downey, Robert J. "An Indentification of the Philosophical Beliefs of Educators in the Field of Health Education." Unpublished Doctor's dissertation, University of Southern California, 1956.

Duncan, Clarence J. "Movement is More Than Moving," Quest, No. 2 (April, 1964), 67-68.

Durant, Will. The Story of Philosophy: The Lives and Opinions of the Great Philosophers of the Western World. Sixth edition. New York: Simon and Schuster, 1961.

Edman, Irwin (ed.). The Philosophy of Schopenhauer. New York: Random House, Inc., 1928.

Edmondson, Cornelia. "A Continuum of Thought on the Value of Health, Physical Education, and Recreation from the Time of John Locke Through the Early Twentieth Century." Unpublished Doctor's dissertation, University of Washington, 1966.

Edwards, Paul (ed.). The Encyclopedia of Philosophy. 8 vols. New York: The Macmillan Co., 1967.

Ehrlich, Robert S. Twentieth Century Philosophers. New York: Monarch Press, Inc., 1965.

Elena, Lugo. "Jose Ortega y Gasset's Sportive Sense of Life: His Philosophy of Man." Unpublished Doctor's dissertation, Georgetown University, 1969.

Ellfeldt, Lois and Metheny, Eleanor. "Movement and Meaning: Development of a General Theory," Research Quarterly, Vol. 29, No. 3 (October, 1958), 264-273.

Elliott, R. K. "Aesthetics and Sport," Readings in the Aesthetics of Sport. H. T. A. Whiting and Don W. Masterson (eds.). London: Lepus Books, 1974.

Ellis, M. J. Why People Play. Englewood Cliffs, N. J.: Prentice-Hall, Inc., 1973.

Elwes, R. H. M. (trans.). The Chief Works of Benedict de Spinoza, Volume II. New York: Dover Publications, Inc., 1951.

Esslinger, Arthur A. "A Philosophical Study of Principles for Selecting Activities in Physical Education." Unpublished Doctor's dissertation, University of Iowa, 1938.

Fahey, Brian W. "Basketball: A Phenomenological Perspective of Lived-Body Experience." Unpublished Master's thesis, University of Washington, 1971.

Fairs, John R. "The Influence of Plato and Platonism on the Development of Physical Education in Western Culture," Quest, No. 11 (December, 1968), 14-23.

Fawcett, Donald F. "Analysis of John Dewey's Theory of Experience: Implications for Physical Education Methodology." Unpublished Master's thesis, University of Southern California, 1966.

Felshin, Janet. More Than Movement: An Introduction to Physical Education. Philadelphia: Lea and Febiger, 1972.

Felshin, Janet. Perspectives and Principles for Physical Education. New York: John Wiley and Sons, 1967.

Felshin, Janet. "Sport and Modes of Meaning," Journal of Health, Physical Education, and Recreation, Vol. 40, No. 5 (May, 1969), 43-44.

Ferm, Vergilius (ed.). History of Philosophical Systems. Paterson, N. J.: Littlefield, Adams and Co., 1961.

Findlay, J. N. Hegel: A Re-examination. London: George Allen and Unwin Ltd., 1958.

Fisher, Marjorie. "Sport as an Aesthetic Experience," Sport and the Body: A Philosophical Symposium. Ellen W. Gerber (ed.). Philadelphia: Lea and Febiger, 1972.

Fogelin, Robert J. "Sport: The Diversity of the Concept." Essay presented at the American Association for the Advancement of Science, Annual Meeting, Dallas, Texas, December, 1968.

Forsythe, Eleanor. "Philosophical Bases for Physical Education Experience Consistent with the Goals of American Education for High School Girls." Unpublished Doctor's dissertation, New York University, 1960.

Fox, Larry. "A Linguistic Analysis of the Concept 'Health' in Sport," Journal of the Philosophy of Sport, Vol. 2 (September, 1975), 31-35.

Fraleigh, Warren P. "The Moving 'I'," The Philosophy of Sport: A Collection of Original Essays. Robert G. Osterhoudt (ed.). Springfield, Ill.: Charles C. Thomas, Publisher, 1973.

Fraleigh, Warren P. "A Prologue to the Study of Theory Building in Physical Education," Quest, No. 12 (May, 1969), 26-33.

Fraleigh, Warren P. "Some Meanings of the Human Experience of Freedom and Necessity in Sport," The Philosophy of Sport: A Collection of Original Essays. Robert G. Osterhoudt (ed.). Springfield, Ill.: Charles C. Thomas, Publisher, 1973.

Fraleigh, Warren P. "Sport-Purpose," Journal of the Philosophy of Sport, Vol. 2 (September, 1975), 74-82.

Fraleigh, Warren P. "Theory and Design of Philosophic Research in Physical Education," 74th Proceedings of the National College Physical Education Association for Men, Annual Meeting (Portland, Oregon, December 27-30, 1970), 28-52.

Fraleigh, Warren P. "Toward a Conceptual Model of the Academic Subject Matter of Physical Education as a Discipline," 70th Proceedings of the National College Physical Education Association for Men, Annual Meeting (San Diego, California, December 28-31, 1966), 31-39.

Fraleigh, Warren P. "On Weiss on Records and on the Significance of Athletic Records," The Philosophy of Sport: A Collection of Original Essays. Robert G. Osterhoudt (ed.). Springfield, Ill.: Charles C. Thomas, Publisher, 1973.

Frankena, William K. Philosophy of Education. New York: The Macmillan Co., 1965.

Frederick, Mary M. "Naturalism: The Philosophy of Jean Jacques Rousseau and Its Implications for American Physical Education." Unpublished Doctor's dissertation, Springfield College, 1961.

Fremantle, Anne J. (ed.). The Age of Belief: The Medieval Philosophers. Boston: Houghton-Mifflin, 1962.

Friedrich, Carl J. (ed.). The Philosophy of Hegel. Second edition. New York: Random House, Inc., 1954.

Friedrich, Carl J. (ed.). The Philosophy of Kant. New York: Random House, Inc., 1949.

Friedrich, John A. and McBride, Frank A. "What Is Your Physical Education Philosophy?" The Physical Educator, Vol. 20, No. 3 (October, 1963), 99-101.

Frost, Reuben B. Physical Education: Foundations, Practices, Principles. Reading, Mass.: Addison-Wesley Publishing Co., 1975.

Gardiner, Patrick L. Nineteenth Century Philosophy. New York: Free Press, 1969.

Gaskin, Geoffrey and Masterson, Don W. "The Work of Art in Sport," Journal of the Philosophy of Sport, Vol. 1 (September, 1974), 36-66.

Geblewicz, Eugeniusz. "The Aesthetic Problems in Physical Education and Sport," Fédération Internationale d'Éducation Physique, No. 3 (1965), 53-59.

Genasci, James E. and Klissouras, Vasillis. "The Delphic Spirit in Sports," Journal of Health, Physical Education, and Recreation, Vol. 38, No. 2 (February, 1966), 43-45.

Gentile, Giovanni. The Reform of Education. Dino Bigongiari (trans.). New York: Harcourt, Brace and Co., 1922.

Gerber, Ellen W. "Arguments on the Reality of Sport," Sport and the Body: A Philosophical Symposium. Ellen W. Gerber (ed.). Philadelphia: Lea and Febiger, 1972.

Gerber, Ellen W. "Identity, Relation and Sport," Quest, No. 8 (May, 1967), 90-97.

Gerber, Ellen W. (ed.). Sport and the Body: A Philosophical Symposium. Philadelphia: Lea and Febiger, 1972.

Gerber, Ellen W. "Three Interpretations of the Role of Physical Education, 1930-1960: Charles Harold McCloy, Jay Bryan Nash and Jesse Feiring Williams." Unpublished Doctor's dissertation, University of Southern California, 1966.

Gewirth, Alan (ed.). Political Philosophy. New York: The Macmillan Co., 1965.

Graves, H. "A Philosophy of Sport," Contemporary Review, Vol. 78 (December, 1900), 877-893.

Gray, Miriam. "The Physical Educator as Artist," Quest, No. 7 (December, 1966), 18-24.

Green, Thomas Hill. Prolegomena to Ethics. A. C. Bradley (ed.). New York: Thomas Y. Crowell Co., 1969.

Greene, Theodore M. "A Liberal Christian Idealist Philosophy of Education," 54th Yearbook of the National Society for the Study of Education. Nelson B. Henry (ed.). Chicago: University of Chicago Press, 1955.

Gregg, Jearald R. "A Philosophical Analysis of the Sports Experience and the Role of Athletics in the Schools." Unpublished Doctor's dissertation, University of Southern California, 1971.

Gulick, Luther Halsey. A Philosophy of Play New York: Association Press, 1920.

Haldane, Elizabeth S. and Ross, G. R. T. (trans.). The Philosophical Works of Descartes, Volume I. London: Cambridge University Press, 1969.

Hampshire, Stuart (ed.). The Age of Reason: The Seventeenth Century Philosophers. Boston: Houghton-Mifflin, 1956.

Harnett, Arthur L. and Shaw, John H. Effective School Health Education. New York: Appleton-Century-Crofts, Inc., 1959.

Harper, William A. "Harper's Reaction to 'Physical Education and Lived Movement'," 74th Proceedings of the National College Physical Education Association for Men, Annual Meeting (Portland, Oregon, December 27-30, 1970), 69-73.

Harper, William A. "Human Revolt: A Phenomenological Description." Unpublished Doctor's dissertation, University of Southern California, 1970.

Harper, William A. "Man Alone," Quest, No. 12 (May, 1969), 57-60.

Harper, William A. "Movement and Measurement: The Case of the Incompatible Marriage," Quest, No. 20 (June, 1973), 92-99.

Harper, William A. "Philosophy of Physical Education and Sport (A Review of the Literature)," Exercise and Sport Science Reviews, Volume II. Jack Wilmore (ed.). New York: Academic Press, 1974.

Harper, William A. "Taking and Giving in Sport." Essay presented at the Symposium on the Philosophy of Sport, Brockport, New York, February 10-12, 1972.

Hegel, Georg W. F. The Phenomenology of Mind. Second edition. J. B. Baillie (trans.). London: Allen and Unwin, 1966.

Hegel, Georg W. F. The Philosophy of History. J. Sibree (trans.). New York: Dover Publications, Inc., 1956.

Heidegger, Martin. Being and Time. John Macquarrie and Edward Robinson (trans.). New York: Harper and Row Publishers, 1962.

Hellison, Donald R. Humanistic Physical Education. Englewood Cliffs, N. J.: Prentice-Hall, Inc., 1973.

Henry, Franklin M. "Physical Education: An Academic Discipline," Anthology of Contemporary Readings: An Introduction to Physical Education. Howard S. Slusher and Aileene S. Lockhart (eds.). Dubuque, Iowa: William C. Brown Co., Publishers, 1966.

Herbart, Johann Friedrich. The Science of Education, Its General Principles Deduced from its Aim, and the Aesthetic Revelation of the World. Henry M. Felkin and Emmie Felkin (trans.). Boston: D. C. Heath and Co., 1902.

Herman, Daniel J. "Mechanism and the Athlete," Journal of the Philosophy of Sport, Vol. 2 (September, 1975), 102-110.

Herrigel, Eugen. Zen in the Art of Archery. R. F. C. Hull (trans.). New York: Random House, Inc., 1971.

Hess, Ford A. "American Objectives of Physical Education from 1900-1957 Assessed in the Light of Certain Historical Events." Unpublished Doctor's dissertation, New York University, 1959.

Hetherington, Clark W. School Program in Physical Education. Yonkers-on-Hudson, N. Y.: World Book Co., 1922.

Hileman, Betty J. "The Emerging Patterns of Thought in Physical Education in the United States: 1956-1966." Unpublished Doctor's dissertation, University of Southern California, 1967.

Hohler, V. "The Beauty of Motion," Readings in the Aesthetics of Sport. H. T. A. Whiting and Don W. Masterson (eds.). London: Lepus Books, 1974.

Holbrook, Leona. "The Teleological Concept of the Physical Qualities of Man," Quest, No. 1 (December, 1963), 13-17.

Holland, George J. and Davis, Elwood Craig. Values of Physical Activity. Dubuque, Iowa: William C. Brown Co., Publishers, 1975.

Horne, Herman Harrell. Idealism in Education. New York: The Macmillan Co., 1910.

Houts, Jo Ann. "Feeling and Perception in the Sport Experience," Journal of Health, Physical Education, and Recreation, Vol. 41, No. 8 (October, 1970), 71-72.

Huelster, Laura J. "The Body of Knowledge in Physical Education--Philosophical," The Physical Educator, Vol. 22, No. 1 (March, 1965), 6-8.

Huelster, Laura J. "The Physical Educator in Perspective," Quest, No. 7 (December, 1966), 62-66.

Huizinga, Johan. Homo Ludens: A Study of the Play-Element in Culture. Boston: The Beacon Press, 1950.

Hume, David. An Inquiry Concerning Human Understanding. Charles W. Hendel (ed.). Indianapolis: The Bobbs-Merrill Co., Inc., 1955.

Husserl, Edmund. Phenomenology and the Crisis of Philosophy. Quentin Lauer (trans.). New York: Harper and Row, Publishers, 1965.

Hyland, Drew A. "Athletic Angst: Reflections on the Philosophical Relevance of Play," Sport and the Body: A Philosophical Symposium. Ellen W. Gerber (ed.). Philadelphia: Lea and Febiger, 1972.

Hyland, Drew A. "Modes of Inquiry in Sport, Athletics and Play," Journal of the Philosophy of Sport, Vol. 1 (September, 1974), 121-128.

Iden, Margaret A. "Substantive Elements About Human Movement." Unpublished Doctor's dissertation, University of California at Los Angeles, 1967.

Jacks, Laurence P. Education Through Recreation. New York: Harper and Brothers, 1932.

James, C. L. R. "The Relationship Between Popular Sport and Fine Art," Readings in the Aesthetics of Sport. H. T. A. Whiting and Don W. Masterson (eds.). London: Lepus Books, 1974.

Jaspers, Karl. "Limits of the Life-Order: Sport," Sport and the Body: A Philosophical Symposium. Ellen W. Gerber (ed.). Philadelphia: Lea and Febiger, 1972.

Jaspers, Karl. Man in the Modern Age. Eden Paul and Cedar Paul (trans.). London: Routledge and Kegan Paul Ltd., 1959.

Jokl, Ernst. "Art and Sport," Readings in the Aesthetics of Sport. H. T. A. Whiting and Don W. Masterson (eds.). London: Lepus Books, 1974.

Jokl, Ernst. "The Future of Physical Education," Anthology of Contemporary Readings: An Introduction to Physical Education. Howard S. Slusher and Aileene S. Lockhart (eds.). Dubuque, Iowa: William C. Brown Co., Publishers, 1966.

Jokl, Ernst. "Sport and Culture," Medical Sociology and Cultural Anthropology of Sport and Physical Education. Ernst Jokl. Springfield, Ill.: Charles C. Thomas, Publishers, 1964.

Jokl, Ernst. "Sport as Leisure," Quest, No. 4 (April, 1965), 37-47.

Jowett, Benjamin (trans.). Aristotle's Politics. New York: Random House, Inc., 1943.

Jowett, Benjamin (trans.). Dialogues of Plato. Fourth edition. 4 vols. Oxford: Clarendon Press, 1953.

Kaech, Arnold. "What Is the Point of Sport?" Recreation, Vol. 50 (December, 1957), 358.

Kaelin, Eugene F. "Being in the Body." Essay presented at the Meeting of the National Association of Physical Education for College Women, Interlochen, Michigan, June 14-19, 1964.

Kaelin, Eugene F. "The Well-Played Game: Notes Toward an Aesthetics of Sport," Quest, No. 10 (May, 1968), 16-28.

Kant, Immanuel. Critique of Practical Reason. Lewis White Beck (trans.). New York: Liberal Arts Press, 1956.

Kant, Immanuel. Critique of Pure Reason. Norman Kemp Smith (trans.). New York: St. Martin's Press, 1965.

Kant, Immanuel. Education. Annette Churton (trans.). Ann Arbor, Michigan: University of Michigan Press, 1966.

Kant, Immanuel. Foundations of the Metaphysics of Morals. Lewis White Beck (trans.). Indianapolis: The Bobbs-Merrill Co., Inc., 1959.

Kaplan, Abraham. The New World of Philosophy. New York: Random House, Inc., 1961.

Kaufmann, Walter. Existentialism from Dostoevsky to Sartre. Cleveland: The World Publishing Co., 1956.

Kaufmann, Walter. Hegel: A Reinterpretation. Garden City, N. Y.: Doubleday and Co., Inc., 1965.

Kaufmann, Walter (trans.). The Portable Nietzsche. New York: The Viking Press, 1954.

Keating, James W. "Athletics and the Pursuit of Excellence," Education, Vol. 85, No. 7 (March, 1965), 428-431.

Keating, James W. "The Ethics of Competition and Its Relation to Some Moral Problems in Athletics," The Philosophy of Sport: A Collection of Original Essays. Robert G. Osterhoudt (ed.). Springfield, Ill.: Charles C. Thomas, Publisher, 1973.

Keating, James W. "The Heart of the Problem of Amateur Athletics," The Journal of General Education, Vol. 16, No. 4 (January, 1965), 261-272.

Keating, James W. "Sartre on Sport and Play." Essay presented at the American Association for Health, Physical Education, and Recreation, Annual Meeting, Chicago, Illinois, March 18-22, 1966.

Keating, James W. "Sportsmanship as a Moral Category," Ethics, Vol. 85, No. 1 (October, 1964), 25-35.

Keating, James W. "The Urgent Need for Definitions and Distinctions," The Physical Educator, Vol. 28, No. 1 (March, 1971), 41.

Keating, James W. "Winning in Sport and Athletics," Thought, Vol. 38, No. 149 (Summer, 1963), 201-210.

Keenan, Francis W. "The Athletic Contest as a 'Tragic' Form of Art," The Philosophy of Sport: A Collection of Original Essays. Robert G. Osterhoudt (ed.). Springfield, Ill.: Charles C. Thomas, Publisher, 1973.

Keenan, Francis W. "The Concept of Doing," The Philosophy of Sport: A Collection of Original Essays. Robert G. Osterhoudt (ed.). Springfield, Ill.: Charles C. Thomas, Publisher, 1973.

Keenan, Francis W. "A Delineation of Deweyan Progressivism for Physical Education." Unpublished Doctor's dissertation, University of Illinois, 1971.

Keenen, Francis W. "Justice and Sport," Journal of the Philosophy of Sport, Vol. 2 (September, 1975), 111-123.

Keller, Hans. "Sport and Art--the Concept of Mastery," Readings in the Aesthetics of Sport. H. T. A. Whiting and Don W. Masterson (eds.). London: Lepus Books, 1974.

Kelly, Darlene A. "Phenomena of the Self-Experienced Body." Unpublished Doctor's dissertation, University of Southern California, 1970.

Kennedy, Charles W. Sport and Sportsmanship. Princeton, N. J.: Princeton University Press, 1931.

Kenyon, Gerald S. "On The Conceptualization of Sub-Disciplines within an Academic Discipline Dealing with Human Movement," 71st Proceedings of the National College Physical Education Association for Men, Annual Meeting (Houston, Texas, January 10-13, 1968), 34-45.

Kierkegaard, Sören. Concluding Unscientific Postscript. David F. Swenson and Walter Lowrie (trans.). Princeton, N. J.: Princeton University Press, 1941.

Kingston, George E. "Towards a Classification of the Theories of Human Play." Unpublished Master's thesis, University of Alberta, Canada, 1968.

Kleinman, Seymour. "The Nature of A Self and Its Relation to An 'Other' in Sport," Journal of the Philosophy of Sport, Vol. 2 (September, 1975), 45-50.

Kleinman, Seymour "Philosophy and Physical Education," Physical Education: An Interdisciplinary Approach. Janet Felshin (ed.). New York: The Macmillan Co., 1972.

Kleinman, Seymour. "Physical Education and Lived Movement," 74th Proceedings of the National College Physical Education Association for Men, Annual Meeting (Portland, Oregon, December 27-30, 1970), 60-66.

Kleinman, Seymour. "The Significance of Human Movement: A Phenomenological Approach," Dimensions of Physical Education. Charles A. Bucher and Myra Goldman (eds.). St. Louis: The C. V. Mosby Co., 1969.

Kleinman, Seymour. "Toward a Non-Theory of Sport," Quest, No. 10 (May, 1968), 29-34.

Kleinman, Seymour. "Will the Real Plato Please Stand Up?" Quest, No. 14 (June, 1970), 73-75.

Kneller, George F. Existentialism and Education. New York: John Wiley and Sons, Inc., 1958.

Kretchmar, R. Scott. "From Test to Contest: An Analysis of Two Kinds of Counterpoint in Sport," Journal of the Philosophy of Sport, Vol. 2 (September, 1975), 23-30.

Kretchmar, R. Scott. "Meeting the Opposition: Buber's 'Will' and 'Grace' in Sport," Quest, No. 24 (Summer, 1975), 19-27.

Kretchmar, R. Scott. "Modes of Philosophic Inquiry and Sport," Journal of the Philosophy of Sport, Vol. 1 (September, 1974), 129-131.

Kretchmar, R. Scott. "Ontological Possibilities: Sport as Play," The Philosophy of Sport: A Collection of Original Essays. Robert G. Osterhoudt (ed.). Springfield, Ill.: Charles C. Thomas, Publisher, 1973.

Kretchmar, R. Scott, "A Phenomenological Analysis of the Other in Sport." Unpublished Doctor's dissertation, University of Southern California, 1970.

Kretchmar, R. Scott and Harper, William A. "Must We Have a Rational Answer to the Question 'Why Does Man Play'?" Journal of Health, Physical Education, and Recreation, Vol. 40, No. 3 (March, 1969), 57-58.

Kroll, Walter P. Perspectives in Physical Education. New York: Academic Press, 1971.

Krug, Orvis C. "The Philosophic Relationship Between Physical Education and Athletics." Unpublished Doctor's dissertation, New York University, 1958.

Kuntz, Paul G. "Aesthetics Applies to Sports as Well as to the Arts," Journal of the Philosophy of Sport, Vol. 1 (September, 1974), 6-35.

Kuntz, Paul G. "The Aesthetics of Sport," The Philosophy of Sport: A Collection of Original Essays. Robert G. Osterhoudt (ed.). Springfield, Ill.: Charles C. Thomas, Publisher, 1973.

Kuntz, Paul G. "The Phenomenology of Bicycling." Essay presented at the Fifth Workshop in Phenomenology, Washington University, June 24, 1972.

Kupfer, Joseph. "Purpose and Beauty in Sport," Journal of the Philosophy of Sport, Vol. 2 (September, 1975), 83-90.

Lane, Valerie B. "Aquatic Movement as an Art Form." Unpublished Master's thesis, University of California at Los Angeles, 1966.

Langerhorst, Christina T. "The Implications of Buytendijk's Work for Physical Education: A Critical Analysis." Unpublished Master's thesis, University of Toledo, 1971.

Larkin, Richard A. "The Influence of John Dewey on Physical Education." Unpublished Master's thesis, Ohio State University, 1936.

Lee, Mabel. The Conduct of Physical Education. New York: A. S. Barnes and Co., 1937.

Leibniz, Gottfried Wilhelm. Monadology and Other Philosophical Essays. Paul Schrecker and Anne Martin Schrecker (trans.). Indianapolis: The Bobbs-Merrill Co., Inc., 1965.

Lenk, Hans. "Alienation, Manipulation, or Emancipation of the Athlete?" Unpublished manuscript, University of Karlsruhe, West Germany, 1974.

Lenk, Hans. "Foundation of a Pluralistic Philosophy of Sport Achievement." Unpublished manuscript, University of Karlsruhe, West Germany, 1974.

Lenk, Hans. Leistungssport: Ideologie oder Mythos? Stuttgart: Verlag W. Kohlhammer, 1972.

Lenk, Hans. "The Philosophy of Sport," The Scientific View of Sport. Organizing Committee for the Games of the XXth Olympiad, Munich (ed.). New York: Springer-Verlag, 1972.

Leonard, Fred E. and Affleck, George B. A Guide to the History of Physical Education. Third edition. Philadelphia: Lea and Febinger, 1947.

Lewis, Clifford G. "Expressed Values of College Women at the University of Georgia Concerning Selected Social Factors Related to Acceptance of and Participation in Physical Education." Unpublished Doctor's dissertation, Columbia University, 1961.

L'Heureux, W. J. "Morality, Sport and the Athlete." Essay presented at the First Canadian Congress for the Multi-Disciplinary Study of Sport and Physical Activity, Montreal, Canada, October 12-14, 1973.

Locke, John. On Education. Peter Gay (ed.). New York: Bureau of Publications, Teachers College, Columbia University, 1964.

Locke, John. An Essay Concerning Human Understanding. A. D. Woozley (ed.). Cleveland: The World Publishing Co., 1964.

Locke, John. On Politics and Education. Toronto: D. Van Nostrand, 1947.

Loy, John W. "The Nature of Sport: A Definitional Effort," Sport, Culture, and Society: A Reader on the Sociology of Sport. John W. Loy and Gerald S. Kenyon (eds.). London: The Macmillan Co., 1969.

Lozes, Jewell H. "The Philosophy of Certain Religious Denominations Relative to Physical Education, and the Effect of this Philosophy on Physical Education in Certain Church-Related Institutions." Unpublished Master's thesis, Pennsylvania State University, 1955.

Lynn, Minnie L. "A Living Legacy," Quest, No. 1 (December, 1963), 1-2.

Lynn, Minnie L. "Major Emphases in Physical Education in the United States." Unpublished Doctor's dissertation, University of Pittsburgh, 1944.

Mack, Mary P. (ed.). A Bentham Reader. New York: Pegasus, 1969.

Maheu, René. "Sport and Culture," International Research in Sport and Physical Education. Ernst Jokl and E. Simon (eds.). Springfield, Ill.: Charles C. Thomas, Publishers, 1964.

Maheu, René. "Sport is Education," The UNESCO Courier (January, 1964), 4-9.

Malina, Robert M. "An Anthropological Perspective of Man in Action," New Perspectives of Man in Action. Roscoe C. Brown and Bryant J. Cratty (eds.). Englewood Cliffs, N. J.: Prentice-Hall, Inc., 1969.

Marcel, Gabriel. The Mystery of Being. 2 vols. Chicago: Henry Regnery Co., 1960.

Marx, Karl. Early Writings. T. B. Bottomore (trans.). New York: McGraw-Hill, 1964.

Masterson, Don W. "Sport and Modern Painting," Readings in the Aesthetics of Sport. H. T. A. Whiting and Don W. Masterson (eds.). London: Lepus Books, 1974.

Matthias, Eugen. The Deeper Meaning of Physical Education. Carl L. Schrader (trans.). New York: A. S. Barnes and Co., 1929.

McBride, Frank. "Toward a Non-Definition of Sport," Journal of the Philosophy of Sport, Vol. 2 (September, 1975), 4-11.

McBride, Peter. The Philosophy of Sport. London: Heath Cranton Ltd., 1932.

McCall, Raymond J. Basic Logic. Second edition. New York: Barnes and Noble, Inc., 1952.

McCloy, Charles H. Philosophical Bases for Physical Education. New York: F. S. Crofts and Co., Inc,, 1940.

McIntosh, Peter C. "Means and Ends in a State of Leisure," Quest, No. 4 (April, 1965), 33-36.

McKeon, Richard P. (ed.). Introduction to Aristotle. New York: Random House, Inc., 1947.

McPherson, Frances A. "Development of Ideas in Physical Education in the Secondary Schools in the United States Between 1889 and 1920." Unpublished Doctor's dissertation, University of Wisconsin, 1965.

Meier, Klaus V. "Authenticity and Sport: A Conceptual Analysis." Unpublished Doctor's dissertation, University of Illinois, 1975.

Meier, Klaus V. "Cartesian and Phenomenological Anthropology: The Radical Shift and Its Meaning for Sport," Journal of the Philosophy of Sport, Vol. 2 (September, 1975), 51-73.

Meier, Klaus V. "An Existential Analysis of Play." Unpublished Master's thesis, University of Western Ontario, Canada, 1971.

Meredith, Lawrence. "The Sensuous Sportsman: An Interpretation of Athletics," 75th Proceedings of the National College Physical Education Association for Men, Annual Meeting (New Orleans, Louisiana, January 9-12, 1972), 39-45.

Merleau-Ponty, Maurice. Phenomenology of Perception. Colin Smith (trans.). London: Routledge and Kegan Paul Ltd., 1959.

Metheny, Eleanor. Connotations of Movement in Sport and Dance. Dubuque, Iowa: William C. Brown Co., Publishers, 1965.

Metheny, Eleanor. "How Does a Movement Mean?" Quest, No. 8 (May, 1967), 1-6.

Metheny, Eleanor. "Man is a Bio-Psycho-Socio-Philosophical Organism Capable of Voluntary Movement," The Physical Educator, Vol. 16, No. 3 (October, 1959), 83.

Metheny, Eleanor. "Metheny's Reaction to 'Theory and Design of Philosophic Research in Physical Education'." 74th Proceedings of the National College Physical Education Association for Men, Annual Meeting (Portland, Oregon, December 27-30, 1970), 57-59.

Metheny, Eleanor. Movement and Meaning. New York: McGraw-Hill Book Co., 1968.

Metheny, Eleanor. "Only By Moving Their Bodies," Quest, No. 2 (April, 1964), 47-51.

Metheny, Eleanor. "Philosophical Methods," Research Methods in Health, Physical Education, and Recreation. Second edition. M. Gladys Scott (ed.). Washington: AAHPER, 1959.

Metheny, Eleanor. "This 'Thing' Called Sport," Journal of Health, Physical Education, and Recreation, Vol. 40, No. 3 (March, 1969), 59-60.

Metheny, Eleanor. "The Unique Meaning Inherent in Human Move-
    ment," The Physical Educator, Vol. 18, No. 1 (March, 1961),
    3-7.

Miller, Donna Mae and Russell, Kathryn R. E. Sport: A Contempo-
    rary View. Philadelphia: Lea and Febiger, 1971.

Mitchell, Elmer D. and Mason, Bernard S. The Theory of Play.
    Revised edition. New York: A. S. Barnes and Co., 1948.

Mitchell, Robert. "Sport as Experience," Quest, No. 24 (Summer,
    1975), 28-33.

Moolenijzer, Nicolaas J. "Implications of the Philosophy of Gaulhofer
    and Streicher for Physical Education." Unpublished Master's
    thesis, University of California at Los Angeles, 1956.

Moore, G. E. Some Main Problems of Philosophy. London: George
    Allen and Unwin, 1953.

Morgan, William J. "An Existential Phenomenological Anslysis of
    Sport as a Religious Experience," The Philosophy of Sport: A
    Collection of Original Essays. Robert G. Osterhoudt (ed.).
    Springfield, Ill.: Charles C. Thomas, Publisher, 1973.

Morgan, William J. "A Philosophical Analysis of the Audience-Ath-
    lete Relationship Utilizing Scheler's Phenomenological Para-
    digm of Sympathy and Love." Essay presented at the First
    Canadian Congress for the Multi-Disciplinary Study of Sport and
    Physical Activity, Montreal, Canada, October 12-14, 1973.

Morgan, William J. "Sport and Temporality: An Ontological Analy-
    sis." Unpublished Doctor's dissertation, University of Minne-
    sota, 1975.

Morland, Richard B. "The Philosophic Method of Research," Re-
    search Methods in Health, Phyiscal Education, and Recreation.
    Third edition. Alfred W. Hubbard (ed.). Washington: AAHPER,
    1973.

Morland, Richard B. "A Philosophical Interpretation of the Educa-
    tional Views Held by Leaders in American Physical Education."
    Unpublished Doctor's dissertation, New York University, 1958.

Morland, Richard B. "The Pragmatism of Clark Hetherington," 72nd
    Proceedings of the National College Physical Education Associ-
    ation for Men, Annual Meeting (Durham, N. C., January 8-11,
    1969), 14-20.

Morris, Van Cleve. Existentialism in Education: What It Means. New York: Harper and Row, Publishers, Inc., 1966.

Morris, Van Cleve. Modern Movements in Educational Philosophy. Boston: Houghton-Mifflin Co., 1969.

Mothersill, Mary (ed.). Ethics. New York: The Macmillan Co., 1965.

Mourant, John A. and Freund, E. Hans (eds.). Problems of Philosophy: A Book of Readings. New York: The Macmillan Co., 1964.

Munrow, A. D. Physical Education: A Discussion of Principles. Baltimore: The Williams and Wilkins Co., 1972.

Murphy, James F. Concepts of Leisure: Philosophical Implications. Englewood Cliffs, N. J.: Prentice-Hall, Inc., 1974.

Nash, Jay B. (ed.). Interpretations of Physical Education: Character Education Through Physical Education, Volume III. New York: A. S. Barnes and Co., Inc., 1932.

Nash, Jay B. (ed.). Interpretations of Physical Education: Mind-Body Relationships, Volume I. New York: A. S. Barnes and Co., Inc., 1931.

Nash, Jay B. Philosophy of Recreation and Leisure. St. Louis: The C. V. Mosby Co., 1953.

Nash, Jay B. Physical Education: Interpretations and Objectives. New York: A. S. Barnes and Co., 1948.

Nash, Jay B. Spectatoritis. New York: Sears Publishing Co., Inc., 1932.

Natan, Alex (ed.). Sport and Society: A Symposium. London: Bowes and Bowes, 1958.

Neal, Patsy. Sport and Identity. Philadelphia: Dorrance and Co., 1972.

Nevins, Allan. The Gateway to History. Garden City, N. Y.: Doubleday and Co., Inc., 1962.

Nixon, John E. and Jewett, Ann E. An Introduction to Physical Education. Seventh edition. Philadelphia: W. B. Saunders Co., 1969.

Oberteuffer, Delbert. "On Learning Values Through Sport," Quest, No. 1 (December, 1963), 23-29.

Oberteuffer, Delbert and Ulrich, Celeste. Physical Education: A Textbook of Principles for Professional Students. Fourth edition. New York: Harper and Row, Publishers, Inc., 1970.

O'Brien, Joseph P. "A Basis in Catholic Thought for Physical Education." Unpublished Master's thesis, Ohio State University, 1958.

Onaga, Takeomo. "Philosophical Concepts of Selected Leaders in Physical Education." Unpublished Master's thesis, Los Angeles State College, 1962.

O'Neill, John. "The Spectacle of the Body," Journal of the Philosophy of Sport, Vol. 1 (September, 1974), 110-122.

O'Neill, Reginald F. Theories of Knowledge. Englewood Cliffs, N. J.: Prentice-Hall, Inc., 1959.

Orringer, Nelson R. "Sport and Festival: A Study of Ludic Theory in Ortega y Gasset." Unpublished Doctor's dissertation, Brown University, 1969.

Osterhoudt, Robert G. "A Descriptive Analysis of Research Concerning the Philosophy of Physical Education and Sport." Unpublished Doctor's dissertation, University of Illinois, 1971.

Osterhoudt, Robert G. "An Hegelian Interpretation of Art, Sport, and Athletics," The Philosophy of Sport: A Collection of Original Essays. Robert G. Osterhoudt (ed.). Springfield, Ill.: Charles C. Thomas, Publisher, 1973.

Osterhoudt, Robert G. "The Kantian Ethic as a Principle of Moral Conduct in Sport," Quest, No. 19 (January, 1973), 118-123.

Osterhoudt, Robert G. "On Keating on the Competitive Motif in Athletics and Playful Activity," The Philosophy of Sport: A Collection of Original Essays. Robert G. Osterhoudt (ed.). Springfield, Ill.: Charles C. Thomas, Publisher, 1973.

Osterhoudt, Robert G. "Modes of Philosophic Inquiry Concerning Sport: Some Reflections on Method," Journal of the Philosophy of Sport, Vol. 1 (September, 1974), 137-141.

Osterhoudt, Robert G. (ed.). The Philosophy of Sport: A Collection of Original Essays. Springfield, Ill.: Charles C. Thomas, Publisher, 1973.

Osterhoudt, Robert G. "A Taxonomy for Research Concerning the Philosophy of Physical Education and Sport," Quest, No. 20 (June, 1973), 87-91.

Osterhoudt, Robert G. "Toward an Idealistic Conception of Physical Education and Sport," The Physical Educator, Vol. 32, No. 4 (December, 1975), 177-179.

Paddick, Robert J. "The Nature and Place of a Field of Knowledge in Physical Education." Unpublished Master's thesis, University of Alberta, Canada, 1967.

Paddick, Robert J. "What Makes Physical Activity Physical?" Journal of the Philosophy of Sport, Vol. 2 (September, 1975), 12-22.

Paplauskas-Ramunas, Anthony. Development of the Whole Man Through Physical Education: An Interdisciplinary Comparative Exploration and Appraisal. Ottawa: University of Ottawa Press, 1968.

Park, Roberta J. "The Human Element in Sports: Play," The Physical Educator, Vol. 28, No. 3 (October, 1971), 122-124.

Park, Roberta J. "The Philosophy of John Dewey and Physical Education," The Physical Educator, Vol. 26, No. 2 (May, 1969), 55-57.

Park, Roberta J. "Raising the Consciousness of Sport," Quest, No. 19 (January, 1973), 78-82.

Paterson, Ann and Hallberg, Edmond C. (eds.). Background Readings for Physical Education. New York: Holt, Rinehart and Winston, 1965.

Patrick, George. "Meaningfulness in the Language of Sport: A Call for Entente." Essay presented at the Symposium on the Philosophy of Sport, Brockport, New York, February 10-12, 1972.

Pearson, Kathleen M. "Deception, Sportsmanship, and Ethics," Quest, No. 19 (January, 1973), 115-118.

Pearson, Kathleen M. "Inquiry Into Inquiry." Unpublished manuscript, University of Illinois, 1968.

Pearson, Kathleen M. "A Proposed Model for Philosophical Conceptual Analysis within the Discipline and/or the Profession of Sport and Physical Activity." Essay presented at the First Canadian Symposium on the Philosophy of Sport and Physical Activity, Windsor, Canada, May 3-4, 1972.

Pearson, Kathleen M. "Some Comments on Philosophic Inquiry into Sport as a Meaningful Human Experience," Journal of the Philosophy of Sport, Vol. 1 (September, 1974), 132-136.

Pelton, Barry C. "A Critical Analysis of Current Concepts Underlying General Physical Education Programs in Higher Education." Unpublished Doctor's dissertation, University of Southern California, 1966.

Pegis, Anton C. (ed.). Introduction to St. Thomas Aquinas. Second edition. New York: Random House, Inc., 1948.

Popkins, Michael. "An Analysis of the Values Asserted by Roger Bannister Concerning Running: Essentialistic-Progressivistic." Unpublished Master's thesis, Western Illinois University, 1972.

Postma, J. W. Introduction to the Theory of Physical Education. Cape Town: A. A. Balkema, 1968.

Progen, Jan. "Man, Nature and Sport," Sport and the Body: A Philosophical Symposium. Ellen W. Gerber (ed.). Philadelphia: Lea and Febiger, 1972.

Pusey, Edward B. (trans.). The Confessions of Saint Augustine. New York: Random House, Inc., 1949.

Quest, The Editors of. "Philosophy--New and Old," Quest, No. 1 (December, 1963), v.

Rajagopalan, K. "A Philosophy for Play," The Physical Educator, Vol. 22, No. 1 (March, 1965), 20.

Randall, John H. and Buchler, Justus. Philosophy: An Introduction. New York: Barnes and Noble, Inc., 1942.

Randall, M. W., Waine, W. K., and Hickling, M. J. Objectives in Physical Education. London: G. Bell and Sons Ltd., 1966.

Rarick, G. Lawrence. "The Domain of Physical Education as a Discipline," Quest, No. 9 (December, 1967), 49-52.

Ratner, Joseph (ed.). Intelligence in the Modern World: John Dewey's Philosophy. New York: Random House, Inc., 1939.

Reid, Louis A. "Sport, the Aesthetic and Art," British Journal of Educational Studies, Vol. 18, No. 3 (October, 1970), 245-258.

Renshaw, Peter. "The Nature of Human Movement Studies and Its Relationship with Physical Education," Quest, No. 20 (June, 1973), 79-86.

Rice, Emmett A., Hutchinson, John L., and Lee, Mabel. A Brief History of Physical Education. Fifth edition. New York: The Ronald Press Co., 1969.

Rickard, Rodger S. "An Explication of the Role of Aesthetic-Value in American Physical Education: A Conceptual Analysis of Physical Education Literature." Unpublished Doctor's dissertation, Stanford University, 1970.

Roberts, Terence J. "An Examination of the Moralities of Athletics and Play." Unpublished Master's thesis, University of Windsor, Canada, 1973.

Roberts, Terence J. "Sport and the Sense of Beauty," Journal of the Philosophy of Sport, Vol. 2 (September, 1975), 91-101.

Roberts, Terence J. and Galasso, P. J. "The Fiction of Morally Indifferent Acts in Sport," The Philosophy of Sport: A Collection of Original Essays. Robert G. Osterhoudt (ed.). Springfield, Ill.: Charles C. Thomas, Publisher, 1973.

Roby, Mary P. "The Power of Sport," Sport and the Body: A Philosophical Symposium. Ellen W. Gerber (ed.). Philadelphia: Lea and Febiger, 1972.

Rogers, Frederick R. The Amateur Spirit in Scholastic Games and Sports. Albany, N. Y.: C. F. Williams and Son, Inc., 1929.

Roochnik, David L. "Play and Sport," Journal of the Philosophy of Sport, Vol. 2 (September, 1975), 36-44.

Rouse, W. H. D. (trans.). The Great Dialogues of Plato. New York: The New American Library, Inc., 1956.

Rousseau, Jean Jacques. Sur le Gouvernement de la Pologne. London: C. Lowndes, 1791.

Royce, Joseph R. The Encapsulated Man: An Interdisciplinary Essay on the Search for Meaning. Princeton, N. J.: D. Van Nostrand Co., Inc., 1964.

Royce, Josiah. Some Relations of Physical Training to the Present Problems of Moral Education in America. Boston: Boston Normal School of Gymnastics, 1908.

Runes, Dagobert D. (ed.). Dictionary of Philosophy. Fifteenth edition. Paterson, N. J.: Littlefield, Adams and Co., 1960.

Runes, Dagobert D. Pictorial History of Philosophy. New York: Bramhall House, 1959.

Sadler, William A. "A Contextual Approach to an Understanding of Competition: A Response to Keating's Philosophy of Athletics," The Philosophy of Sport: A Collection of Original Essays. Robert G. Osterhoudt (ed.). Springfield, Ill.: Charles C. Thomas, Publisher, 1973.

Sanborn, Marion A. "Major Issues in Physical Education." Unpublished Doctor's dissertation, Ohio State University, 1958.

Sanborn, Marion A. and Hartman, Betty G. Issues in Physical Education. Revised edition. Philadelphia: Lea and Febiger, 1970.

Santayana, George. "Philosophy on the Bleachers," Harvard Monthly, Vol. 18, No. 5 (July, 1894), 181-190.

Sartre, Jean-Paul. Being and Nothingness: An Essay on Phenomenological Ontology. Hazel E. Barnes (trans.). New York: Washington Square Press, 1953.

Sartre, Jean-Paul. "Play and Sport," Sport and the Body: A Philosophical Symposium. Ellen W. Gerber (ed.). Philadelphia: Lea and Febiger, 1972.

Schacht, Richard L. Alienation. Garden City, N. Y.: Doubleday and Co., Inc., 1970.

Schacht, Richard L. "On Weiss on Records, Athletic Activity and the Athlete," The Philosophy of Sport: A Collection of Original Essays. Robert G. Osterhoudt (ed.). Springfield, Ill.: Charles C. Thomas, Publisher, 1973.

Schiller, Friedrich. On the Aesthetic Education of Man. Reginald Snell (trans.). New York: Frederick Ungar Publishing Co., 1965.

Schmitz, Kenneth L. "Sport and Play: Suspension of the Ordinary." Essay presented at the American Association for the Advancement of Science, Annual Meeting, Dallas, Texas, December, 1968.

Schutte, Fred M. "Objectives of Physical Education in the United States: 1870-1929." Unpublished Master's thesis, New York University, 1930.

Scott, Harry A. Competitive Sports in Schools and Colleges. New York: Harper and Brothers, 1951.

Seidel, Beverly L. and Resick, Matthew C. Physical Education: An Overview. Reading, Mass.: Addison-Wesley Publishing Co., 1972.

Shadduck, Ione G. "A Philosophical Base for a Physical Education Program Design." Unpublished Doctor's dissertation, Michigan State University, 1967.

Shapiro, Herman (ed.). Medieval Philosophy. New York: Random House, Inc., 1964.

Shapiro, Herman and Curley, Edwin M. (eds.). Hellenistic Philosophy. New York: Random House, Inc., 1965.

Sharman, Jackson R. Modern Principles of Physical Education. New York: A. S. Barnes and Co., Inc., 1937.

Sheehan, Thomas J. "Sport: The Focal Point of Physical Education," Quest, No. 10 (May, 1968), 59-67.

Shepard, Natalie M. "Democracy in Physical Education: A Study of the Implications for Educating for Democracy Through Physical Education." Unpublished Doctor's dissertation, New York University, 1953.

Shepard, Natalie M. Foundations and Principles of Physical Education. New York: The Ronald Press Co., 1960.

Sherman, Atara P. "Theoretical Foundations of Physical Education in the United States: 1886-1930." Unpublished Doctor's dissertation, University of Southern California, 1965.

Shivers, Jay S. "An Analysis of Theories of Recreation." Unpublished Doctor's dissertation, University of Wisconsin, 1958.

Shivers, Jay S. "Play, Leisure, and Recreation: Views of Goethe and Schiller," The Physical Educator, Vol. 22, No. 1 (March, 1965), 31-34.

Shvartz, Esar. "Nietzsche--Philosopher of Fitness," Quest, No. 8 (May, 1967), 83-89.

Shvartz, Esar. "Romanticism in Physical Education," The Physical Educator, Vol. 23, No. 3 (October, 1966), 111-113.

Siedentop, Daryl. Physical Education: Introductory Analysis. Dubuque, Iowa: William C. Brown Co., Publishers, 1972.

Siedentop, Daryl. "What Did Plato Really Think?" The Physical Educator, Vol. 24, No. 1 (March, 1968), 25-26.

Slater, Morris B. "An Identification and Comparison of Some Philosophical Beliefs in the Area of Physical Education Held by Elementary School Teachers." Unpublished Master's thesis, University of Oregon, 1966.

Slatton, Yvonne L. "The Philosophical Beliefs of Undergraduate and Graduate Physical Education Major Students and the Physical Education Faculty at the University of North Carolina at Greensboro." Unpublished Master's thesis, University of North Carolina at Greensboro, 1964.

Slusher, Howard S. "The Existential Function of Physical Education." Essay presented at the Meeting of the National Association of Physical Education for College Women, Interlochen, Michigan, June 14-19, 1964.

Slusher, Howard S. "Existentialism and Physical Education," The Physical Educator, Vol. 20, No. 4 (December, 1963), 153-156.

Slusher, Howard S. Man, Sport and Existence: A Critical Analysis. Philadelphia: Lea and Febiger, 1967.

Slusher, Howard S. "To Test the Wave is to Test Life," Journal of Health, Physical Education, and Recreation, Vol. 40, No. 5 (May, 1969), 32-33.

Smith, John E. (ed.). Philosophy of Religion. New York: The Macmillan Co., 1965.

Smith, William (trans.). The Popular Works of Johann Gottlieb Fichte, Volume II. Fourth edition. London: Trubner and Co., 1889.

Spears, Betty M. "Philosophical Bases for Physical Education Experiences Consistent with the Goals of General Education for College Women." Unpublished Doctor's dissertation, New York University, 1956.

Spence, Dale. "Analysis of Selected Values in Physical Education as Identified by Professional Personnel." Unpublished Doctor's dissertation, Louisiana State University, 1966.

Spence, Dale. "What is the Deeper Meaning of Physical Education," The Physical Educator, Vol. 21, No. 2 (May, 1964), 68-69.

Spencer, Herbert. Education: Intellectual, Moral, and Physical. New York: D. Appleton and Co., 1920.

Spencer-Kraus, Peter. "The Application of 'Linguistic Phenomenology' to the Philosophy of Physical Education and Sport." Unpublished Master's thesis, University of Illinois, 1969.

Staley, Seward C. Sports Education: The New Curriculum in Physical Education. New York: A. S. Barnes and Co., 1939.

Staley, Seward C. The World of Sport. Champaign, Ill.: Stipes Publishing Co., 1955.

Stanley, Sheila. Physical Education: A Movement Orientation. Toronto: McGraw-Hill Co. of Canada Ltd., 1969.

Stone, Roselyn E. "Assumptions About the Nature of Human Movement," The Philosophy of Sport: A Collection of Original Essays. Robert G. Osterhoudt (ed.). Springfield, Ill.: Charles C. Thomas, Publisher, 1973.

Stone, Roselyn E. "Meanings Found in the Acts of Surfing and Skiing." Unpublished Doctor's dissertation, University of Southern California, 1969.

Stroup, Francis. "Physical Education and the Liberal Arts," The Physical Educator, Vol. 16, No. 4 (December, 1959), 129-130.

Studer, Ginny. "From Man Moving to Moving Man," Quest, No. 20 (June, 1973), 104-107.

Suits, Bernard. "The Elements of Sport," The Philosophy of Sport: A Collection of Original Essays. Robert G. Osterhoudt (ed.). Springfield, Ill.: Charles C. Thomas, Publisher, 1973.

Suits, Bernard. "The Grasshopper; A Thesis Concerning the Moral Ideal of Man," The Philosophy of Sport: A Collection of Original Essays. Robert G. Osterhoudt (ed.). Springfield, Ill.: Charles C. Thomas, Publisher, 1973.

Suits, Bernard. "What Is A Game?" Philosophy of Science, Vol. 34 (June, 1967), 148-156.

Sundly, Jerry A. "The Desire to Win: A Phenomenological Description." Unpublished Doctor's dissertation, University of Southern California, 1971.

Taggart, Gladys M. "A Study of the Relationships Between the Goals of Physical Education and Higher Education: with Implications for the Achievement of These Goals at the University of Wichita." Unpublished Doctor's dissertation, New York University, 1959.

Thévenaz, Pierre. What Is Phenomenology? and Other Essays. James M. Edie (ed.). Chicago: Quadrangle Books, 1962.

Thilly, Frank and Wood, Ledger. A History of Philosophy. Third edition. New York: Holt, Rinehart and Winston, 1957.

Thomas, Carolyn E. "Do You 'Wanna' Bet: An Examination of Player Betting and the Integrity of the Sporting Event," The Philosophy of Sport: A Collection of Original Essays. Robert G. Osterhoudt (ed.). Springfield, Ill.: Charles C. Thomas, Publisher, 1973.

Thomas, Carolyn E. "The Perfect Moment: An Aesthetic Perspective of the Sport Experience." Unpublished Doctor's dissertation, Ohio State University, 1972.

Thomas, Carolyn E. "Science and Philosophy: Peaceful Coexistence," Quest, No. 20 (June, 1973), 99-104.

Thomas, Carolyn E. "Toward an Experiental Sport Aesthetic," Journal of the Philosophy of Sport, Vol. 1 (September, 1974), 67-91.

Thompson, Merritt M. (ed.). The Educational Philosophy of Giovanni Gentile. Los Angeles: University of Southern California Press, 1934.

Thomson, Patricia L. "Ontological Truth in Sport: A Phenomenological Analysis." Unpublished Doctor's dissertation, University of Southern California, 1967.

Thomson, Patricia L. "Thomson's Reaction to 'Physical Education and Lived Movement'," 74th Proceedings of the National College Physical Education Association for Men, Annual Meeting (Portland, Oregon, December 27-30, 1970), 66-69.

Torkildsen, George E. "Sport and Culture." Unpublished Master's thesis, University of Wisconsin, 1967.

Tunis, John R. Democracy and Sport. New York: A. S. Barnes and Co., 1941.

Turnbull, George H. (trans.). The Educational Theory of Johann Gottlieb Fichte. Liverpool: The University Press of Liverpool Ltd., 1926.

Twomey, Jeremiah J. Christian Philosophy and Physical Education. Liverpool, England: Kilburns Ltd., 1958.

Ueberweg, Friedrich. History of Philosophy from Thales to the Present Time. 2 vols. George S. Morris (trans.). New York: C. Scribner's Sons, 1887.

Ulrich, Celeste. The Social Matrix of Physical Education. Englewood Cliffs, N. J.: Prentice-Hall, Inc., 1968.

Updyke, Wynn F. and Johnson, Perry B. Principles of Modern Physical Education, Health and Recreation. New York: Holt, Rinehart and Winston, Inc., 1970.

Van Dalen, Deobold B. "Philosophical Profiles for Physical Education," Anthology of Contemporary Readings: An Introduction to Physical Education. Howard S. Slusher and Aileene S. Lockhart (eds.). Dubuque, Iowa: William C. Brown Co., Publishers, 1966.

Van Dalen, Deobold B., Mitchell, Elmer D. and Bennett, Bruce L. A World History of Physical Education: Cultural, Philosophical, Comparative. Englewood Cliffs, N. J.: Prentice-Hall, Inc., 1953.

VanderZwaag, Harold J. "Delineation of an Essentialistic Philosophy of Physical Education." Unpublished Doctor's dissertation, University of Michigan, 1962.

VanderZwaag, Harold J. "Distinguishing Characteristics of Sport," 77th Proceedings of the National College Physical Education Association for Men, Annual Meeting (Kansas City, Mo., December 26-29, 1973), 70-78.

VanderZwaag, Harold J. "Essentialism and Physical Education," The Physical Educator, Vol. 20, No. 4 (December, 1963), 147-149.

VanderZwaag, Harold J. "Sport: Existential or Essential?" Quest, No. 12 (May, 1969), 47-56.

VanderZwaag, Harold J. "Sports Concepts," Journal of Health, Physical Education, and Recreation, Vol. 41, No. 3 (March, 1970), 35-36.

VanderZwaag, Harold J. Toward a Philosophy of Sport. Reading, Mass.: Addison-Wesley Publishing Co., 1972.

Wachholz, William H. "The Nature of Man and the Nature of Competition in Sport and Athletics." Unpublished Master's thesis, University of Minnesota, 1974.

Wagner, Ann L. "A Concept of Physical Education," The Physical Educator, Vol. 21, No. 4 (December, 1964), 169-170.

Wagner, Ann L. "The Concept of Physical Education in Selected Liberal Arts Colleges." Unpublished Master's thesis, State University of Iowa, 1963.

Walsh, John H. "A Fundamental Ontology of Play and Leisure." Unpublished Doctor's dissertation, Georgetown University, 1968.

Warren, William E. "An Application of Existentialism to Physical Education." Unpublished Doctor's dissertation, University of Georgia, 1970.

Warren, William E. "Physical Education and Death," The Physical Educator, Vol. 28, No. 3 (October, 1971), 127-128.

Watson, John. Schelling's Transcendental Idealism: A Critical Exposition. Chicago: S. C. Griggs and Co., 1882.

Wayman, Agnes. A Modern Philosophy of Physical Education. Philadelphia: W. B. Saunders Co., 1938.

Webster, Randolph W. Philosophy of Physical Education. Dubuque, Iowa: William C. Brown Co., Publishers, 1965.

Weiss, Paul. "Records and the Man," The Philosophy of Sport: A Collection of Original Essays. Robert G. Osterhoudt (ed.). Springfield, Ill.: Charles C. Thomas, Publisher, 1973.

Weiss, Paul. Sport: A Philosophic Inquiry. Carbondale, Ill.: Southern Illinois University Press, 1969.

Weiss, Paul. "Strategems and Competition." Essay presented at the Inaugural Meeting of the Philosophic Society for the Study of Sport, Boston, Massachusetts, December 28, 1972.

Wenkart, Simon. "The Meaning of Sports for Contemporary Man," Journal of Existential Psychiatry, Vol. 3, No. 12 (Spring, 1963), 397-404.

Wheelwright, Philip E. (ed.). The Presocratics. New York: Odyssey Press, 1966.

White, David A. " 'Great Moments in Sport:' The One and the Many," Journal of the Philosophy of Sport, Vol. 2 (September, 1975), 124-132.

White, Morton G. (ed.). The Age of Analysis: Twentieth Century Philosophers. Boston: Houghton-Mifflin, 1955.

Whitehead, Alfred North. The Aims of Education. New York: The New American Library, 1949.

Whiting, H. T. A. and Masterson, Don W. (eds.). Readings in the Aesthetics of Sport. London: Lepus Books, 1974.

Wild, John. "Education and Human Society: A Realistic View," 54th Yearbook of the National Society for the Study of Education. Nelson B. Henry (ed.). Chicago: University of Chicago Press, 1955.

Williams, Jesse F. The Principles of Physical Education. Eighth edition. Philadelphia: W. B. Saunders Co., 1964.

Williams, Jesse F. and Hughes, William L. Athletics in Education. Philadelphia: W. B. Saunders Co., 1930.

Williams, Jesse F. and Nixon, Eugene W. The Athlete in the Making. Philadelphia: W. B. Saunders Co., 1932.

Wilton, Wilton M. "A Comparative Analysis of Theories Related to Moral and Spiritual Values in Physical Education." Unpublished Doctor's dissertation, University of California at Los Angeles, 1956.

Wilton, Wilton M. "John Locke's Thoughts Concerning Health, Physical Education and Recreation," The Physical Educator, Vol. 20, No. 2 (May, 1963), 72-73.

Windelband, Wilhelm. A History of Philosophy. 2 vols. James H. Tufts (trans.). New York: Harper and Row, Publishers, 1958.

Wittich, W. J. "What Is Your Philosophy of Health and Physical Education?" The Physical Educator, Vol. 7, No. 1 (March, 1950), 21.

Wood, Thomas D. and Cassidy, Rosalind. The New Physical Education: A Program of Naturalized Activities for Education Toward Citizenship. New York: The Macmillan Co., 1927.

Wright, Willard H. (ed.). The Philosophy of Nietzsche. Second edition. New York: Random House, Inc., 1954.

Zeigler, Earle F. "An Analysis of the Claim that 'Physical Education' Has Become a 'Family Resemblance' Term." Essay presented at the First Canadian Congress for the Multi-Disciplinary Study of Sport and Physical Activity, Montreal, Canada, October 12-14, 1973.

Zeigler, Earle F. "The Implications of Experimentalism for Physical, Health and Recreation Education," The Physical Educator, Vol. 20, No. 4 (December, 1963), 147-149.

Zeigler, Earle F. "A Philosophical Analysis of Amateurism, Semi-professionalism, and Professionalism in Competitive Sport," School Activities, Vol. 35, No. 7 (March, 1964), 199-203.

Zeigler, Earle F. "A Philosophical Analysis of Recreation and Leisure," Quest, No. 5 (December, 1965), 8-17.

Zeigler, Earle F. "Philosophical Foundations and Educational Leadership," The Physical Educator, Vol. 20, No. 1 (March, 1963), 15-18.

Zeigler, Earle F. Philosophical Foundations for Physical, Health, and Recreation Education. Englewood Cliffs, N. J.: Prentice-Hall, Inc., 1964.

Zeigler, Earle F. "Philosophy of Physical Education in a New Key," The Australian Journal of Physical Education, No. 26 (October-November, 1962), 5-8.

Zeigler, Earle F. "The Pragmatic (Experimentalistic) Ethic as It Relates to Sport and Physical Education," The Philosophy of Sport: A Collection of Original Essays. Robert G. Osterhoudt (ed.). Springfield, Ill.: Charles C. Thomas, Publisher, 1973.

Zeigler, Earle F. Problems in the History and Philosophy of Physical Education and Sport. Englewood Cliffs, N. J.: Prentice-Hall, Inc., 1968.

Zeigler, Earle F. "The Rationale for Philosophical Analysis (and Language Analysis)," Illinois Journal of Health, Physical Education and Recreation, Vol. 1 (Winter, 1970), 17.

Zeigler, Earle F. "The Role of Physical Education in the Educational Structure," The Australian Journal of Physical Education, No. 35 (October-November, 1965), 5-11.

Zeigler, Earle F. "A True Professional Needs a Consistent Philosophy," The Physical Educator, Vol. 19, No. 1 (March, 1962), 17-18.

Zeigler, Earle F. "Zeigler's Reaction to 'Theory and Design of Philosophic Research in Physical Education'," 74th Proceedings of the National College Physical Education Association for Men, Annual Meeting (Portland, Oregon, December 27-30, 1970), 52-57.

Zeigler, Earle F., Howell, Maxwell L. and Trekell, Marianna. Research in the History, Philosophy, and International Aspects of Physical Education and Sport: Bibliographies and Techniques. Champaign, Ill.: Stipes Publishing Co., 1971.

Zeigler, Earle F. and VanderZwaag, Harold J. Physical Education: Progressivism or Essentialism? Revised edition. Champaign, Ill.: Stipes Publishing Co., 1968.

Ziff, Paul. "A Fine Forehand," Journal of the Philosophy of Sport, Vol. 1 (September, 1974), 92-109.